ALL NEW 100 MATHS LESSONS

Licence

YEAR 4

Contents

Introduction	3 – 5
Term 1	**6**
Term 1 planning grid	6 – 7
Units 1–6	8 – 43
Units 8–13	44 – 83
Term 2	**84**
Term 2 planning grids	84 – 85
Units 1–6	86 – 117
Units 8–12	118– 147
Term 3	**148**
Term 3 planning grids	148 – 149
Units 1–6	150 – 184
Units 8–13	185 – 224

Published by
Scholastic Ltd
Villiers House
Clarendon Avenue
Leamington Spa
Warks. CV32 5PR

© Scholastic Ltd, 2005
Text © Clare Tuthill and Ann Montague-Smith, 2005
Printed by Bell & Bain
1 2 3 4 5 6 7 8 9   5 6 7 8 9 0 1 2 3 4

Series Consultant
Ann Montague-Smith

Authors
Claire Tuthill and
Ann Montague-Smith

Editors
Sara Wiegand and
Robin Hunt

Assistant Editors
Aileen Lalor and
Victoria Paley

Series Designer
Joy Monkhouse

Designers
Andrea Lewis,
Catherine Mason and
Micky Pledge

Illustrations
Adrian Barclay and
Andy Keylock
(Beehive Illustration)

CD development
CD developed in association
with Footmark Media Ltd

Visit our website at
www.scholastic.co.uk

Acknowledgements

Extracts from the National Numeracy Strategy *Framework for Teaching Mathematics* © Crown copyright. Reproduced under the terms of HMSO Guidance Note 8.

Designed using Adobe Inc. InDesign™ v2.0.1

British Library Cataloguing-in-Publication Data
A catalogue record for this book is available from the British Library.
ISBN 0-439-98470-X
ISBN 9780-0-439-98470-6

Every effort has been made to trace copyright holders for the works reproduced in this book and the publishers apologise for any inadvertent omissions.

Due to the nature of the web, we cannot guarantee the content or links of any sites featured. We strongly recommend that teachers check websites before using them in the classroom.

About the series

100 Maths Lessons is designed to enable you to provide clear teaching, with follow-up activities that are, in the main, practical activities for pairs of children to work on together. These activities are designed to encourage the children to use the mental strategies that they are learning and to check each other's calculations. Many of the activities are games that they will enjoy playing, and that encourage learning.

About the book

This book is divided into three termly sections. Each term begins with a **Medium-term plan** ('Termly planning grid') based on the National Numeracy Strategy's *Medium-term plans* and *Framework for Teaching Mathematics*. Each term's work is divided into a number of units of differentiated lessons on a specific subject.

Note: Because the units in this book follow the structure of the National Numeracy Strategy's *Framework for Teaching Mathematics*, the units in each term jump from Unit 6 to Unit 8. The Strategy suggests you put aside the time for Unit 7 for Assess and review.

Finding your way around the lesson units

Each term is comprised of up to 12 units. Each unit contains:
- a short-term planning grid
- three to five lesson plans
- photocopiable activity sheets.

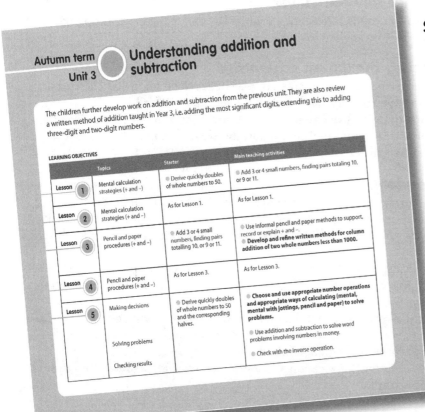

Short-term planning grids

The short-term planning grids ('Learning objectives') provide an overview of the objectives for each unit. The objectives come from the Medium-term plan and support clear progression through the year. Key objectives are shown in bold, as in the Yearly Teaching Programme in the NNS *Framework for Teaching Mathematics*.

Lesson plans

The lessons are structured on the basis of a daily maths lesson following the NNS's three-part lesson format: a ten-minute **Starter** of oral work and mental maths, a **Main teaching activities** session with interactive teaching time and/or group/individual work and a **Plenary** round-up including **Assessment** opportunities. In some lessons, differentiated tasks are supplied for more able and less able pupils.

However, this structure has not been rigidly applied. Where it is appropriate to concentrate on whole-class teaching, for example, the lesson plan may not include a group-work session at all. The overall organisation of the lesson plan varies from unit to unit depending on the lesson content. In some units all the plans are separate, though they provide different levels of detail. Elsewhere you may find a bank of activities that you can set up as a 'circus', or instruction and support for an extended investigation, either of which the children will work through over the course of several days.

Most units of work are supported with activity pages provided in the book, which can also be found on the accompanying CD. In addition to these core activity sheets, the CD contains differentiated versions for less able and more able ability levels. Some are available as blank templates, to allow you to make your own further differentiated versions.

How ICT is used

Ideas for using ICT are suggested wherever appropriate in *100 Maths Lessons*. We have assumed that you will have access to basic office applications, such as word-processing, and can email and research using the Internet. The QCA's *ICT Scheme of Work for Key Stages 1 and 2* has been used as an indicator of the skills the children will be developing formally from Year 1 and their progression in the primary years.

While some lessons use dataloggers or floor robots, we have avoided suggesting specific software, except for the games and interactive teaching programs (ITPs) provided by the NNS. If you do not already have them, these can be downloaded from the NNS website at:
http://www.standards.dfes.gov.uk/primary/mathematics

How to use the CD-ROM

System requirements

Minimum specification:
- PC with a CD-ROM drive and at least 32 MB RAM
- Pentium 166 MHz processor
- Microsoft Windows 98, NT, 2000 or XP
- SVGA screen display with at least 64K colours at a screen resolution of 800 x 600 pixels

100 Maths Lessons **CD-ROMs are for PC use only.**

Setting up your computer for optimal use

On opening, the CD will alert you if changes are needed in order to operate the CD at its optimal use. There are two changes you may be advised to make:

Viewing resources at their maximum screen size

To see images at their maximum screen size, your screen display needs to be set to 800 x 600 pixels. In order to adjust your screen size you will first need to **Quit** the program.

If using a PC, select **Settings**, then **Control Panel** from the **Start** menu. Next, double click on the **Display** icon and then click on the **Settings** tab. Finally, adjust the **Screen area** scroll bar to 800 x 600 pixels. Click **OK** and then restart the program.

Adobe® Acrobat® Reader®

Acrobat® Reader® is required to view Portable Document Format (PDF) files. All of the unit resources are PDF files. It is not necessary to install Acrobat Reader on your PC. If you do not have it installed, the application will use a 'run-time' version for the CD, i.e. one which only works with the 100 Maths Lessons application.

However if you would like to install **Acrobat® Reader®**, version 6 can be downloaded from the CD-ROM. To do this, right-click on the **Start** menu on your desktop and choose **Explore**. Click on the + sign to the left of the CD drive entitled '100 Maths Lessons' and open the folder called **Acrobat Reader Installer.** Run the program contained in this folder to install **Acrobat® Reader®.**
If you experience any difficulties viewing the PDF files, try changing your **Acrobat® Reader®** preferences. Select **Edit**, then **Preferences**, within **Acrobat® Reader®**. You will then be able to change your viewing options. For further information about **Adobe® Acrobat® Reader®**, visit the **Adobe®** website at www.adobe.com.

Getting started

The *100 Maths Lessons CD-ROM* program should auto run when you insert the CD-ROM into your CD drive. If it does not, use **My Computer** to browse the contents of the CD-ROM and click on the '100 Maths Lessons' icon.

From the start up screen there are three options: Click on **Credits** to view a list of acknowledgements. You must then read the **Terms and conditions**. If you agree to these terms then click **Next** to continue. **Continue** on the start up screen allows you to move to the Main menu.

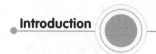

Main menu

Each *100 Maths Lessons* CD contains:
- core activity sheets – with answers, where appropriate, that can be toggled by pressing the 'on' and 'off' buttons on the left of the screen
- differentiated activity sheets for more and less able pupils (though not necessarily both more and less able sheets in every instance)
- blank core activity sheets for selected core activity sheets – these allow you to make your own differentiated sheets by printing and annotating.
- general resource sheets designed to support a number of activities.

You can access the printable pages on the CD by clicking:
- the chosen term ('Autumn','Spring' or 'Summer')
- the unit required (for example,'Unit 2: Addition and subtraction)
- the requisite activity page (for example,'Numbers to 10';'Less able').

To help you manage the vast bank of printable pages on each CD, there is also a 'Practical assessment record sheet' provided on the CD that you can use to record which children have tackled which pages. This could be particularly useful if you would like less able children to work through two or three of the differentiated pages for a lesson or topic.

CD navigation

Back: click to return to the previous screen. Continue to move to the **Menu** or start up screens.
Quit: click **Quit** to close the menu program. You are then provided with options to return to the start up menu or to exit the CD.
Help: provides general background information and basic technical support. Click on the **Help** button to access. Click **Back** to return to the previous screen.
Alternative levels: after you have accessed a CD page, you will see a small menu screen on the left-hand side of the screen. This allows you to access differentiated or template versions of the same activity.

Printing

There are two print options:
- The **Print** button on the bottom left of each activity screen allows you to print directly from the CD program.
- If you press the **View** button above the **Print** option, the sheet will open as a read-only page in **Acrobat® Reader®**. To print the selected resource from **Acrobat® Reader®**, select **File** and then **Print**. Once you have printed the resource, minimise or close the **Adobe®** screen using _ or **x** in the top right-hand corner of the screen.

Viewing on an interactive whiteboard or data projector

The sheets can be viewed directly from the CD. To make viewing easier for a whole class, use a large monitor, data projector or interactive whiteboard.

About Year 4

In Year 4 the children develop their use of pencil and paper procedures for addition and subtraction. While these methods are taught and practised, the emphasis must be upon a suitable method for the numbers involved, so that mental, mental with jottings, and paper and pencil procedures are used appropriately. Pencil and paper procedures are introduced for multiplication and division. Children are encouraged to make the links between fractions and decimals, and simple proportion. By the end of the year, children are expected to know the 2-, 3-, 4-, 5- and 10-times tables, and to use this knowledge, for example, when using intervals labelled in 2s, 5s or 10s when compiling bar charts.

EVERY DAY: Practise and develop oral and mental skills (for example, counting, mental strategies, rapid recall of × and ÷ facts)

- Read and write whole numbers to at least 10 000 in figures and words, and know what each digit represents.
- Add/subtract 1, 10 or 100 to/from any integer.
- Count on or back in tens or hundreds from any whole number up to 10 000.
- Consolidate knowing by heart addition and subtraction facts for all numbers to 20.
- Derive quickly doubles of all whole numbers to 50, and the corresponding halves.
- Add 3 or 4 small numbers, finding pairs totalling 10, or 9 or 11.
- **Use known number facts and place value to add or subtract mentally, including any pair of two-digit whole numbers, crossing the 10 (but not the 100) boundary.**
- **Know by heart multiplication facts for 2-, 3-, 4-, 5- and 10-times tables.**
- **Derive quickly division facts corresponding to 2-, 3-, 4-, 5- and 10-times tables.**
- Multiply any integer up to 1000 by 10 and understand the effect.
- **Round any positive integer less than 1000 to the nearest 10 or 100.**

Units	Days	Topics	Objectives
1	3	Place value, ordering and rounding (whole numbers)	Read and write whole numbers to 10 000 in figures and words, and know what each digit represents. Partition numbers into thousands, hundreds, tens and ones. Read and write the vocabulary of estimation and approximation. Make and justify estimates up to about 250 and estimate a proportion.
		Measures	Record estimates and readings from scales to a suitable degree of accuracy.
2–3	10	Understanding addition and subtraction	Consolidate understanding of relationship between addition and subtraction. Understand the principles (not the names) of the commutative and associative laws as they apply (or not) to addition and subtraction.
		Mental calculation strategies (+ and −)	Count on or back in repeated steps of 1, 10, 100. Identify near doubles, using known doubles. Add 3 or 4 small numbers, finding pairs totalling 10, or 9 or 11.
		Pencil and paper procedures (+ and −)	Use informal pencil and paper methods to support, record or explain additions and subtractions. **Develop and refine written methods of column addition of two whole numbers less than 1000.**
		Problems involving 'real life' and money	Use all four operations to solve word problems involving numbers in 'real life' and money, using one or more steps.
		Making decisions and checking results	**Choose and use appropriate number operations and appropriate ways of calculating (mental, mental with jottings, pencil and paper) to solve problems.** Check with the inverse operation.
		Solving problems	Use addition and subtraction to solve word problems involving numbers in money.
4–6	13	Measures	Use, read and write standard metric units (km, m, cm), including their abbreviations, and imperial units (mile). **Know and use the relationships between familiar units of length.** Convert up to 1000 centimetres to metres, and vice versa. Suggest suitable units and measuring equipment to estimate or measure length. Measure and calculate the perimeter of rectangles and other simple shapes. Record estimates and readings from scales to a suitable degree of accuracy.
		Making decisions	**Choose and use appropriate number operations and appropriate ways of calculating (mental, mental with jottings, pencil and paper) to solve problems.**
		Solving problems	Use all four number operations to solve word problems involving measures.
		Shape and space	Describe and visualise 2-D shapes, including the heptagon. Recognise equilateral and isosceles triangles. **Classify polygons using criteria such as number of right angles, whether or not they are regular, symmetry properties.** Recognise positions and directions: for example, describe and find the position of a point on a grid of squares where the lines are numbered. Make and investigate a general statement about familiar shapes by finding examples that satisfy it.
		Reasoning about numbers	Explain methods and reasoning about numbers orally and in writing.
7	2	Assess and review	

EVERY DAY: Practise and develop oral and mental skills (for example counting, mental strategies, rapid recall of + and – facts)

- Read and write whole numbers up to at least 10 000 in figures and words, and know what each digit represents.
- Count on or back in tens, hundreds or thousands from any whole number up to 10 000.
- **Round any positive integer less than 1000 to the nearest 10 or 100.**
- Consolidate knowing by heart addition and subtraction facts for all numbers to 20.
- **Use known number facts and place value to add or subtract mentally, including any pair of two-digit whole numbers, crossing the 10 (but not the 100) boundary.**
- Know by heart multiplication facts for 2-, 3-, 4-, 5- and 10-times tables.
- Derive quickly division facts corresponding to 2-, 3-, 4-, 5- and 10-times tables.
- Derive quickly doubles of all whole numbers to 50, and the corresponding halves.
- Use known number facts and place value to multiply integers by 10.

Units	Days	Topics	Objectives
8	5	Properties of numbers and number sequences	Recognise and extend number sequences formed by counting from any number in steps of constant size, extending beyond zero when counting back: for example, count on in steps of 25 to 500, and then back to, say, –100. Recognise odd and even numbers up to 1000, and some of their properties, including the outcome of sums or differences of pairs of odd/even numbers.
		Reasoning about numbers	Solve mathematical problems or puzzles, recognise and explain patterns and relationships, generalise and predict. Suggest extensions by asking 'What if...?' Make and investigate a general statement about familiar numbers by finding examples that satisfy it.
9–10	10	Understanding × and ÷	Extend understanding of × and ÷ and their relationship to each other and to + and –.
		Mental calculation strategies (× and ÷)	Use doubling and halving, starting from known facts. For example: to multiply by 4, double, then double again; to multiply by 5, multiply by 10 then halve; to multiply by 20, multiply by 10 then double; find the 8-times table facts by doubling the 4-times table.
		Pencil and paper procedures (× and ÷)	Approximate first. Use informal pencil and paper methods to support, record or explain multiplications and divisions. Develop and refine written methods for TU × U, TU ÷ U.
		Problems involving 'real life', money and measures	Use all four operations to solve word problems involving numbers in 'real-life', money and measures, using one or more steps, including converting pounds to pence, and metres to centimetres and vice versa.
		Making decisions	**Choose and use appropriate number operations and appropriate ways of calculating (mental, mental with jottings, pencil and paper) to solve problems.**
		Checking results	Check with an equivalent calculation.
11	5	Fractions and decimals	Use fraction notation. Recognise simple fractions that are several parts of a whole, such as 2/3 or 5/8, and mixed numbers, such as 53/4; recognise the equivalence of simple fractions (for example, fractions equivalent to 1/2, 1/4 or 3/4). Begin to relate fractions to division and find simple fractions such as 1/2, 1/3, 1/4, 1/5, 1/10 of numbers or quantities. Find fractions such as 2/3, 3/4, 3/5, 7/10… of shapes.
12	5	Understanding + and –	Consolidate understanding of relationship between + and –.
		Mental calculation strategies (+ and –)	Find a small difference by counting up (for example, 5003 – 4996). Continue to use the relationship between addition and subtraction.
		Pencil and paper procedures (+ and –)	**Develop and refine written methods for column subtraction of two whole numbers less than 1000.**
		Measures	Use, read and write the vocabulary related to time. Read the time from an analogue clock to the nearest minute, and from a 12-hour digital clock. Use am and pm and the notation 9:53.
		Problems involving 'real-life', money and measures	Use all four operations to solve word problems involving time, using one or more steps.
13	5	Handling data	Solve a problem by collecting quickly, organising, representing and interpreting data in tables, charts, graphs and diagrams, including those generated by a computer, for example: tally charts and frequency tables; pictograms – symbol representing 2, 5, 10 or 20 units; bar charts – intervals labelled in 2s, 5s, 10s or 20s.
14	2	Assess and review	

Reading, writing and estimating numbers

In this first unit, children consolidate work on reading and writing whole numbers in figures and in words and extend it to include numbers up to 10 000. They also further develop their estimation skills, estimating the number of words on a page and the number of pages in a book and estimating proportions.

LEARNING OBJECTIVES

		Topics	Starter	Main teaching activities
Lesson	1	Place value, ordering and rounding (whole numbers)	● Read whole numbers to at least 10 000.	● Read and write whole numbers to at least 10 000 in figures and words, and know what each digit represents. ● Partition numbers into thousands, hundreds, tens and ones.
Lesson	2	Place value, ordering and rounding (whole numbers)	● Write whole numbers to at least 10 000.	● Read and write the vocabulary of estimation and approximation. Make and justify estimates up to about 250, and estimate a proportion.
Lesson	3	Measures	● Read and write whole numbers to at least 10 000.	● Record estimates and readings from scales to a suitable degree of accuracy.

Lessons overview

Preparation
Use food colouring to colour the water used for the main teaching activity in Lesson 3.

Learning objectives
Starter
● Read and write whole numbers to at least 10 000.
Main teaching activities
● Read and write whole numbers to at least 10 000 in figures and words, and know what each digit represents.
● Partition numbers into thousands, hundreds, tens and ones.
● Read and write the vocabulary of estimation and approximation. Make and justify estimates up to about 250, and estimate a proportion.
● Record estimates and readings from scales to a suitable degree of accuracy.

Vocabulary
thousands, ten thousand, hundred thousand, million, numeral, guess, estimate, approximate, round

You will need:
Photocopiable pages
'A bigger place?' (page 11) for each child.

CD pages
'Numeral cards 0–20' (see General resources); 'A bigger place?'; 'Partition party' and 'Dots before your eyes' core, less able and more able versions.

Equipment
OHP calculator; OHP; individual whiteboards and pens; reading books; measuring cylinders; jugs; beakers marked in ml and litres; tall, thin litre cylinder marked in ml; water; dial scales; Plasticine; food colouring.

Lesson

Starter

Give the children copies of activity sheet 'A bigger place'. Explain that you will draw three numeral cards at random from a 0–9 pack, and after each card is drawn the children should write that digit in either the H, T or U section of the first box on their worksheets. Their aim is to make the highest possible three-digit number. Repeat this several times.

Main teaching activities

Whole class: Using the OHP calculator, ask a child to enter a number up to 1000. Ask the rest of the class to read out the number. Point to each of the digits and ask its value. Partition the number on the OHP/board: for example, '346 = 300 + 40 + 6'. Now introduce the thousands place. Write 1352 on the board with the word 'thousand' and ask the children to say the value of each digit. Repeat this for numbers up to 5000. When the children are confident with numbers up to 9999, introduce the ten thousands place and write the number 10 000 on the board.

Individual work: Give the children copies of activity sheet 'Partition party'. Explain that they have to partition the remaining nine numbers in a similar way to the example given.

Differentiation

Less able: Use the version of the activity sheet that has smaller numbers to partition.
More able: Use the version of the activity sheet that has larger numbers to partition.

Plenary & assessment

Tell the children that you are thinking of a four-digit number, and the sum of the digits (ignoring their place value) is 22. *What possible number could it be?* (4639, for example.) Allow the children to work in pairs for about five minutes to find as many different answers as they can. Ask each pair to write one of their numbers on the board. Then ask the class questions such as: *What is the smallest number? What is the largest number? What number is closest to 1200?*

Assess which children can read the numbers without hesitation. Those who struggle will need further experience of reading and partitioning three- and then four-digit numbers.

Lesson

Starter

Say aloud a range of numbers below 10 000 for the children to write on their whiteboards or on paper. Ask them to hold up their work. They can write the numbers in digits, then go on to write them in digits and in words.

Main teaching activities

Whole class: Talk about what an estimate is, and how our 'guess' needs to be as close to the real answer as possible, if it is to be an 'estimate' and not a 'guess'.

Draw a number line on the board like this:

0 ——————————————————————— 200

Ask a child to come out and mark 100 on the line. Ask: *Why is it easy to find roughly where 100 goes?* (It's half 200, and you can see roughly where half is.) Rub out the 100 and ask another child to estimate where 130 should go. Do the class agree? Ask the child how he or she worked it out. Repeat this with other numbers less than 200, asking the children to justify their positioning.

Give each pair of children the same reading book. Tell them to open the book at random and working *individually* estimate the number of words on that page. Emphasise they should not count every word, but they might need to count a small number of the words, such as those on one line, to help them make an estimate. When they have finished, the pair can share their estimates. Encourage them to justify their estimates to each other and discuss their methods. Then ask the children to count the number of words on the page to see how close they were. Share ideas, and then let them choose another page and repeat the process, having refined their estimation skills. Ask: *Did anyone get really close with their estimate? What strategies did you use to make your estimate?*
Group work: Give the children copies of the activity sheet 'Dots before your eyes' and ask them to find a good strategy for estimating the number of dots on the page (there are 100 of them).

Differentiation

Less able: Repeat the book activity with a reading book that does not have too many words on each page. Use the version of the activity sheet that has only has 50 dots.
More able: Use the version of the activity sheet that has 200 dots. Counting them can be quite a challenge! Look for grouping strategies.

Plenary & assessment

Draw comparisons between the estimates the children have made. Ask questions such as:
- *What strategies did you use to make your estimate of the number of dots?*
- *Did anyone get really close with their estimate? How?*
- *Did you think of a better way to estimate the number of dots after you had counted them?*

Lesson

Repeat the Starter from Lesson 1, this time including four-digit numbers.
For the main teaching activity, pour some coloured water into a tall, thin measuring cylinder and ask: *How much water is there? Can you be exact?* Agree a measurement will be only a 'reasonable approximation'. Try other amounts of water, each time inviting a child to record 'how much' on the board, in ml. Repeat this with a piece of Plasticine on a dial scale.

For the main teaching activity ask the children to work in groups of four. Provide the groups with either a dial scale and some Plasticine, or capacity measuring vessels and water. Ask them to divide into pairs in their group. One pair puts water into the vessel (or Plasticine onto the scale), takes a reading and writes it down; the other pair takes a reading and then the pairs compare their measurements. Then the pairs swap tasks. Groups can swap equipment. Decide whether to work with the less able children as a group. Challenge the more able to record using fractions or decimals.

During the plenary, ask the children to decide the mass of some Plasticine on the scales: *Is this just over… under…? How much more Plasticine do you think we need to make the dial reach 1… 2… 3… kilograms?* Encourage the children to use the vocabulary of estimation and approximation, such as: *It is nearly… just over…*

Name		Date	

A bigger place?

**As your teacher calls out a number name,
write it in one of the three boxes.**

Try to make the largest number you can each time.

1.

2.

3.

4.

5.

6.

7.

8.

9.

10.

Addition and subtraction

Children are encouraged to use appropriate methods of calculation when adding or subtracting with the focus on mental methods or mental methods supported by jottings. They also consolidate their understanding of the relationship between addition and subtraction and the principles of the commutative and associative laws as they are asked to think of different ways to partition a range of additions.

LEARNING OBJECTIVES

	Topics	Starter	Main teaching activities
Lesson 1	Understanding addition and subtraction Checking results	● Add/subtract 1, 10, 100 to/from any whole integer.	● Consolidate understanding of relationship between + and −. ● Understand the principles (not the names) of the commutative and associative laws as they apply (or not) to addition and subtraction. ● Check with the inverse operation.
Lesson 2	Understanding addition and subtraction Problems involving 'real life', money	As for Lesson 1.	● Understand the principles (not the names) of the commutative and associative laws as they apply (or not) to addition and subtraction. ● Use all four operations to solve word problems involving numbers in 'real life', and money, using one or more steps.
Lesson 3	Mental calculation strategies (+ and −)	● Count on or back in repeated steps of 1, 10 or 100.	● Count on or back in repeated steps of 1, 10 or 100. ● Identify near doubles, using known doubles.
Lesson 4	Making decisions	● Consolidate knowing by heart addition and subtraction facts for all numbers up to 20.	**● Choose and use appropriate number operations and appropriate ways of calculating (mental, mental with jottings, pencil and paper) to solve problems.**
Lesson 5	Making decisions	As for Lesson 4.	As for Lesson 4.

Lessons   overview

Preparation
For the Starter in Lessons 1 and 2, enlarge a copy of 'Numbers grid' to A3 size or make it into an OHT and display it where all the children can see it.

Learning objectives
Starter
● Add/subtract 1, 10, 100 to/from any whole integer.
Main teaching activities
● Consolidate understanding of relationship between + and −.
● Understand the principles (not the names) of the commutative and associative laws as they apply or not to addition and subtraction.
● Check with the inverse operation.
● Use all four operations to solve word problems involving numbers in 'real life', and money, using one or more steps.

Vocabulary
more, add, sum, total, altogether, increase, equals, sign, inverse

You will need:
Photocopiable pages
A copy of 'Let's get checking!' (page 17) and 'The sweet Sweet Shop' (page 18) for each child

CD pages
'Numbers grid' (see General resources); 'Let's get checking!', core, less able and more able versions; 'The sweet Sweet Shop!', core and template versions.

Lesson

Starter

Ask the children to add 1, 10 and 100 to each number you point to on the enlarged 'Numbers grid' and call out the three answers each time. Tell them that this is a time challenge, so they have to do it as quickly as they can, ask individual children to repeat some of the additions as a spot check on their understanding and involvement. You may prefer the least able to add only 1 or 10 to two-digit numbers.

Main teaching activities

Whole class: Write on the board '75 + 26 = ❑ '. Ask: *What is the answer?* (101) *What strategy did you use to work it out?* The children will use a range of strategies including counting on in 10s, or partitioning as (for example) 75 + 20 + 6 or 70 + 20 + 5 + 5 + 1. While there is no such thing as a 'best' method, partitioning the numbers mentally is good preparation for learning written methods that involve partitioning. Ask: *Does it matter which way round we add the numbers?* (No. This is the commutative aspect of addition, with which the children should be familiar from Year 3.) Then continue: *If we know that 75 add 26 equals 101, what else do we know?* (26 + 75 = 101 by commutation, and by using the inverse 101 – 75 = 26 and 101 – 26 = 75.) Write the four different number facts that relate to 75 + 26 on the board: 75 + 26, 26 + 75; 101 – 26; 101 – 75. Highlight that the order in which we do subtraction matters, but the order in which we do addition does not.

Write on the board '70 + 20 + 10 + 1 = ❑ '. Ask: *How would you solve this addition?* If the children have not solved it by adding two of the numbers together first, model this on the board: 70 + 20 or 10 + 20. Highlight that it doesn't matter how the numbers are paired (the associative aspect of addition), and that this can help with recombining numbers after partitioning them.

Individual work: Give the children copies of activity sheet 'Let's get checking!'. Explain that they can find the answers mentally or make jottings to help. They should then check their answers by subtraction and write down the check calculation they used in the 'check box'. When the children get to Question 7, encourage them to try to be systematic in finding the totals (example answers are given on the CD page).

Differentiation

Less able: Use the version of the activity sheet that has smaller (TU) numbers to add. Encourage the children to make as many jottings as they like.
More able: Use the version of the activity sheet that has larger numbers (HTU) and missing number questions.

Plenary & assessment

Discuss Question 7 from the activity sheets. Ask questions such as:
● *How many different solutions did you find?*
● *What strategy did you use to find the solutions?*
● *How can you be certain that you have found all the answers?*

Lesson

As a starter, ask the children to subtract 1, 10 and 100 from each of the numbers on the enlarged 'Numbers grid' as you point to them. Encourage the children to call out the three numbers as quickly as they can.

For the main teaching activity, write three two-digit numbers (less than 50) on the board. Ask the children what strategies they could use to add these numbers. Encourage them to recall efficient strategies, such as pairing numbers, adding all the tens first, and so on. Ask the children to work with a partner and add up the numbers. Now repeat this, using amounts of money such as 50p and 65p, then extend to pounds and pence, such as £1.87 + £2.28. Provide activity sheet 'The sweet Sweet Shop!' and ask the children to complete this individually. A blank version of the sheet is available for you to enter appropriate amounts of money to spend for the more and less able children.

In the plenary, ask the children to work out how much all of the sweets would cost. Ask: *How did you work that out?* Highlight efficient addition strategies. If necessary, show how to add the numbers by combining pairs, then re-combining these until the sweet prices have been totalled.

Lessons   overview

Preparation
Copy 'Double number cards' onto card, laminate them and cut them up. The blank cards are for you or the children to add larger or smaller numbers later.

Learning objectives
Starter
- Count on or back in repeated steps of 1, 10 or 100.
- Consolidate knowing by heart addition and subtraction facts for all numbers up to 20.

Main teaching activities
- Count on or back in repeated steps of 1, 10 or 100.
- Identify near doubles, using known doubles.
- **Choose and use appropriate number operations and appropriate ways of calculating**
   (mental, mental with jottings, pencil and paper) to solve problems.

Vocabulary
counting on, counting back, plus, subtract, doubles, near doubles, operation, sign, symbol, number sentence, equation

You will need:
Photocopiable pages
'In your head 1' and 'In your head 2' (pages 19 and 20) for each child.

CD pages
'Double number cards' (see General resources); 'Doubles I know', core version; 'In your head', core, less able and more able versions; 'Write a problem' core version.

Equipment
Whiteboards; markers; wipers.

Lesson

Starter
Give the children a start number (say, 25) and ask the children to count up in 10s. Choose one child to say 'STOP!' whenever he or she wants to. Once the shout has been given, the children have to count back in 10s to the original start number. Repeat this with other start numbers. Ask: *How could we solve 39 add 40 by counting like this?* Encourage the children to chant from 39: 49, 59, 69, 79. Give the children a range of similar questions about adding and subtracting 10s and 100s from 'near multiples' such as 51 or 28.

Main teaching activities
Whole class: Explain that you are going to look at a way of adding involving near doubles. Write on the board '39 + 40 = ☐ '. Ask: *How can we solve this? How could we use doubles to help us?*

Model this on the board, using a number line: 39 is one less than 40, double 40 is 80, so double 40 less 1 will be the same as 39 + 40. (See below.) Repeat this for other near doubles.

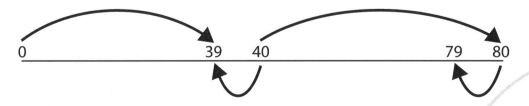

Group work: With the children working in pairs, give them each a set of cards made from 'Double number cards' and activity sheet 'Doubles I know'. Ask them to put the cards face down and choose two of them. They should try to add the numbers, using known doubles to help them. Emphasise that 'near doubles' might not be the best way for them to do the sums, and that if they think another method is more efficient they should use it.

Differentiation

Less able: Only give the children the two-digit number cards. It would be helpful to allow them to use number lines.

More able: Only let the children use the three-digit number cards. There are also two blank cards on which the children could write other three- or four-digit numbers to challenge themselves.

Plenary & assessment

Review the lesson by asking questions such as:

● *Who can tell me some sums to which they found the answers by using near doubles?*
● *Who can tell me some calculations where they used another method? What was that method? Why was it better?*
● *What was the hardest calculation?*
● *What was the easiest?*
● *What have you learned about using near doubles today?*

Lesson

As a starter, explain that you will write a number sentence on the board and would like the children to tell you the other three related facts. Begin with 13 + 7.

For the main teaching activity, write '434 + 175 = ☐ ' on the board and invite the children to work out the answer. Ask the children to suggest a number story or word problem for this number sentence. Repeat this for other addition and subtraction sentences that use two- or three-digit numbers. Provide copies of activity sheet 'In your head' for the children to work at individually. This is available in differentiated versions.

For the plenary, ask the children to read out their solutions and compare the way they did it with the others' methods. Ask questions such as:

● *Did anyone else do it this way?*
● *What is the most efficient way?*
● *Now that we have talked about it, can you think of another way to do it?*

Lesson

Starter

Repeat the Starter from Lesson 4, but this time ask the children to write all four number sentences onto their individual whiteboards. When you say: *Show me,* the children hold up their boards. Keep the pace of this sharp to encourage rapid recall.

Main teaching activities

Whole class/Paired work: Explain that you would like the children to work in pairs to think of a word problem that involves adding two numbers, such as: *Two children went collecting conkers. One child collected 45 conkers, the other 21. How many conkers did they collect altogether?* Ask the children to discuss in pairs what their problem is going to be, write it down, and find the answer in any way they like. Invite some children from each ability group to read out their problems for the others in the class to solve. Ask: *How did you work it out? Who used a different strategy? Which strategy do you think is best for this problem? Why do you think that?* Give each of the children a copy of activity

sheet 'Write a problem' each and ask them to choose the box on the sheet to write their problem in, depending on how they solved it.

Now ask them to take turns in their pairs to give each other a new problem. This is written onto the sheet in the appropriate box, and solved. Encourage the children to use larger numbers and, over the duration of the paired work, to move to including subtraction problems.

Differentiation

Less able: Make sure the children are grouped with others of similar ability. It would be appropriate to ask these children just to give you addition problems.

More able: Specify the size of the numbers you want the children to use (HTU or ThHTU, perhaps). Ask them for problems involving multiplication and division.

Plenary & assessment

Select children to read out some of their problems from 'Write a problem', and explain to the class how they were solved. After each problem, ask:

- *Would anyone else do it that way?*
- *Can anyone think of another way of solving this problem?*
- *Who thinks they have written the hardest problem?*

Look for children who perhaps relied on jottings or pencil and paper a little too much. Discuss together what mental strategies others might have used.

Name	Date

Let's get checking!

Find the answers to these sums.

You can work mentally or make jottings to help.

Check your answers by subtraction and show the calculation in the check box.

1. 86 + 38 =

Jottings box	**Check box**

2. 79 + 34 =

Jottings box	**Check box**

3. 27 + 96 =

Jottings box	**Check box**

4. 76 + 58 =

Jottings box	**Check box**

5. 87 + 99 =

Jottings box	**Check box**

6. Add together 56, 78 and 97. What is the total?

Jottings box	**Check box**

7. Find all the different totals you can by using three of these numbers. **Be sure to check your answers!**

97   183   56   212   107

Name	Date

The sweet Sweet Shop!

Choose four different sweets.

Write each price in the chart.

Total the sweets.

Write the change from £5.00

Repeat this four times, choosing different combinations of sweets each time.

Little lollies 45p

Chews 32p

Choco crisp 83p

Peppermints 91p

Toffees 98p

Rainbow licks 20p

Glow in the
dark drops 57p

Sparkle bars 75p

Fruity frogs 49p

Magic drops 85p

Sweet prices	Cost	Check	Change from £5.00

Name	Date

In your head 1

Answer these problems.

If you can do them in your head, just write the answer.

If necessary, show your workings in the box.

1. A house has 7 rooms in it, including 2 bathrooms.
   How many rooms would 5 houses have?
   How many would 15 houses have?

2. When you mix paint you need 4 spoonfuls of water to 2 spoonfuls of paint.
   How many spoonfuls of water would be required to mix
   12 spoonfuls of paint?

3. A sweet packet can hold 80 sweets.
   10 of the sweets are red, the rest are yellow.
   If you eat 18, how many are left?
   Out of those sweets that are left, what would be the most
   you could give each of 6 children?
   How many sweets would there be in 10 packets?

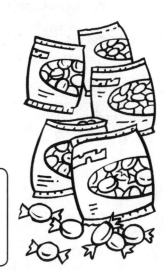

4. I am thinking of a number. When I subtract 15 from it, I get 34.
   What's my number?

Name	Date

In your head 2

Answer these problems.

If you can do them in your head, just write the answer.

If necessary, show your workings in the box.

1. I used to collect stamps and I had 120 of them.

    I gave one quarter away to my sister. How many have I left?

2. A minibus holds 17 passengers and one driver. It has 18 seat belts.

    How many people would be in 7 full minibuses?

    How many seats for two people would there be on the minibus?

    How many minibuses would be needed to hold 100 passengers?

3. Make up some number stories for these number sentences.

    You will have to work out the answers first!

    a) 546 + 112 =

    b) 87 − 23 =

    c) 80 × 5 =

    d) 69 ÷ 3 =

Understanding addition and subtraction

The children further develop work on addition and subtraction from the previous unit. They also review a written method of addition taught in Year 3, ie adding the most significant digits, extending this to adding three-digit and two-digit numbers.

LEARNING OBJECTIVES

	Topics	Starter	Main teaching activities
Lesson 1	Mental calculation strategies (+ and –)	● Derive quickly doubles of whole numbers to 50.	● Add 3 or 4 small numbers, finding pairs totalling 10, or 9 or 11.
Lesson 2	Mental calculation strategies (+ and –)	As for Lesson 1.	As for Lesson 1.
Lesson 3	Pencil and paper procedures (+ and –)	● Add 3 or 4 small numbers, finding pairs totalling 10, or 9 or 11.	● Use informal pencil and paper methods to support, record or explain + and –. ● **Develop and refine written methods for column addition of two whole numbers less than 1000.**
Lesson 4	Pencil and paper procedures (+ and –)	As for Lesson 3.	As for Lesson 3.
Lesson 5	Making decisions Solving problems Checking results	● Derive quickly doubles of whole numbers to 50 and the corresponding halves.	● **Choose and use appropriate number operations and appropriate ways of calculating (mental, mental with jottings, pencil and paper) to solve problems.** ● Use addition and subtraction to solve word problems involving numbers in money. ● Check with the inverse operation.

Lessons overview

Learning objectives
Starter
● Derive quickly doubles of all whole numbers to 50 and the corresponding halves.
Main teaching activities
● Add 3 or 4 small numbers finding pairs totalling 10, or 9 or 11.

Vocabulary
add, addition, more, plus, increase, sum, total, altogether

You will need:
Photocopiable pages
'Adding small numbers' (page 26) for each child.

CD pages
'Numeral cards 0–20' for each pair (see General resources); 'Adding small numbers', core, less able and more able versions.

Equipment
Individual whiteboard and pen for each child.

Lesson

Starter

Explain to the children that you will say a number that you would like them to double. Ask them to write the number onto their whiteboard and to hold that up when you say: *Show me.* Use numbers between 1 and 20 initially, then extend to 30… 40… 50. Say, for example: *What is double 5? How many sweets would there be in two packs of 25?* so that some of the questions include problems.

Main teaching activities

Whole class: Explain to the children that today they will be adding three or four small numbers. On the board write '2 + 3 + 8 + 5 = ❑' and ask: *How shall we begin?* Children may remember from Year 3 that it is helpful to make a 10 when possible, so that here they would combine the 2 and the 8. Rewrite the addition:'2 + 8 + 3 + 5 = 10 + 8 = 18'. Repeat this for another example, such as '6 + 14 + 9 + 7 = ❑'. Here children may say:'6 + 4 is 10, so 6 + 14 is 20. Then 9 + 7 is 16. And 20 + 16 is 36.'

Write up '7 + 12 + 9 + 4 = ❑'. Here children may notice that they can make 11 (7 + 4), 19 (7 + 12) or 21 (12 + 9). Complete the example both ways:'7 + 12 + 9 + 4 = 19 + 13 = 32'; and '12 + 9 + 7 + 4 = 21 + 11 = 32'. Discuss how another strategy can be to look for pairs that make 9, 11, 19, 21… and adjust by 1. Remind the children that yet another strategy (which they should have met in Year 3) is to begin with the largest number. Write up '13 + 4 + 8 + 9 = ❑'. Children may suggest combining 13 and 8 (21) then 9 and 4 (13) to total 34.

Explain that all three of these strategies are useful and that the children should look carefully at the small numbers to be combined to decide which one would be the most appropriate. Write the three strategies onto the board to remind the children:

- **Look for pairs that make 10 or 100 and do those first.**
- **Begin with the largest number.**
- **Look for pairs that make 9 or 11 and adjust by 1.**

Group work: Ask the children to work in pairs. Each pair will need a set of 0 to 20 numeral cards. Ask the children to sort out the cards for 1 to 12 and to work with these. They take turns to take the top four cards from the shuffled pack. Then they decide how to total the numbers. They write an addition sentence, and the total.

Differentiation

Less able: The children can work in pairs with the 1 to 9 cards, taking three cards each time to total.
More able: The children can use all the cards from 1 to 19, taking four each time.

Plenary & assessment

Ask children from each ability group, in turn, to write one of their addition sentences onto the board. Invite the other children to work mentally to find the total. Ask the child doing the demonstration: *How did you work this out?* and then open the debate up to the whole class: *Who used a different method?* Repeat this until at least two number sentences from each ability group have been checked by the whole class.

Lesson

Repeat the Starter from Lesson 1, this time including halves, such as: *What is half of 50? Half of 30? Half of 26?*

For the main teaching activity, review addition of small numbers from Lesson 1. Write an example on the board such as '3 + 8 + 9 + 2 = ?' and ask the children to work mentally to discover the total. Ask: *How did you work this out?* Remind the children of the three strategies they considered in the previous lesson. Provide copies of activity sheet 'Adding small numbers' and ask the children to work independently, making sure they understand what to do. They should work mentally to total the numbers and write the sum to show which strategy they decided to use. The sheet is available in differentiated form for the less and more able.

For the plenary, review the version of 'Adding small numbers' that most of the class were using and invite all the children to decide how to work out each question. Encourage the children to explain why they chose a particular strategy and assess their ability to choose an effective and efficient one.

Lessons   overview

Preparation
Numeral cards made from CD page 'Numeral cards 0–20'.

Learning objectives
Starter
● Add three or four small numbers finding pairs totalling 10, or 9 or 11.
Main teaching activities
● Use informal pencil and paper methods to support, record or explain additions and subtractions.
● **Develop and refine written methods for column addition of two whole numbers less than 1000.**

Vocabulary
add, addition, more, plus, increase sum, total, altogether, subtract, equals, sign, inverse

You will need:
Photocopiable pages
'Vertical addition' (page 27) for each child.

CD pages
'Numeral cards 0–20' (see General resources); 'Vertical addition', core, less able and more able versions; a copy of 'Missing numbers' for the teacher/LSA.

Equipment
Individual whiteboard and pen for each child.

Lesson

Starter
Explain that you will say, slowly, three or four numbers that you would like the children to add together mentally. When you say: *Show me*, ask the children to use their whiteboards to show the answer. Say, for example: *3 + 7 + 4 + 6* (20), *9 + 2 + 5 + 1* (17), and so on. Ask questions such as: *What strategy did you use? Who made a 10? Who used a rolling total?*

Main teaching activities
Whole class: Remind the children of the informal written strategy that they learned in Year 3. Write on the board '45 + 68 = ☐' and ask: *How can we solve this?* Invite a child to show how to solve it. For example, they might write: 40 + 60 + 5 + 8 = 100 + 13 = 113. Now rewrite the same addition sentence, this time presenting it vertically like this:

```
  45
+ 68
```

Explain that this is another way of writing what they have just done, and that they should again start with the most significant figures – that is, the tens:

```
   45
+  68
  100
+  13
  113
```

Discuss how the tens digits are lined up underneath each other, and similarly the units digits.

Work through another example, such as 58 + 74. Again, ask a child to do this horizontally, then repeat this working vertically. When the children are confident with this, introduce a third example, this time adding a three-digit number to a two-digit number, such as 615 + 59.

Individual work: Give the children copies of activity sheet 'Vertical addition' and ask them to work through the questions, changing the format of each and finding the total. Check that they record the question properly by lining the digits up underneath each other. This is a very important skill that children need to learn to do for themselves.

Differentiation

Less able: Give the children the version of the activity sheet that has two-digit numbers to add. Ask the children to try mental methods or jottings first, then to write the same addition sentences in vertical form.

More able: Give the children the version of the activity sheet that has addition sentences that are all of the three-digit add two-digit number variety. Encourage them to complete these as quickly as they can.

Plenary & assessment

Write on the board '257 + 63 = ☐' and invite the children to think about how they would work this out using the vertical method. Invite a child to come to the board and to write up the first line of 200, then another to total the tens, and so on. Encourage the children to work mentally. As you work through this number sentence with the children, ask:

● *How many hundreds are there? How can you tell that?*
● *How many tens? How do you know that?*
● *What about the units? What is 7 + 3? So, what is the total?*

Repeat this for another example, such as 165 + 79.

Lesson ④

Starter

Repeat the Starter from Lesson 3, this time writing the additions on the board, leaving out one of the numbers, and writing the total, like this: '1 + 9 + ☐ + 6 = 23'. Ask the children to work out the missing number. Repeat for other examples such as '2 + 4 + 7 + ☐ = 22'.

'Missing numbers' is a handy sheet of examples for teacher use. Ask questions such as: *How did you work this out? Who used a different way?*

Main teaching activities

Whole class: Remind the children how they solved addition problems yesterday by writing the sums vertically. Work through an example with the children, such as 156 + 85. If necessary, provide another example for the children to do, to check that they are confident with this method.

Group work: The children can work in pairs with two sets of set of 0–9 numeral cards from CD page 'Numeral cards 0–20'. Ask them to shuffle the numeral cards and then to take the top five cards from the stack. They turn the cards over and decide how to arrange the cards to make a three- and a two-digit number. They take turns, one writing an addition sentence in horizontal form and calculating the answer, while the other child works in vertical form. They compare answers to check their working. Ask the children to complete ten addition sentences in this way.

Differentiation

Less able: Ask the children to draw just four cards each time, to make two two-digit numbers. They both work in horizontal form, then in vertical form, and check their answers.

More able: Ask the children to complete five additions of a two- and a three-digit number, then five addition sentences of two three-digit numbers in the same way.

Plenary & assessment

Invite children from each group to write one of their addition sentences onto the board. Challenge the other children to complete these as quickly as possible, in vertical form. Invite a child to write in the workings and answers when everyone has finished the first question. Ask questions such as: *What do you do first? How many hundreds/tens/units are there? How do you know that?*

Lesson overview

Learning objectives
Starter
● Derive quickly doubles of whole numbers to 50 and the corresponding halves.
Main teaching activities
● **Choose and use appropriate number operations and appropriate ways of calculating (mental, mental with jottings, pencil and paper) to solve problems.**
● Use addition and subtraction to solve word problems involving numbers in money.
● Check with the inverse operation.

You will need:
CD pages
'At the fair', core, less able and more able versions.

Lesson

Starter

Divide the class into two groups. One group has to double, the other group has to halve. Point to the first group and say the number 14; the group has to shout out the double (28). Point to the second group and say the number 24; the group has to shout out the half (12). Repeat this for other numbers up to 50.

Main teaching activities

Whole class: The children will find it useful to have paper and pencils handy to make jottings as they work. Explain to the children that today they will be solving problems involving money. Begin by saying: *Comics cost 45p each. James has £2. How many comics can he buy? How much money will he have left?* Invite the children to explain how they solved the problem. Some may have doubled 45, then doubled again. Others may have repeatedly subtracted 45 from 200. Now ask: *What is the total cost of a £3.70 book and a £5.20 game?* When the children have explained how they arrived at the answer of £8.90, ask: *How could we check that our answer is correct?* Encourage the children to check by using an inverse procedure, such as £8.90 – £3.70. Remind the children that if it helps, they can partition the amounts of money into pounds and pence, and then find the total.

Group work: Ask the children to work in pairs to complete the money word problem on activity sheet 'At the fair'. This covers totalling and finding change from £10. Both children should work out a solution, then use inverse operations to check their results.

Differentiation

Less able: Use the version of the activity sheet that covers totalling and finding change from £5. Work with this group and solve the problems together, discussing the strategies used.
More able: Use the version of the activity sheet that covers totalling and finding change from £20.

Plenary & assessment

Use the activity sheet that most of the class worked on and discuss with the children how they solved the problems. Ask questions such as: *What is the important information in this problem? What is not important in this problem? What method did you use to calculate the answer? How did you check your answer?*

Name	Date

Adding small numbers

1   4   5   7   8   9   11   12   14   15

Choose four of the above numbers to add each time.

Decide how you will add them.

Write the sum into the box for the strategy you will use.

Write the answer.

Repeat this until there are four addition sentences in each box.

Look for pairs that make 10 and do this first.	Start with the largest number.	Look for pairs that make 9 or 11; total by adding 10 and adjusting by 1.

Name	Date

Vertical addition

Write these additions vertically.

Write the answers.

1. 76 + 67 =

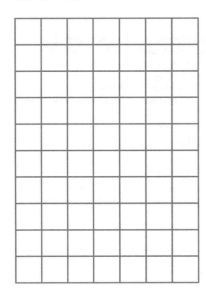

2. 72 + 39 =

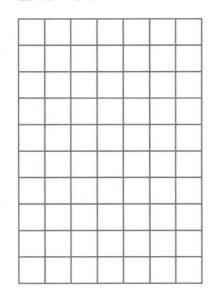

3. 68 + 89 =

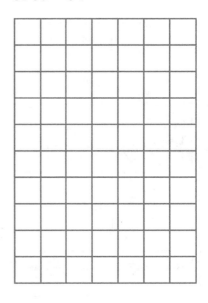

4. 162 + 79 =

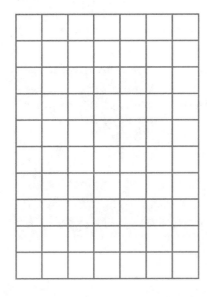

5. 291 + 58 =

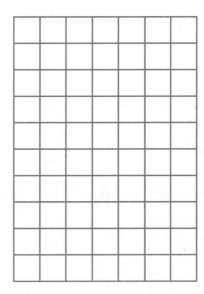

6. 369 + 82 =

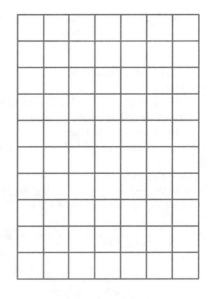

Shape and space

Children are challenged to visualise polygons and describe them using a range of mathematical vocabulary. They go on to classify them in a variety of ways and to investigate general statements about different shapes.

LEARNING OBJECTIVES

	Topics	Starter	Main teaching activities
Lesson **1**	Shape and space	● **Use known number facts and place value to add or subtract mentally, including any pair of two-digit whole numbers**.	● Describe and visualise 2-D shapes, including the heptagon.
Lesson **2**	Shape and space	As for Lesson 1.	● **Classify polygons using criteria such as number of right angles, whether or not they are regular, symmetry properties.** ● Recognise equilateral and isosceles triangles. ● Make and investigate a general statement about familiar shapes by finding examples that satisfy it.
Lesson **3**	Shape and space	As for Lesson 1.	As for Lesson 2.
Lesson **4**	Shape and space	● **Know by heart multiplication facts for 2-, 3-, 4-, 5- and 10-times tables.** ● **Derive quickly division facts corresponding to 2-, 3-, 4-, 5-, and 10-times tables.**	● Make and investigate a general statement about familiar shapes by finding examples that satisfy it.
Lesson **5**	Shape and space	As for Lesson 4.	As for Lesson 4.

Lesson overview

Learning objectives
Starter
● **Use known number facts and place value to add or subtract mentally, including any pair of two-digit whole numbers**.
Main teaching activities
● Describe and visualise 2-D shapes, including the heptagon.

Vocabulary
triangle, quadrilateral, rectangle, oblong, square, pentagon, hexagon, heptagon, octagon, polygon, right angle, vertex, cube

You will need:
Equipment
Individual whiteboard and pen for each child.

Lesson

Starter

Ask the children 'quickfire' questions such as: *23 + 46* (69); *62 + 13* (75); *56 + 12* (68); *45 + 21* (66); *12 + 32* (44); *89 – 71* (18); *57 – 23* (34); *38 – 17* (21); *67 – 43* (24); *87 – 56* (31). The children can respond with their whiteboards. Ask: *How did you work that out? Who used a different strategy?* Refer back to the ideas explored in Units 2 and 3.

Main teaching activities

Whole class: On the board, draw a regular shape with seven sides and write 'heptagon' alongside it. Explain to the children that any seven-sided 2-D shape is called a heptagon. Invite the children to use their whiteboards and draw a heptagon. When you say: *Show me*, they hold up their boards for you to see. Now write the words 'polygon' and 'oblong' on the board and explain that a polygon is any closed and flat shape with three or more sides, and an oblong is another name that is sometimes used for a rectangle. Ask the children each to draw any polygon on their board, and to write its mathematical name underneath it, then hold up their boards when you say: *Show me* again. Now say: *I will describe a shape. If that shape is on your board, hold it up.* Take into account the shapes that the children have drawn and describe some of them. For example: *Hold up your board if you have drawn a shape with more than four sides; a shape that has four right angles…*

Group work: Ask the children to work in groups of four. They take turns to give instructions to the others in their group for a shape for them to draw on their whiteboard. Encourage the children to say more than the name of the shape, instead describing the properties of the shape.

Differentiation

Less able: Work with this group. Begin by giving descriptions for the children to draw. As they become more confident, the children can take turns to describe a shape.

More able: When the children have tried this activity a few times in their groups, suggest that they write some descriptions for the others to try during the plenary.

Plenary & assessment

Invite some of the more able children to read out their descriptions for the others to draw. The children can hold up their boards to show you their responses. Ask questions such as:
- *What shape do you think was described?*
- *What other shapes could fit that description?*

Lessons   overview

Preparation

Prepare an OHT from CD page '2-D shapes – polygons'.

Learning objectives

Starter
- **Use known number facts and place value to add or subtract mentally, including any pair of two-digit whole numbers.**

Main teaching activities
- **Classify polygons using criteria such as number of right angles, whether or not they are regular, symmetry properties.**
- Recognise equilateral and isosceles triangles.
- Make and investigate a general statement about familiar shapes by finding examples that satisfy it.

Vocabulary

equilateral triangle, isosceles triangle, quadrilateral, rectangle, oblong, square, pentagon, hexagon, heptagon, octagon, polygon, right angle

You will need:

Photocopiable pages
'Carroll diagrams' (page 32) for each child.

CD pages
At least one copy of 'Carroll diagrams' for each child and one set of 2-D shapes from '2-D shapes – polygons' (see General resources).

Equipment
Individual whiteboard and pen for each child.

Lesson ②

Starter
Repeat the Starter from Lesson 1. Encourage the children to compare their mental methods in groups of four, so that they hear various ways of calculating mentally.

Main teaching activities
Whole class: Put up the OHT produced from '2-D shapes – polygons' and ask the children to look carefully and name each of the shapes. Now discuss the fact that some of the shapes are regular (that is, all of their sides are the same length) and some are irregular. Invite the children to decide which of the shapes on the OHT are regular and which are irregular. Now point to the equilateral triangle, name it and explain that all the sides are equal and all the angles are the same size. Then point to the isosceles triangle and ask the children to decide what is special about this triangle. (Two sides the same length, and the two angles formed by those sides and the base are the same.)

Tell the children that they are going to sort the shapes according to certain criteria. Ask the children to suggest some criteria to you and then write them on the board (number of sides; number of angles; regular/irregular; number of lines of symmetry; number of right angles). Ensure the criteria are mathematical and based on properties of shape. Spend some time with the class defining what we mean by each criterion.

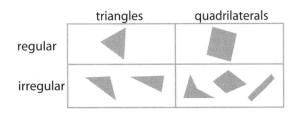

Now draw a Carroll diagram on the board. Explain to the children that they can use a diagram like this to sort their shapes.
Group work: Explain that the activity for this lesson and the next is to sort all the shapes on '2-D shapes – polygons' by any criteria they like from the list on the board. After each sort they draw the shapes onto their copies of activity sheet 'Carroll diagrams' and label the diagrams appropriately.

Differentiation
Less able: Adapt the activity by suggesting that the children begin with the criteria of 'triangles' and 'not triangles'; 'regular' and 'irregular'. When the children are confident with this, suggest that they use their own criteria.
More able: Encourage the more able children to cover as many different sorting criteria as possible in the time available.

Plenary & assessment
Ask the children to explain their shape sorts. Ensure that children are using correct mathematical vocabulary for the names of the shapes and their properties. Ask questions such as:
● *How many sides has a pentagon… hexagon… heptagon…?*
● *What is a quadrilateral?*
● *Tell me some regular polygons.*
● *Is an isosceles triangle a regular or an irregular polygon? Why is that?*

Lesson ③

Repeat the Starter from Lesson 1, this time encouraging the children to explain to their partner how they find the answer. This will give the children ideas about other strategies that they might use.

For the main teaching activity, review the names and properties of the shapes from activity sheet '2-D shapes – polygons', then ask the children to continue with the sorting activity from Lesson 2. Towards the end of the work time, prepare to talk about favourite sorts of polygons.

During the plenary, ask children from each group to describe their favourite sort. Then invite the children to describe shapes by asking questions such as: *What is a polygon? What is a vertex?* (A corner.) *Tell me a polygon with 3… 4… vertices.*

Lessons overview

Learning objectives

Starter
- **Know by heart multiplication facts for 2-, 3-, 4-, 5- and 10-times tables.**
- **Derive quickly division facts corresponding to 2-, 3-, 4-, 5-, and 10-times tables.**

Main teaching activities
- Make and investigate a general statement about familiar shapes by finding examples that satisfy it.

You will need:

Equipment
Individual whiteboards and pens.

Lesson

Starter
Ask the children to write the answers to some table fact questions on their whiteboards, and to show you. Ask, for example: *What is 3 × 5; 10 × 4; 35 ÷ 5; 8 × 2; 90 ÷ 10?* Include some word problems such as: *If I share 36 sweets among nine children, how many will they have each?*

Main teaching activities
Whole class: Explain to the children that you will describe a shape. Ask them to shut their eyes, listen carefully to the description and then, when they know what the shape is, put their hands up. Say, for example: *I am thinking of a flat shape. It has seven sides.* (A heptagon.) Or: *I am thinking of a shape with four sides. The sides are not all the same length. The angles are not all right angles.* (An irregular quadrilateral.) Repeat this for other shapes.
Paired work: Ask the children, working in pairs to take turns to make a statement about a shape for their partner to draw.

Differentiation
Less able: Suggest to the children that they begin with easier shapes to describe, such as squares, rectangles or triangles.
More able: Encourage the children to think of more complex shapes and to describe these.

Plenary & assessment
Invite a child from each group, in turn, to describe a shape for the others to draw. Ask questions:
- *What shape is it?*
- *What sentence told you which shape it was?*

Now draw a concave quadrilateral (such as an arrowhead) on the board. Invite the children to take turns to describe this shape. Then ask: *Who can say a sentence that will describe all quadrilaterals?*

Lesson

Repeat the Starter from Lesson 4, asking different table fact questions.

During the main teaching activity, describe a quadrilateral by saying: *It has four sides, but none of the sides are the same length. What could this shape be?* Encourage children to draw what they think the shape is and to name it. During the group activity, ask the children to work in pairs and to think of some statements they could make about a 2-D shape. You may want to put the children into groups for this, with particular shapes from activity sheet '2-D shapes' assigned to a group.

During the plenary, ask children to take turns to read out their descriptions. The other children draw and write the name of the shape they think is being described on their whiteboards. They hold their whiteboards up for checking. Ask: *Was that a good description of a…? Why was that? How could we make the description even better?*

Name	Date

Carroll diagrams

Decide how you will sort the shapes.

Draw your sorting onto a Carroll diagram. Label the criteria.

Now find different ways of sorting the shapes.

Solving problems, making decisions and reasoning about numbers

This unit includes a range of problem solving activities, some of which are focused on standard units of measure. The children use all four operations to solve word problems about measurements and to choose appropriate operations and methods of solving these problems. Throughout the unit, they are encouraged to explain their methods and reasoning orally and in writing.

LEARNING OBJECTIVES

	Topics	Starter	Main teaching activities
Lesson 1	Measures	● Consolidate knowing by heart addition and subtraction facts for all numbers up to 20.	● Use, read and write standard metric units (km, m, cm, mm), including their abbreviations, and imperial units (mile). ● **Know and use the relationships between familiar units of length.** ● Convert up to 1000 centimetres to metres, and vice versa.
Lesson 2	Measures	As for Lesson 1.	● Suggest suitable units and measuring equipment to estimate or measure length.
Lesson 3	Measures	As for Lesson 1.	As for Lesson 2.
Lesson 4	Solving problems Making decisions Reasoning about numbers	● Multiply any integer up to 1000 by 10 and understand the effect.	● Use all four number operations to solve word problems involving measures. ● **Choose and use appropriate number operations and appropriate ways of calculating (mental, mental with jottings, pencil and paper) to solve problems.** ● Explain methods and reasoning about numbers orally and in writing.
Lesson 5	Solving problems Making decisions Reasoning about numbers	As for Lesson 4.	As for Lesson 4.

Lesson ① overview

Learning objectives
Starter
● Consolidate knowing by heart addition and subtraction facts for all numbers up to 20.
Main teaching activities
● Use, read and write standard metric units (km, m, cm, mm), including their abbreviations, and imperial units (mile).
● **Know and use the relationships between familiar units of length.**
● Convert up to 1000 centimetres to metres, and vice versa.

Vocabulary
unit, standard unit, metric unit, imperial unit, kilometre, metre, centimetre, millimetre, mile

You will need:

Photocopiable pages
'Metric units for length' (page 37) for each child.

CD pages
'Metric units for length', core, less able and more able versions.

Equipment
Rulers marked in mm and cm; measuring tapes; individual whiteboard and pen for each child.

Lesson 1

Starter

Explain that you will ask an addition sentence with an answer that will be between 0 and 12. Ask the children to write the answer onto their whiteboards and, when you say: *Show me,* they hold up their boards for you to see. Keep the pace of this sharp, and for some number sentences ask questions such as: *How did you find the answer?* Encourage rapid recall. Ask, for example: *6 + 5, 12 − 8, 3 + 8…*

Main teaching activities

Whole class: Write on the board:'km, m, cm'. Choose children to come to the board to write the full word next to each abbreviation. Ask the children to read each word correctly and check the spelling of the word. Then write up 'mm' and ask if anyone knows what this stands for. Write the word 'millimetre' on the board. Explain about millimetres and their use in measuring small lengths.

Provide rulers marked in millimetres to pairs of children and invite them to use the rulers to measure, for example, the width of their pencil. Ask: *How wide was your pencil?* Invite children from each group to write their answer onto the board, using the shortened form 'mm'. Ask questions such as: *How many metres are there in a kilometre? How many centimetres in a metre? How many millimetres in a centimetre?* Write the relationships on the board:'1 kilometre = 1000 metres'; '1 metre = 100 centimetres';'1 centimetre = 10 millimetres'.

Discuss the fact that longer distances in Britain (such as road journeys) are measured in miles, and that this is an imperial unit. In the rest of Europe the standard unit is a kilometre, which is a metric unit. Tell them that one mile is longer than one kilometre, but shorter than two.

Group work: Provide copies of the activity sheet 'Metric units for length'. Ask the children to complete the questions about converting measurements, then to measure the lines on the page. For the final question, they can draw lines of the required length on the back of the sheet.

Differentiation

Less able: Decide whether to provide the version of the activity sheet that asks children to draw lines measuring in centimetres.

More able: Decide whether to provide the version of the activity sheet that asks children to draw lines measuring in millimetres. They may need to approximate the lengths of their drawings.

Plenary & assessment

Using the core version of the activity sheet, review the answers to the questions. Encourage all of the children to join in responding to the questions. Ask:
- *How many metres is 300 centimetres? How do you know?*
- *What is 4 metres in centimetres? How did you work it out?*

Lessons   overview

Learning objectives
Starter
- Consolidate knowing by heart addition and subtraction facts for all numbers up to 20.

Main teaching activities
- Suggest suitable units and measuring equipment to estimate or measure length.

Vocabulary
measure, measurement, unit, standard unit, metric unit, kilometre, metre, centimetre, millimetre, mile, estimate, roughly, nearly, about, approximately

You will need:
Photocopiable pages
'Standard units for length' (page 38) for each child.

CD pages
'Standard units for length', core version.

Equipment
Individual whiteboards and pens; metre sticks; rulers marked in millimetres; measuring tapes.

Lesson ②

Starter
Repeat the Starter for Lesson 1, this time concentrating on subtraction questions, up to 12 – 12.

Main teaching activities
Whole class: Ask the children to work in pairs. Ask: *How tall do you think your partner is? What units would you use? Why would you choose those?* Discuss how they made their estimate and the units chosen, and whether these seem sensible. Now invite each pair to measure each other in their chosen units and to see how close they were to their estimate. Ask: *How close was the measurement to the estimate? Were the chose units sensible?*

Group work: Invite the children to continue to work in their pairs. Write on the board a list of classroom items which they can estimate and then measure, choosing their units appropriately.

Differentiation
Less able: Encourage children to use the vocabulary of estimation and measurement, putting into a sentence each estimate they make, and checking the accuracy of this with the measurement.
More able: Work outside to make larger measurements such as the dimensions of the playground.

Plenary & assessment
Invite children from each group to give their estimates and measurements and to discuss how accurate their original estimate was.

Lesson ③

Repeat the Starter from Lesson 1, this time extending to include addition and subtraction questions that lie within the whole range from 0 to 20. Keep the pace sharp to encourage rapid recall.

For the main teaching activity, review estimation and measurement for length, and ask questions such as: *What units would you use to measure the height of a bungalow; the width of your thumb…?* Discuss measuring distances and how we still use the standard imperial units of miles in Britain, while in Europe kilometres are used. Provide copies of activity sheet 'Standard units for length'. This invites the children to make estimates of lengths, and to suggest what could be measured in specific units. This sheet is not differentiated, so you may wish to work with the less able children, and complete the sheet together. When they have finished the sheet, challenge the more able children to add to the list of items that they would measure with specific units.

During the plenary, review the children's responses to the questions. Ask: *Why did you decide to use those units? Do others agree? Why/why not?*

Lessons ④ ⑤ overview

Learning objectives
Starter
● Multiply any integer up to 1000 by 10, and understand the effect.
Main teaching activities
● Use all four number operations to solve word problems involving measures.
● **Choose and use appropriate number operations and appropriate ways of calculating (mental, mental with jottings, pencil and paper) to solve problems.**
● Explain methods and reasoning about numbers orally and in writing.

Vocabulary
kilometre, metre, centimetre, millimetre, operation, sign, symbol, number sentence, difference

You will need:
Photocopiable pages
'Length word problems' (page 39) for each child.

CD pages
'Length word problems', core, less able and more able versions.

Equipment
OHP calculator; individual whiteboards and pens.

Lesson 4

Starter

Enter a number less than 100 into the OHP calculator and tell the children that you are going to multiply the number by 10. The children have to write what they think is the answer on their whiteboards. When you have entered × 10 and pressed =, ask how many children got the correct answer. Ask the children what happened to the original number. Repeat this for other two-digit numbers.

Main teaching activities

Whole class: Explain that for the next two lessons, the children will be engaged in solving word problems about measurements. Say: *In the school sports day, two children did the standing long jump. Ali jumped 76 centimetres and he was 120 centimetres tall. Daisy jumped 88 centimetres but she was only 110 centimetres tall. Who jumped further? How much further?*
Then ask the children to discuss the following questions:
- *What is the important information in the problem?*
- *What is the information that doesn't help you solve the problem?*
- *What is the answer to the problem?*
- *How did you work it out?*

Invite a child to write a number sentence on the board to show the answer to the problem. Talk about how sometimes in word problems there can be information that is not useful in solving the problem.
Group work: Ask the children to work in pairs to answer the problems on activity sheet 'Length word problems'. Explain that the children should not expect to finish all of these problems in one session.

Differentiation

Less able: Use the version of the activity sheet that uses smaller numbers and just centimetres.
More able: Use the version that uses larger numbers and requires more conversions of units.

Plenary & assessment

Review the first problem from the core version of the activity sheet and question the children:
- *What was the hardest problem. Why?*
- *What was the easiest problem. Why?*
- *What methods of calculation did you use?*
- *Who used a different method?*

Lesson 5

Repeat the Starter from Lesson 4, this time extending the numbers to be multiplied to beyond 100.
During the main teaching activity, invite children to provide suggestions for word problems for number sentences such as 56 + 37, 198 + 47, 93 − 48… Children can continue to work in groups on the activity sheet 'Length word problems'.
During the plenary, review Question 6 from each version of the activity sheet 'Length word problems', inviting children to suggest possible word problems for the number sentences given. Ask: *Which number operations would you need to use to solve these word problems?*

Name   Date

Metric units for length

Answer these questions.

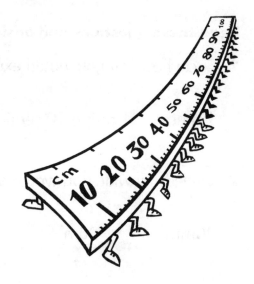

1. How many millimetres in a centimetre?

2. How many centimetres in a metre?

3. How many metres in a kilometre?

4. How many metres in 500 centimetres?

5. How many metres in 1000 centimetres?

6. Measure these lines carefully.
   Write your answers in millimetres.

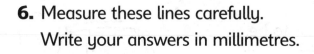

7. On the back of this sheet draw these lines.

   6cm   25mm   45mm

Name	Date

Standard units for length

Read these questions and answer them.

1. Circle how tall you would expect an adult man to be.

    I metre   I metre 80 centimetres   3 metres

3m

2. Circle how wide you would expect your big toe to be.

    20mm   20m   20cm

3. Write about how long you would expect a car to be.

4. Write which metric unit you would choose to measure these:

The distance from Manchester to Birmingham

The height of a bus stop

The depth of water in a sink

The width of a knitting needle

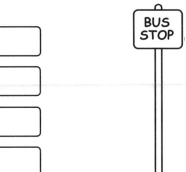

BUS STOP

5. Write some things in each box that you would measure using these units.

Metres	Kilometres	Centimetres	Millimetres	Miles

Name	Date

Length word problems

Answer these questions.

In the boxes, show how you and your partner worked out the answers.

1. During the school sports day two children did the standing long jump. Ravi jumped 89cm and he was 120cm tall. Kylie jumped 94cm and she was 110cm tall. How far were both jumps together?

   How we worked it out

2. Justin went out for a drive. He was 24 years old. He stopped after 24 miles for something to eat. He then drove another 45 miles and got home at 7 o'clock. How far did he drive?

   How we worked it out

3. A carpenter was putting up a shelf. The shelf needed to be 71cm long but the piece of wood she had was 1 metre long. Her saw was 45cm long. How much did she have to cut off the piece of wood?

   How we worked it out

The children extend their understanding of the relationship between different metric units. They are engaged in some practical measuring activities to find the perimeter of rectangles and other simple shapes. They also look at co-ordinates and use these to find the position of points on numbered grids.

LEARNING OBJECTIVES

	Topics	Starter	Main teaching activities
Lesson 1	Measures	● **Know by heart multiplication facts for 2-, 3-, 4-, 5- and 10-times tables.**	● Measure and calculate the perimeter of rectangles and other simple shapes. ● **Know and use the relationships between familiar units of length.** ● Convert up to 1000 centimetres to metres, and vice versa.
Lesson 2	Shape and space Measures	● **Derive quickly division facts corresponding to 2-, 3-, 4-, 5-, and 10-times tables.**	● Recognise positions and directions: for example, describe and find the position of a point on a grid of squares where the lines are numbered. ● Measure and calculate the perimeter of rectangles and other simple shapes.
Lesson 3	Measures	● **Round any positive integer less than 1000 to the nearest 10 or 100.**	● Suggest suitable units and measuring equipment to estimate or measure length. ● Record estimates and readings from scales to a suitable degree of accuracy.

Lessons   overview

Preparation
Copy 'Co-ordinates' onto an OHT sheet.

Learning objectives
Starter
● **Know by heart multiplication facts for 2-, 3-, 4-, 5- and 10-times tables.**
● **Derive quickly division facts corresponding to 2-, 3-, 4-, 5- and 10-times tables.**
● **Round any positive integer less than 1000 to the nearest 10 or 100.**
Main teaching activities
● Measure and calculate the perimeter of rectangles and other simple shapes.
● **Know and use the relationships between familiar units of length.**
● Recognise positions and directions: for example, describe and find the position of a point on a grid of squares where the lines are numbered.
● Suggest suitable units and measuring equipment to estimate or measure length.
● Record estimates and readings from scales to a suitable degree of accuracy.

Vocabulary
perimeter, distance, position, direction, co-ordinates, grid, vertical, horizontal, origin, diagonal, axis, axes, measurement, unit, standard unit, metric unit, measuring scale, division, estimate

You will need:
Photocopiable pages
'Find the perimeter' (page 43) for each child.

CD pages
'Find the perimeter', 'Co-ordinates' and 'Measures of length', core versions.

Equipment
Individual whiteboards and pens; rulers; squared centimetre paper; 2-D regular and irregular shapes; soluble OHP pens; rulers marked in cm and mm; metre sticks marked in cm; measuring tapes.

Lesson 1

Starter

Begin by reciting the multiplication tables for 2, 3, 4, 5 and 10. Keep the pace sharp. Now explain that you will say a multiplication or division fact. Ask the children to write their answers on their whiteboards and to hold up their boards when you say: *Show me*. Keep the pace of this sharp to encourage rapid recall.

Main teaching activities

Whole class: Draw a rectangle on the board and discuss its properties. Highlight the fact that pairs of sides are of equal length and therefore it is not necessary to measure all the sides. Ask the children to imagine that the rectangle on the board is a farmer's field full of bulls, and that he wants to put a fence around the field to keep the bulls in. Ask questions such as: *How could we find out how much fence is needed? Do we have to measure all the sides? Why not?*

Write the word 'perimeter' on the board and explain that it is the measurement of length all the way around a shape. Put some measurements on the rectangle, such as 80 metres and 60 metres, and ask the children to calculate the perimeter of the field. Ask: *How did you work that out?* Check that the children used an efficient method. They may have multiplied each measurement by two then totalled, or they may have added the measurements of the four sides. Say together: *Perimeter*. Repeat this with rectangles of other sizes, such as a football pitch, a playground…

Group work: Ask the children to work in pairs. Explain that you would like them to find ten rectangular items in the classroom, such as the top of their table, a book… They should find the length and breadth of each one and then calculate the perimeter. They can record their work on activity sheet 'Find the perimeter'. Explain that they can use rulers, metre sticks and measuring tapes. Give the children about 20 minutes to complete this work, and remind them when there are five minutes left.

Differentiation

Less able: Work with this group. Agree as a group which item to measure first, then compare measurements. Work together to find the perimeter so that the children are sure of how to do this.
More able: If the children finish the group work above, suggest that they search for more unusual shapes with straight sides, and find the perimeters of those.

Plenary & assessment

Ask the children for the sizes of the rectangles they found in the second part of the lesson. Show on the board how to find a quick solution by doubling each side and then adding together. Hold up some regular 2-D shapes and ask the children for a quick way to calculate the perimeter. If the children do not use the term 'multiplication', use it to show them how to find the answer. Hold up an irregular shape and ask if you could find the perimeter of this shape by multiplication. Look for children who have used 'quick' methods to calculate the perimeter. Ask: *How can you find the perimeter of this shape? Is this the quickest way? Why/why not?*

Lesson 2

Starter

Repeat the Starter from Lesson 1, but this time ask the children division facts. Again, keep the pace sharp to encourage rapid recall. If the children are unsure, remind that if a multiplication fact such as 6 × 3 = 18 is known, then 3 × 6, 18 ÷ 6 and 18 ÷ 3 can be derived too.

Main teaching activities

Whole class: Use activity sheet 'Co-ordinates' as an OHT, with soluble OHP pens to show the children how to find co-ordinates. Explain that the vertical and horizontal outer lines are called 'axes' and are numbered, with zero being common to both axes; this point is called the 'origin'. Explain that in co-ordinates, the horizontal line number is given first, then the vertical. Now invite a child to put a small cross on given co-ordinates such as (1, 4). Repeat this for co-ordinates such as (1, 1), (4, 1) and (4, 4) and ask: *If we join these points, what shape will we make?*

Clean the grid and invite children from different groups to come to the front and label the grid. Say: *Put zero at the origin. Put the numbers 1 to 5 up the vertical axis, then along the horizontal axis.* Give other sets of co-ordinates, such as (1, 3), (3, 1) and (5, 3) and ask: *What shape is this?*

Group work: Ask the children to work in pairs on activity sheet 'Co-ordinates'. One child draws a shape (in pencil) on their grid without the other child seeing the shape; this child then gives the co-ordinates to the second child. They compare and measure their shapes and find the perimeter.

Differentiation

Less able: The children can begin with simpler shapes such as rectangles and squares.
More able: The children can go on to try more complex shapes.

Plenary & assessment

Decide on co-ordinates at which treasure might be hidden. Put the OHT of 'Co-ordinates' up again and explain that the grid represents a treasure map. Ask the children to suggest co-ordinates of where the treasure might be, and to mark these spots on the map grid. The child who 'finds' the treasure can then decide where they have treasure hidden on the map, and repeat the activity.

Lesson

Starter

Explain that you will say a number between 1 and 100. Ask the children to work out on their whiteboards what the number becomes after rounding to the nearest 10, and to hold up their whiteboards when you say: *Show me.* Keep the pace of this sharp. When the children are confident with this, extend the number range to 1000.

Main teaching activities

Whole class: Discuss the classroom bookcase: *How long do you think one shelf is? Why do you think that? How long would two or three of the shelves be in total? How did you work that out?* Invite two children to measure one of the shelves while the others watch. Ask: *What measuring equipment will you use? Why do you think that is a good choice? Do you all agree?* Discuss the units chosen and how close to the estimate the measure is. Ask a child to write the measurement onto the board.

Group work: Choose from the selection of practical tasks on activity sheet 'Measures of length'. These are suitable for children to complete in pairs.

Differentiation

Less able: The children could work as a group on a chosen activity on 'Measures of length'. Encourage them to begin by saying which units they will need, and why.
More able: Challenge the children to suggest their own measuring problem to solve.

Plenary & assessment

Choose one of the activities that most of the children have completed. Ask questions such as:
● *What units did you choose? Was this a good choice? Why/why not?*
● *Which measuring equipment did you choose? Was this a good choice? Why?*
Remind the children how measuring is always approximate, and that we use rounding to record.

Name   Date

Find the perimeter

You will need rulers, tapes, metre sticks.

Work with a partner.

Find 10 things in the classroom that have a rectangular shape.

Measure them.

Calculate their perimeter.

Record your findings in the table.

We chose	Length and breadth	Perimeter

Properties of numbers and reasoning about numbers

Autumn term

Unit 8

The children recognise and extend number sequences using a variety of steps and extending beyond zero when counting back. They make and investigate statements about numbers, in particular the properties of odd and even numbers.

LEARNING OBJECTIVES

	Topics	Starter	Main teaching activities
Lesson 1	Properties of numbers and number sequences	● Count on or back in repeated steps of 1, 10 or 100.	● Recognise and extend number sequences formed by counting from any number in steps of constant size, extending beyond zero when counting back: for example, count on in steps of 25 to 500, and then back to, say, –100.
Lesson 2	Properties of numbers and number sequences	As for Lesson 1.	As for Lesson 1.
Lesson 3	Properties of numbers	● Count on or back in thousands from any whole number up to 10 000.	● Recognise odd and even numbers up to 1000, and some of their properties, including the outcome of sums or differences of pairs of odd/even numbers.
Lesson 4	Reasoning about numbers	● Read and write whole numbers up to at least 10 000 in figures and words, and know what each digit represents.	● Solve mathematical problems or puzzles, recognise and explain patterns and relationships, generalise and predict. Suggest extensions by asking 'What if…?' ● Make and investigate a general statement about familiar numbers by finding examples that satisfy it.
Lesson 5	Properties of numbers	As for Lesson 4.	As for Lesson 4.

Lessons   overview

Learning objectives

Starter
● Count on or back in repeated steps of 1, 10 or 100.
● Count on or back in thousands from any whole number up to 10 000.

Main teaching activities
● Recognise and extend number sequences formed by counting from any number in steps of constant size, extending beyond zero when counting back: for example, count on in steps of 25 to 500, and then back to, say, –100.
● Recognise odd and even numbers up to 1000, and some of their properties, including the outcome of sums or differences of pairs of odd/even numbers.

Vocabulary

consecutive, sequence, predict, pattern, rule, relationship, extend

You will need:

Photocopiable pages
'Counting patterns' (page 49) for each child.

CD pages
'Counting patterns' and 'Odd and even numbers', core, less able and more able versions; 'Numeral cards 0–20' (see General resources).

Equipment
OHP calculator; calculators.

Lesson ①

Starter

Split the class into four groups. Give the children a start number such as 345. Each group takes a turn to count up in tens from that number. The groups keep going until you shout: *Back,* when the children should start counting back in tens. Keep the pace of this sharp, and change from group to group for continuing the count to keep everyone on their toes!

Main teaching activities

Whole class: Use the OHP calculator to add on in twos. (Usually, '2 + + =' will generate the required pattern.) Ask the children to shout out what the next number will be before you press the equals key. Ask questions such as:

● *How did you work out what the next number would be?*
● *If we keep going, will 409 come up on the calculator? Why?* (No. It's an odd number and this is an even number pattern.)

Repeat this for counting back (inputting '2 – – ='), and again for other generated patterns, such as counting in 5s, starting on 3, 4… Then repeat for larger increments, such as counting in 20s, then 25s. Ask questions such as:

● *Are we going to get to zero? What will happen then?*
● *Will we get to –78? How do you know that?*

Group work: The children work in pairs with one calculator between each pair. They take turns to think of a number in which they want to count, and input it to the calculator. One child has to predict the next number and the other has to check with the calculator. They can record their sequence of numbers on a sheet of paper. They then choose a different number and repeat the process.

Differentiation

Less able: Suggest to the children that they begin with one-digit numbers.
More able: Challenge the children to produce more complex and challenging sequences.

Plenary & assessment

Invite children from each ability group to say the beginning of one of their sequences of numbers. Ask the other children to say what the counting on number was. Keep the pace of this sharp. Ask:

● *How did you work out the counting on number?*
● *What if we started the sequence on…? What would the next number be?*

Lesson ②

Repeat the Starter from Lesson 1, this time extending the counting to include counting on and back in hundreds.

During the main teaching activity, provide further opportunities for extending counting patterns, such as counting in 20s, 30s and so on. On the board, write '36, 45, 54, 63' and ask: *What is the pattern? How did you work it out?* Repeat this for other examples, where the increase or decrease is a one-digit number. Provide copies of activity sheet 'Counting patterns' and ask the children to complete these individually. There are differentiated versions of this sheet.

Review the sheets during the plenary, writing questions from each of the sheets in turn onto the board for all the children to think about the answers. Ensure that children from your lower ability group have an opportunity to respond about their work.

Lesson ③

Starter

Split the class into four groups and give them a start number such as 275. Each group takes a turn to count up and back in thousands.

Main teaching activities

Whole class: Explain to the children that today's lesson is about odd and even numbers. Ask: *What is an odd number? What is an even number? How can you tell whether any number is odd or even?* (Even numbers can be halved or divided by two to give a whole number.) Encourage the children to explain that any odd number has 1, 3, 5, 7 or 9 in its units, and any even number has 0, 2, 4, 6 or 8 in its units. Write a three-digit even number on the board, such as '246', and ask questions such as:

● *Is this number odd or even?*
● *Who can tell me a three-digit odd number?*

Repeat this for other numbers.

Group work: Give the children copies of activity sheet 'Odd and even numbers'. There is a practical sorting activity of three-digit numbers into odd and even, and a challenge to complete.

Differentiation

Less able: Decide whether to use the version of the activity sheet that has two-digit numbers to sort.
More able: Decide whether to use the version of the activity sheet that has four-digit numbers to sort.

Plenary & assessment

Write 'Odd' and 'Even' in two boxes on the board and invite children from each group to write in the appropriate box a number. Ask them to explain why their number is odd or even. Review the three questions at the end of the activity sheets. Invite children to explain their thinking and to read out the sentences they wrote. Ask the children questions such as:

● *How do you know if a number is odd or even?*
● *What happens when we add two even numbers? Why is that?*

Lessons ④ ⑤ overview

Learning objectives

Starter
● Read and write whole numbers up to at least 10 000 in figures and words, and know what each digit represents.

Main teaching activities
● Solve mathematical problems or puzzles, recognise and explain patterns and relationships, generalise and predict. Suggest extensions by asking 'What if…?'
● Make and investigate a general statement about familiar numbers by finding examples.

Vocabulary

pattern, puzzle, calculate, consecutive

You will need:

CD pages
'Is this true?', core version; 'Numeral cards 0–20' for each pair (see General resources).

Equipment
Individual whiteboards and pens.

Lesson 4

Starter

Explain to the children that you will say some words that you would like them to write in numerals on their whiteboards. Begin with three-digit numbers, such as 345, 612 and 705, and then extend this to four-digit numbers. Keep the pace sharp. Where one of the place holders in a number is a zero, check that the children have understood this and written the number correctly. Ask questions such as: *Which digit represents the units… tens… hundreds… thousands? What does this digit represent in this number?*

Main teaching activities

Whole class: Write on the board '1, 2, 3, 4' and '27, 28, 29, 30', and ask the children what they notice about these sequences of numbers. Discuss how these are 'next door' or consecutive numbers. Write the word 'consecutive' on the board. Invite children from each ability group to come to the board and write a sequence of four consecutive numbers. Check that the children understand the term 'consecutive'.

Now explain the problem that all of them will tackle in this lesson: *Is it possible to total consecutive numbers to make all of the numbers from 1 to 20? This is your task today, to find different ways of making 1, 2, 3… to 20, using only addition of two or more consecutive numbers.* Each pair may find it useful to have a set of 0 to 20 numeral cards so that they can combine pairs and trios of consecutive card numbers as a starting point. Stress that zero is allowed.

Group work: Ask the children to begin work on the task immediately. Encourage them to be systematic and to make jottings as they work, so that they have a record of what they have tried.

Differentiation

Less able: The children may find it beneficial to work in pairs, then come together in fours to share what they have found out so far.

More able: If the children find a solution before the end of this session, challenge them to find which totals have more than one solution.

Plenary & assessment

Invite the children to share their results. Begin with 1, 2, 3… and ask the less able children to contribute their responses. On the board, draw up a table that you can fill in as the children give their results (see rights). As children give results, they will find that some numbers have more than one solution. Record the other results, too. When there is a solution for all possible totals, ask:

● *Which numbers cannot be made using consecutive numbers?*

● *What is special about these numbers?* (They are powers of 2. Children may comment that they are some of the two-times table numbers.)

● *What patterns can you see?*

Total	Ways to make this total using consecutive numbers		
1 =	0 + 1		
2 =			
3 =	0 + 1 + 2		
4 =			
5 =	2 + 3		
6 =	1 + 2 + 3		
7 =	3 + 4		
8 =			
9 =	4 + 5	2 + 3 + 4	
10 =	1 + 2 + 3 + 4		
11 =	5 + 6		
12 =	3 + 4 + 5		
13 =	6 + 7		
14 =	2 + 3 + 4 + 5		
15 =	7 + 8	4 + 5 + 6	1 + 2 + 3 + 4 + 5
16 =			
17 =	8 + 9		
18 =	5 + 6 + 7	3 + 4 + 5 + 6	
19 =	9 + 10		
20 =	2 + 3 + 4 + 5 + 6		

Discuss the patterns that emerge. For example, for odd totals there is always a solution using just two consecutive numbers. For three-times table totals there is always a solution using three-numbers. Discuss how important it is, when carrying out an investigation like this, to search for patterns. Pattern spotting can help with finding more solutions.

Invite children to discuss how they went about the task, and how they recorded their results. Stress the importance of recording what has been tried, even if it 'did not work', as this will act as a reminder of what has been tried. Finally, congratulate the children on their hard work.

Lesson ⑤

Repeat the Starter from Lesson 4 but this time, say a number and ask the children to write it in words on their individual whiteboards.

During the main teaching activity, ask the children to think about odd and even numbers. Ask: *How can you tell an even number is even? An odd number is odd? What is the rule?* Ask the children to work individually from activity sheet 'Is this true?'. This asks them to read a statement and to find some number sentences that show the statement is true. Decide whether to work with the less able children as a group to consider each statement. Challenge the more able children to use larger numbers to demonstrate each sentence.

During the plenary, invite children from each ability group to give number sentences that demonstrate each statement. Ask: *How did you work this out? Is this always true?*

Name   Date

Counting patterns

Write in the missing numbers, then write the rule underneath.

1. [15] [21] [   ] [   ] [   ] [45]

_____

2. [   ] [   ] [   ] [11] [7] [3]

_____

3. [   ] [75] [78] [81] [   ] [   ]

_____

4. [91] [87] [   ] [   ] [   ] [71]

_____

Write some counting patterns of your own. Write the rule underneath.

5. [   ] [   ] [   ] [   ] [   ] [   ]

The rule is _____

6. [   ] [   ] [   ] [   ] [   ] [   ]

The rule is _____

7. [   ] [   ] [   ] [   ] [   ] [   ]

The rule is _____

8. [   ] [   ] [   ] [   ] [   ] [   ]

The rule is _____

On the back of this sheet:

9. Write a pattern for the rule 'Start on 13 and increase by 5 each time'.

10. Write a pattern for the rule 'Start on 84 and decrease by 6 each time'.

Multiplication and division

In this unit children move from developing mental strategies to working with written methods of multiplication and division. They use the grid method for multiplications of TU by U and use multiples of divisors in division. Throughout the unit, they are encouraged to discuss, explain and compare methods of calculation.

LEARNING OBJECTIVES

	Topics	Starter	Main teaching activities
Lesson 1	Understanding × and ÷	● Derive quickly doubles of all whole numbers to 50, and the corresponding halves.	● Extend understanding of the operations of × and÷, and their relationship to each other and to + and −.
Lesson 2	Mental calculation strategies (× and ÷)	As for Lesson 1.	● Use doubling or halving, starting from known facts. For example, to multiply by 4, double, then double again; to multiply by 5, multiply by 10 then halve; to multiply by 20, multiply by 10 then double; find the 8-times table facts by doubling the 4-times table.
Lesson 3	Pencil and paper procedures (× and ÷) Checking results	● **Know by heart multiplication facts for 2-, 3-, 4-, 5- and 10-times tables.**	● Approximate first. Use informal pencil and paper methods to support, record or explain × and ÷. ● Develop and refine written methods for TU × U, TU ÷ U. ● Check with an equivalent calculation.
Lesson 4	Pencil and paper procedures (× and ÷) Checking results	As for Lesson 3.	As for Lesson 3.
Lesson 5	Pencil and paper procedures (× and ÷) Checking results	As for Lesson 3.	As for Lesson 3.

Lesson overview

Learning objectives
Starter
● Derive quickly doubles of all whole numbers to 50, and the corresponding halves.
Main teaching activity
● Extend understanding of the operations of × and ÷, and their relationship to each other and to + and −.

Vocabulary
times, multiply, multiplied by, product, multiple, inverse, share, group, divided by, divided into, divisible by, factor, remainder

You will need:

CD pages
'Multiplication and division', core, less able, more able and template versions.

Lesson

Starter

Explain that you will say a number between 1 and 50. Ask the children to call out the double for that number quietly. Keep the pace sharp. If the children falter with any number, discuss how they could mentally calculate the double.

Main teaching activities

Whole class: Explain that the work this week will be about multiplication and division. Write on the board '8 + 8 + 8 = ☐' and ask: *How could we work this out?* Some children will say: 'Add 8 and 8, then add 16 and 8'. Others will suggest: 'Multiply 8 by 3'. Discuss with the children that 8 + 8 + 8 is equivalent to 8 × 3.

Now write up '24 – 8 – 8 – 8 = ☐' and ask the children to explain how this could be worked out. If nobody suggests the link with division, write up '24 ÷ 8 = 3', and discuss how division can also be seen as repeated subtraction. Ask for suggestions for all four linked multiplication and division facts for 8, 3 and 24, and write these on the board: '8 × 3 = 24'; '3 × 8 = 24'; '24 ÷ 3 = 8'; '24 ÷ 8 =3'. Write up another example, such as '6 + 6 + 6 + 6 = ☐', and repeat this exercise.

Ask: *How can we check multiplication with division? How can we check division with multiplication?* Ensure that the children understand that, for example, they can check that 6 × 4 = 24 by trying 24 ÷ 4 = 6.

Individual work: Give the children activity sheet 'Multiplication and division'. Explain to them that they are to follow exactly the workings you have written on the board for each calculation.

Differentiation

Less able: Give the children the version of the activity sheet that asks the children to add fewer numbers.

More able: Give the children the version of the activity sheet that asks the children to add more numbers, and to add larger numbers (TU × U).

Plenary & assessment

Go through the activity sheet that most of the class have completed, all the time emphasising the correct mathematical language. Encourage all of the children to respond to the questions. Invite a child to come to the board each time, and to write the relevant addition or multiplication sentences, and the corresponding division sentences for checking. Say, for example:

● *If I know 8 × 4, what other multiplication and division sentences can I work out?*
● *Tell me another way to write 4 + 4 + 4.*

Lesson overview

Learning objectives

Starter

● Derive quickly doubles of all whole numbers to 50, and the corresponding halves.

Main teaching activities

● Use doubling or halving, starting from known facts. For example, to multiply by 4, double, then double again; to multiply by 5, multiply by 10 then halve; to multiply by 20, multiply by 10 then double; find the 8-times table facts by doubling the 4-times table.

Vocabulary

times, multiply, multiplied by, product, multiple, inverse, share, group, divided by, divided into, divisible by, factor, remainder, double, half

You will need:

CD pages

A set of 'Numeral cards 10–20' (see General resources) for each pair and a set of 'Numeral cards 21–30' (see General resources) for more able pairs.

Lesson ②

Starter
Repeat the Starter from Lesson 1. This time, explain that you will say an even number between 2 and 100. Ask the children to call out the half of this number quietly. Again, keep the pace sharp.

Main teaching activities
Whole class: Write on the board '16 × 4 = ❏' and ask: *Who can tell me a way of working this out that uses doubling?* Write up '16 × 2 + 16 × 2 = 32 + 32 = 64'. Explain that it can be possible to work out unknown multiplication facts from those that you know, such as using doubling and halving methods. Write on the board '13 × 20 = ❏'. Ask the children to think how they could work this out using doubles. Invite a child to write their response: 13 × 10 + 13 × 10 = 130 + 130 = 260. Repeat this for some more examples.

Now ask: *How could you work out multiplication by 8?* Agree that it can be done by multiplying by 2, then doubling and doubling again. Ask the children to calculate 15 × 8 by this method. Discuss how, in order to multiply by 5, it can be useful to multiply by 10 and then halve the result. Ask: *How could we multiply by 20?* Children will probably suggest multiplying by 10, then doubling that result.

Group work: Ask the children to work in pairs with a set of 11–19 numeral cards. They take turns to choose a card, then multiply the card number by 2, 4, 8, 5 and 20, using doubling and halving methods. Ask them to record this on a sheet of paper, and to show how they calculated each one.

Differentiation
Less able: Decide whether to limit the children to multiplying the numbers 1–9.
More able: Challenge the children to use the numbers 21–29. A set of 'Numeral cards 21–30' have been provided for this purpose.

Plenary & assessment
Invite children from each group to give an example for the others to try. Invite the child to explain how they carried out the calculation on the board. Ask:
● *How did you work that out?*
● *Who used a different method?*

Lessons ③ ④ ⑤ overview

Preparation
Enlarge a copy of 'Blank number lines' to A3 and pin it to the board.

Learning objectives
Starter
● **Know by heart multiplication facts for 2-, 3-, 4-, 5- and 10-times tables.**
Main teaching activities
● Approximate first. Use informal pencil and paper methods to support, record or explain multiplications and divisions.
● Develop and refine written methods for TU × U, TU ÷ U.
● Check with an equivalent calculation.

You will need:
Photocopiable pages
'Grid method multiplication' (page 55) and 'Division' (page 56) for each child.

CD pages
'Blank number lines' (see General resources); 'Grid method multiplication', 'Division', core, less able, more able and template versions.

Equipment
Squared paper and/or individual whiteboards and pens.

Lesson ③

Starter

Play multiplication bingo. Provide the children with squared paper and ask them to draw a 3 × 3 grid on it. Explain that you will be calling out multiplication questions from the 2- or 3-times tables. Ask them to fill each square of the grid with an answer number. Start to pose questions from the 2- or 3-times tables. If the answer to a question is on a child's sheet, tell them to cross it out. The first child to complete their card shouts 'Times table bingo'. Keep the pace of this sharp. Ask questions at the end of the game, such as: *Which numbers did you choose? Why did you choose those? What about numbers that are in both the 2- and the 3-times tables, such as 6, 12…?*

Main teaching activities

Whole class: Show the children how to do multiplication by the grid method. Write on the board '26 × 3 = ❑' Ask the children what they think the rough (approximate) answer would be, and how they worked that out (25 × 3). Write on the board:

×	20	6
3		

and then fill in the gaps. Write underneath: '60 + 18 = 78'.

Demonstrate another example, such as 34 × 4. Now provide an example, such as 27 × 5, for the children to try for themselves, working in pairs on paper or individual whiteboards. Review this together, with a confident child writing out the grid method on the board.

Individual work: Give the children activity sheet 'Grid method multiplication', and tell them they have to write down their approximations and then use the grid method to find the answers.

Differentiation

Less able: Provide the version of the activity sheet that involves multiplying teens numbers by single-digit numbers.

More able: Provide the version that asks the children to use the grid method for HTU × U.

Plenary & assessment

Review some of the examples from each of the three levels of the activity sheet, asking children to take turns to write the grid method onto the board. Check that the children have given an approximation and ask how they worked it out. Target some children during this time, and ask: *How did you work out the approximation?* Choose one of the questions and invite the children to invent a word problem using those numbers.

Lesson ④

Starter

Repeat the Starter from Lesson 3, but this time for multiplication facts from the 4-, 5- and 10-times tables.

Main teaching activities

Whole class: Use the enlarged version of 'Blank number lines' and write up '40 ÷ 5 = ❑'. Invite the children to suggest an approximate answer, and to explain how they worked this out. Ask: *What multiplication facts do you know with these numbers?* Agree that 8 × 5 and 5 × 8 both equal 40. On one of the blank number lines, mark in jumps of 5 from 40 back to 0:

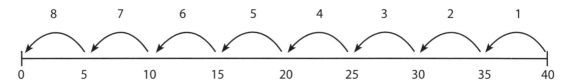

Discuss the fact that each time there is a jump back along the number line, 5 is subtracted, and that this happens eight times.

Now ask the children, working in pairs, to try 36 ÷ 4. Provide general resources sheet 'Blank number lines' for them to record their jumps on the number line. Review this example with the class to check that they understand how to use this method. When the children are confident with this, explain that there is another way of writing out division, using repeated subtraction. Write '36 ÷ 4' on the board, and then the working (see left).

```
      36
    − 20   5 × 4
      16
    − 16   4 × 4
       0
36 ÷ 4 = 9
```

Explain to the children how 5 groups of 4, then 4 groups of 4 have been subtracted. Provide another example of this for the children to try in pairs: 42 ÷ 3. Ask them to write an approximate answer first. When the children have worked through this, invite a pair to write their solution onto the board. Remind the children that it can be useful to subtract in multiples of 10, where possible (see left).

```
      42
    − 30   10 × 3
      12
    − 12    4 × 3
       0
42 ÷ 3 = 14
```

Now provide an example where there is a remainder, such as 45 ÷ 4. Again, ask the children to work through this example in pairs, beginning with an approximate answer. Review this on the board (see left).

```
      45
    − 40   10 × 4
       5
     − 4    1 × 4
       1
45 ÷ 4 = 11   (r 1)
```

Group work: Ask the children to work in pairs and to write and answer five division questions of their own. Remind the children to try an approximation first. Give them about ten minutes to work on these, then ask them to join with another pair and to try each others' questions.

Differentiation
Less able: Decide whether to work as a larger group and to work through some more examples together. Try 30 ÷ 5; 24 ÷ 3; 42 ÷ 3; 56 ÷ 4; 37 ÷ 3.
More able: Challenge the children to write three more division questions, each of which has an answer that includes 'remainder 2'.

Plenary & assessment
Invite children from each group to give examples of division questions for the others to try. Ask your able group to provide an example with an answer that includes remainder 2. Ask: *How did you work these out? Was your answer close to your approximation? How did you approximate the answer?*

Lesson

Repeat the Starter from Lesson 3, this time for the multiplication tables 2, 3, 4, 5 and 10. For the main activity explain to the children that you would like them to practise what they have learned about division. Write '65 ÷ 5 = ?' on the board and invite the children to find an approximate answer, and to explain how they worked that out. Now ask them to help you to divide by the 'chunking' method. Repeat this for an example with a remainder, such as 73 ÷ 5. Provide the activity sheet 'Division' for the children to complete individually. This sheet is available in differentiated versions. During the plenary, review some of the examples from each version of the activity sheet, inviting children to write on the board to show how they worked out the answer.

Name		Date	

Grid method multiplication

Write each multiplication out using the grid method.

Write your estimate of the answer. Write the answer.

1. 47 × 4 =

I estimate the answer is approximately

Answer = [　　]

2. 29 × 3 =

I estimate the answer is approximately

Answer = [　　]

4. 59 × 4 =

I estimate the answer is approximately

Answer = [　　]

3. 61 × 5 =

I estimate the answer is approximately

Answer = [　　]

5. 14 × 7 =

I estimate the answer is approximately

Answer = [　　]

Name	Date

Division

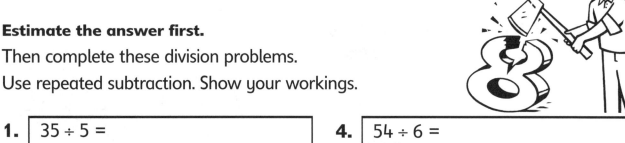

Estimate the answer first.

Then complete these division problems.

Use repeated subtraction. Show your workings.

1. | $35 \div 5 =$
Approximate answer =

4. | $54 \div 6 =$
Approximate answer =

2. | $30 \div 10 =$
Approximate answer =

5. | $84 \div 7 =$
Approximate answer =

3. | $48 \div 6 =$
Approximate answer =

6. | $133 \div 4 =$
Approximate answer =

Making decisions, checking results: problems involving 'real life'

There is a focus within this unit on problem solving. Children are asked to choose and use appropriate number operations in a variety of number sentences. They move on to solve single-step and multi-step money and measurement problems.

LEARNING OBJECTIVES

	Topics	Starter	Main teaching activities
Lesson 1	Making decisions Checking results	● Use known number facts and place value to add or subtract mentally any pair of two-digit whole numbers.	● Choose and use appropriate number operations and appropriate ways of calculating (mental, mental with jottings, pencil and paper) to solve problems. ● Check with an equivalent calculation.
Lesson 2	Making decisions Checking results	As for Lesson 1.	As for Lesson 1.
Lesson 3	Making decisions Checking results	As for Lesson 1.	As for Lesson 1.
Lesson 4	Problems involving 'real life', money and measures	● Consolidate knowing by heart addition and subtraction facts for all numbers to 20.	● Use all four operations to solve word problems involving numbers in 'real-life', money and measures, using one or more steps, including converting pounds to pence and metres to centimetres and vice versa.
Lesson 5	Problems involving 'real life', money and measures	As for Lesson 4.	As for Lesson 4.

Lessons   overview

Learning objectives
Starter
● Use known number facts and place value to add or subtract mentally any pair of two-digit whole numbers.
Main teaching activities
● Choose and use appropriate number operations and appropriate ways of calculating (mental, mental with jottings, pencil and paper) to solve problems.
● Check with an equivalent calculation.

Vocabulary
add, sum, total, altogether, increase, subtract, decrease, difference between, multiplied by, divided by, answer, right, wrong, number sentence, sign, operation, symbol, equation

You will need:
Photocopiable pages
'Number equations' (page 61) for each child.

CD pages
'Number equations', core, less able, more able and template versions; '1 to 20' for each pair.

Equipment
OHP calculator; individual whiteboards and pens.

Lesson

Starter

Explain that you will input a two-digit number into the OHP calculator. Ask the children to decide what number must be added to the number on the calculator to make a total of 100. Ask the children to put up their hands, and then input the addition of the number of the child you choose to respond. Check by showing the total. Keep the pace of this sharp. Use numbers such as 20, 35, 49, 21, 37…

Main teaching activities

Whole class: Explain that the focus of this unit of work is on solving problems. On the board, write '18 ❏ 22 = 40' and ask: *What operation is this number sentence?* Check that the children understand that the symbol ❏ in the number sentence, or 'equation', stands for an operation. Ask: *How did you work out that it is an add number sentence?* Repeat this for other operations: subtraction (such as 71 ❏ 28 = 43), multiplication (such as 70 ❏ 6 = 420) and division (such as 32 ❏ 2 = 16).

Group work: Give out copies of activity sheet 'Number equations' and ask the children to work individually to find which operation signs are needed. There is space on the sheet for the children to invent their own missing symbol questions to give to a partner.

Differentiation

Less able: Decide whether to use the version of the activity sheet that uses simpler number equations.

More able: Decide whether to use the version of the activity sheet that uses harder number equations.

Plenary & assessment

Invite children from each group to set one of their own number sentences for the others to try. Keep the pace of this sharp. Ask questions such as:
● *How did you decide which operation it was?*
● *Who worked this out another way?*
Some children may by now be able to look at an equation and, without working it out, recognise which operation is needed by the size of the numbers. Praise those who can do this.

Lesson

Starter

Explain that you have subtracted a two-digit number from 100 and have the answer. The children are to work out what number was subtracted. They can respond by writing a subtraction sentence on their whiteboards and holding these up when you say: *Show me*. Keep the pace sharp. Say numbers such as 63, 57, 12…

Main teaching activities

Whole class: Write a number sentence on the board, for example: '81 ❏ 6 = 486'. Ask: *What is the missing sign? How do you know that?* Ask the children to check with an equivalent calculation to be sure that they have the correct sign, for example: 81 × 6 = 480 + 6 = 486.

Group work: Ask the children to work in pairs, using activity sheet '1 to 20'. This asks them to find a way to make all the numbers from 1 to 20, just using the numbers 1, 2, 3 and 4 and the operations +, −, × or ÷ (or a combination of these). The children should write equivalent calculations to check their answers each time.

Differentiation

Less able: Decide whether to ask these children to work as a group, and work together to solve this problem.

More able: Challenge these children to find different ways of making each number.

Plenary & assessment

Invite children from each group to give examples of how 1, 2, 3… 20 can be made. Write these on the board. Ask questions such as: *What strategies did you use? How did you decide which operation/s to use? What equivalent calculation did you use to check?*

Lesson ③

Starter

Use a combination of questions from the starters for Lessons 1 and 2, asking the children to record their answers on their whiteboards. Keep the pace sharp.

Main teaching activities

Whole class: Write '80 × 4 = 320' on the board, and ask: *What number story might this represent?* Invite the children to suggest possible number stories. Repeat this for 81 ÷ 3 = 27.

Group work: Ask the children to work in pairs. On the board, write three each of addition, subtraction, multiplication and division questions for the children to solve. Remind the children to approximate first, then to find the answer. Ask them to invent a number story for each question.

Differentiation

Less able: Decide whether to work with these children in a larger group to help them solve the problems.

More able: Ask these children to come up with some entertaining number stories!

Plenary & assessment

Review how the children solved the questions and ask for examples of a number story from some of the pairs. Ask: *How did you approximate the answer first? How did you find the answer? What checking strategies did you use?*

Lessons ④ ⑤ overview

Learning objectives

Starter
- Consolidate knowing by heart addition and subtraction facts for all numbers to 20.

Main teaching activities
- Use all four operations to solve word problems involving numbers in 'real life', money and measures, using one or more steps, including converting pounds to pence and metres to centimetres and vice versa.

Vocabulary

money, pounds, pence, note, price, cost, cheaper, more expensive, pay, change, total, value amount, metres, centimetres, convert, distance

You will need:

Photocopiable pages
'Money problems' (page 62) and 'Deepham Primary School' (page 63) for each child.

CD pages
'Money problems' and 'Deepham Primary School', core, less able, more able and template versions.

Equipment
Pencils and paper.

Lesson ④

Starter
Ask the children each to choose six numbers between 1 and 20, and to write these on a piece of paper. Tell the children that you will say some addition and subtraction number sentences. For each one, ask the children to work out the answer and, if the answer is one of their numbers, to cross it through. The first child to cross through all six numbers wins the game. Keep the pace of this sharp. This can be repeated, with the children choosing six new numbers for each new game. Use as wide a variety of calculation vocabulary as possible, for example: *What is 5 plus 4? 19 subtract 13? The difference between 12 and 6?*

Main teaching activities
Whole class: Begin by asking the children some conversion questions such as these:
- *How many pence in £1.20… £2.50… £5.60?* (Keep the amounts below £10.00.)
- *How many pounds in 145p… 295p… 729p?* (Keep the amounts below £10.00.)
- *How many centimetres in 1.56m… 2.18m… 8.10m?* (Keep the distances below 10m.)
- *How many metres in 182cm… 451cm… 790cm?* (Keep the distances below 10m.)

Ask the children to explain how they converted from one kind of unit to another. (By dividing or multiplying by 10 or 100.) Now say: *James has £10.00. He spent a fifth of his money on a comic. How much did he spend? How did you work out the answer?* Discuss how, to find a fifth of £10.00, we can divide 10 by 5.

Now set this problem: *A CD costs £6.00. Ali saves 30p a week. How many weeks must Ali save up in order to buy the CD?* Discuss with the children how they can find the answer. They will need to convert £6.00 into pence, then consider what to divide 600 by in order to get an answer of 20.

Group work: Explain to the children that for the next two lessons they are going to be solving problems. Give out activity sheet 'Money problems' to pairs of children. This has money problems to solve. Remind the children to read each of the problems carefully first, and then to decide on the relevant information and what operation to use to find the solution.

Differentiation
Less able: There is a version of the activity sheet that has simpler questions to solve.
More able: Decide whether to use the version of the activity sheet with harder questions to solve.

Plenary & assessment
Select a problem from each of the differentiated activity sheets and ask groups of children to explain how they solved the problems. Ask the children to tell you which problems they found hardest and which ones were easiest, and why that was. Look for children who can confidently convert pounds into pence and vice versa. Ask questions such as:
- *How did you work this out?*
- *How did you know that you needed to use addition… subtraction… multiplication… division?*

Lesson ⑤

Repeat the Starter from Lesson 4, but this time ask the children to choose eight numbers between 1 and 20 to play with.

For the main teaching activity, review conversions of measures: km to m, m to cm, cm to mm. Explain to the children that you would like them to solve some word problems about measurements of length. Provide a copy of activity sheet 'Deepham Primary School' to each pair of children. This is available in differentiated versions.

During the plenary, invite children from each group to explain how they solved one of their problems. Discuss which operation they chose, and why. Ask the children to explain which units they used, and why they used them.

Name	Date

Number equations

Decide whether the number sentence involves addition, subtraction, multiplication or division.

Write in the missing sign.

1. 16 △ 57 = 73

2. 360 △ 10 = 36

3. 94 △ 67 = 27

4. 46 △ 4 = 184

5. 423 △ 324 = 747

Now make up five missing operation sign sentences.

Swap these with a partner and try to work them out.

Name	Date

Money problems

Work with a partner.

Write the answers to these questions.

Show your workings.

1. The Great Choc Bar costs 35p.

How many of them could you buy if you had £2.00?

2. It costs 50p to go on a fairground ride.

How much would it cost for six children to go on the ride?

3. Rupinder has been saving his pocket money to buy a game.

The game costs £9.00. He gets £1.50 pocket money a week.

How many weeks will he need to save for?

4. Mrs Chalk is a very kind teacher.

She spends £3.00 on six chocolate bars for her class.

How much did each bar cost?

5. Kylie spent £1.45 in a shop. Her mum had given her £2.00.

How much change should Kylie have?

6. Jamie was going on a sponsored walk. The walk was 10 miles.

He collected 75p from his dad,

£1.00 from his mum and 89p from his sister.

How much did he collect altogether?

Name	Date

Deepham Primary School

The children at Deepham Primary School have been designing some playground games.

Write the answers to each of these.

Show your working.   **Answer**

1. Each square on this ladder has sides that are 20cm long. What is the perimeter of the whole ladder?

2. The children measured the perimeter of this square, which was 2m 40cm. How many 30cm rulers would it take to measure this all the way round?

3. One side of this pitch is 10m long, while the other is 12.5m long. What is the perimeter of the pitch?

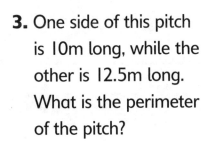

4. The longest ladder is 1m 34cm long and the shortest snake is 70cm long. What is the difference between these measurements?

5. The children at school measured the distance around the front playground. It was 1000cm wide and 2000cm long. How many metre sticks would it take to measure all the way around the playground?

Children start to develop and refine their understanding of fractions. They consolidate their understanding of fractions that are several parts of a whole as well as mixed number fractions. Finally, they begin to relate fractions to division and find simple fractions of numbers and quantities. Throughout the unit they are encouraged to use appropriate fraction notation.

LEARNING OBJECTIVES

	Topics	Starter	Main teaching activities
Lesson 1	Fractions and decimals	● **Use known number facts and place value to multiply integers by 10.**	● Use fraction notation. ● **Recognise simple fractions that are several parts of a whole,** such as 2/3 or 5/8, **and mixed numbers,** such as 53/4; **recognise the equivalence of simple fractions** (for example, fractions equivalent to 1/2, 1/4 or 3/4). ● Find fractions such as 2/3, 3/4, 3/5, 7/10… of shapes.
Lesson 2	Fractions and decimals	As for Lesson 1.	● Use fraction notation. ● **Recognise simple fractions that are several parts of a whole,** such as 2/3 or 5/8, **and mixed numbers,** such as 53/4; **recognise the equivalence of simple fractions** (for example, fractions equivalent to 1/2, 1/4 or 3/4).
Lesson 3	Fractions and decimals	● **Round any positive integer less than 1000 to the nearest 10 or 100.**	● Use fraction notation. ● Begin to relate fractions to division and find simple fractions such as 1/2, 1/3, 1/4, 1/5, 1/10… of numbers or quantities.
Lesson 4	Fractions and decimals	As for Lesson 3.	As for Lesson 3.
Lesson 5	Fractions and decimals	As for Lesson 3.	As for Lesson 3.

Lessons overview

Preparation
Photocopy 'Fraction cards' onto thin card and cut out the fraction cards. Enlarge copies of each differentiated version of activity sheet 'Fractions of shapes' to A3, or make them into OHTs.

Learning objectives
Starter
● **Use known number facts and place value to multiply integers by 10.**
Main teaching activities
● Use fraction notation.
● **Recognise simple fractions that are several parts of a whole,** such as 2/3 or 5/8, **and mixed numbers,** such as 53/4; **recognise the equivalence of simple fractions** (for example, fractions equivalent to 1/2, 1/4 or 3/4).
● Find fractions such as 2/3, 3/4, 3/5, 7/10… of shapes.

Vocabulary
fraction, equivalent, mixed numbers, half, quarter, eighth, third, sixth, fifth, tenth, twentieth

You will need:
Photocopiable pages
'Fractions of shapes' (page 69) for each child.

CD pages
'Fractions of shapes', core, less able and more able versions; a teaching set of 'Fraction cards' (see General resources).

Equipment
Individual whiteboards and pens.

Lesson

Starter

Explain that you will say a two-digit number greater than 20. Ask the children to multiply it by 10 and write the answer on their whiteboards. Write the original number on the board and the new number underneath it. Ask the children: *What has happened to our numbers?* Discourage 'add a zero' responses, and encourage the idea of changes in place value and digits moving relative to the decimal point. Repeat this for other two-digit numbers.

Main teaching activities

Whole class: Draw a 0 to 1 number line on the board, or use a washing line. Using the prepared fraction cards, ask a child to place the '1/2' card on the line. Then ask other children to place other cards equivalent to a half on the line (2/4, 3/6…). Discuss with the children why these cards all go at the same point on the line. If possible, suspend two (or more) equivalent cards in a sort of chain, one under another. Use the cards equivalent to 1/4 and repeat the activity. Then ask the children to discuss their ideas with their partner and write down fractions equivalent to 3/4. Discuss with the children the answers they have recorded.

Ask the children to draw a rectangle on squared paper and to shade in 3/4 of it. Discuss different outcomes (for example, 18 of 24 squares or 9 of 12 squares). Each of these fractions is equivalent to 3/4 of the total shape.

Individual work: Give the children copies of activity sheet 'Fractions of shapes', which asks them to shade in each shape according to the fraction shown. Make sure the children realise that the first five shapes will all show 1/2, and the other three are all pictures of 3/4.

Differentiation

Less able: Decide whether to use the version of the activity sheet that has simpler fractions to identify.

More able: Decide whether to use the version of the activity sheet that has harder fractions.

Plenary & assessment

Review the fractions on the activity sheet presented as an OHT, or using the enlarged version pinned to the board. Discuss how many sections need to be shaded, and why. Where simpler equivalent fractions are possible, such as 4/8 or 1/2, ask the children to say the simpler fraction. Ask questions such as:

- *What fraction is equivalent to…?*
- *What is another way of writing…?*

Invite children to write equivalent fractions onto the board.

Lesson

Starter

Repeat the Starter from Lesson 1. This time, ask the children to say the multiples of 10 together, as a chant, when you hold up your hand. Give a very small amount of thinking time, as children should be beginning to have rapid recall of multiples of 10.

Main teaching activities

Whole class: Ask the children to suggest any fractions that they can think of that are equivalent to 1/2. Write these on the board, listing them in a ringed set headed 'Half'. Repeat this for 1/4, then for 3/4. Now ask the children to look for the 'family' of fractions linked to 4/8 and write them on the board: '4/8 = 2/4 or 1/2'. Ask: *What is the equivalent fraction for 6/8?* Write on the board: '6/8 = 3/4'. Now ask them to write down some mixed numbers, such as 6 1/2, 2 3/4 and so on, and to suggest where they might find these fractions in everyday life. They might suggest whole and half oranges, or two bars of chocolate and 3/4 of a bar. Make sure they understand that, for example, 2 3/4 is two whole ones and 3/4 of another whole one.

Group work: Ask the children to work in small groups of four or five , with one child in each group acting as scribe. On the board, write up 'families' such as tenths and fifths, sixths and twelfths, and so on. Invite the children to write down the equivalent fractions that they can think of for the different families. When the children have done this, write some of the fractions that they suggest on the board.

Differentiation

All the children should be able to participate at their own level within the group activity.

Plenary & assessment

Begin by inviting children from each of the ability groups to contribute to the fraction families by writing suggestions onto the board. Discuss the equivalence of these fractions. Ask: *What fractions belong to the tenths family? And the twelfths family? How can you tell?* Now ask the children to suggest some mixed numbers. Ask them to suggest occasions when these fractions might occur in everyday life, for example: 3 1/2 pints of milk, 2 whole pizzas and 3/8 of a pizza…

Lessons   overview

Learning objectives
Starter
● **Round any positive integer less than 1000 to the nearest 10 or 100.**
Main teaching activities
● Use fraction notation.
● Begin to relate fractions to division and find simple fractions such as 1/2, 1/3, 1/4, 1/5, 1/10… of numbers or quantities.

Vocabulary
fraction, equivalent, mixed numbers, half, quarter, eighth, third, sixth, fifth, tenth, twentieth

You will need:
Photocopiable pages
'Finding fractions' (page 70) and 'Fractions of money' (page 71) for each child.

CD pages
'Finding fractions', 'Fractions of money' and 'Fractions of measures', core less able and more able versions.

Equipment
Individual whiteboards and pens.

Lesson ③

ROUNDING RULES
Rounding to nearest 10: if a number ends in 5 or higher, round UP.
Rounding to nearest 100: if a number ends in 50 or higher, round UP.

Starter

Remind the children of the rules for rounding numbers up or down (see above) Give the children questions like these, for rounding to the nearest 10. Ask the children to put their hands up to respond:

● *I am thinking of a three-digit number. When I round it down, it becomes 380. What could my starting number be?* (381–384)

● *I am thinking of a three-digit number. When I round it up, it becomes 870. What could my starting number be?* (865–869)

Main teaching activities

Whole class: Select a group of six children to come to the front of the class. Ask questions such as these and, after each question, actually split the group up into the fraction and write the operation on the board.

● *If we split the group into half, how many children would there be in each group?* $6 \div 2 = 3$
● *How many children would there be one third of the group?* $6 \div 3 = 2$
● *How many children would two-thirds be?* Discuss how 1/3 of 6 is 2, so 2/3 is double 2 = 4.

Now invite a group of ten children to come to the front and repeat the process. Ask questions relating to fifths and tenths.

Talk to the children about the relationship between fractions and division. Ask questions such as: *How would we find one quarter of 16? How could we find one tenth of 50?* Model some of the children's suggestions on the board. They may suggest finding one quarter of 16 by dividing 16 by 4, and finding one tenth of 50 by dividing 50 by 10. Discuss how division can be useful to find fractions of quantities.

Individual work: Give the children copies of activity sheet 'Finding fractions', which asks them to find fractions of quantities.

Differentiation

There are differentiated versions of activity sheet 'Finding fractions'.

Plenary & assessment

Ask the children to tell you which questions they found hardest and why. Review these together, using the board to record. Invite the children to explain how they found the answers. Remind the children that division is useful to find a fraction of a quantity. Ask the children questions such as:

● *Which would you rather have, half of £1.50 or a quarter of £3.00? Why?*
● *Which would you rather have, seven tenths of £1.00 or fifth of £2.00? Why?*

Look for children who can demonstrate a clear understanding of the way to calculate fractions of quantities and easily make the link with division.

Lesson

Repeat the Starter from Lesson 3, this time asking the children to round to the nearest 100.

During the main teaching activity, review with the children how to find a fraction of an amount of money by division, for example finding a quarter of 80p. Say: *To find a quarter of 80p, divide 80p by 4. So quarter of 80p is 20p*. Provide activity sheet, 'Fractions of money' for the children to complete individually. This asks them to find fractions of quantities of money, then to say what fraction one amount is of another. The sheet is available in differentiated versions.

During the plenary, invite children from each ability group to show how they calculated to find the answers. Ask questions such as: *How did you work that out? Who used a different strategy?* Again, check that children have made the link between division and finding fractions of quantities.

Lesson

Starter

Repeat the starters for Lessons 3 and 4, this time asking a combination of questions involving rounding to the nearest 10 or 100.

Main teaching activities

Whole class: Explain that today the children will be finding fractions of measures. Begin by reviewing how many centimetres in a metre (100); grams in a kilogram (1000); millilitres in a litre (1000). Invite the children to explain how to work out half a metre, expressing the answer in centimetres. Discuss how using division is helpful when finding fractions of quantities. For example, to find a quarter of 1 metre, we can divide 100cm (which is equivalent to 1 metre) by 4.

Individual work: Provide each child with a copy of activity sheet 'Fractions of measures'. This contains questions about fractions of measures. Explain that we usually use full numbers of appropriate units rather than fractions when we are actually measuring (for example 25cm rather than 1/4 m), so that we can read the numbers on a scale.

Differentiation

Less able: Decide whether to provide the version of the activity sheet that contains simpler questions, all about fractions of a metre.

More able: Use the version of the activity sheet that contains more complex fractions of measures.

Plenary & assessment

Take a question from each of the differentiated activity sheets in turn, and invite a child from the relevant group to explain how they found the solution. Invite children to write on the board, showing how they worked out the answer. Ask questions such as: *What is a quarter of 1 kilogram? How did you work that out? What units did you use in your answer?* Discuss the equivalence of 0.25kg = 1/4 kg = 250g, for example. Again, check that children have made the link between division and finding fractions of quantities.

Name	Date

Fractions of shapes

Shade in the fraction of the shape.

$\dfrac{2}{4}$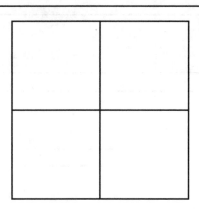

$\dfrac{4}{8}$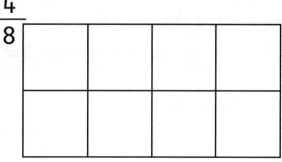

$\dfrac{1}{2}$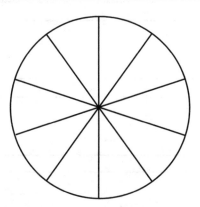

$\dfrac{6}{12}$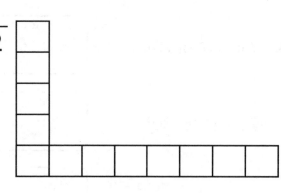

$\dfrac{7}{14}$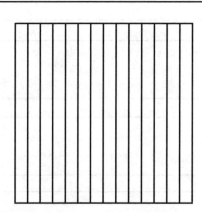

$\dfrac{6}{8}$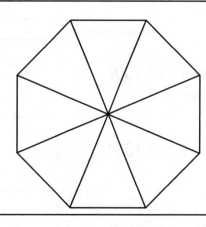

$\dfrac{9}{12}$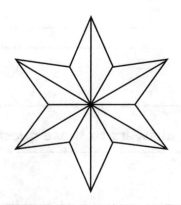

$\dfrac{3}{4}$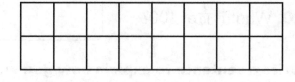

Name	Date

Finding fractions

Write the answers. Show your working.

1. What is $\frac{1}{2}$ of 20?

2. What is $\frac{1}{2}$ of 30?

3. What is $\frac{1}{4}$ of 20?

4. What is $\frac{1}{10}$ of 20?

5. What is $\frac{1}{10}$ of 30?

6. What is $\frac{1}{3}$ of 30?

7. What is $\frac{1}{2}$ of 100?

8. What is $\frac{1}{4}$ of 100?

9. What is $\frac{3}{4}$ of 100?

10. What is $\frac{2}{10}$ of 100?

Write a sentence to explain how you worked out the answers to these questions.

Name	Date

Fractions of money

Write the answers to these questions.

Show your working.

1. What is $\frac{1}{2}$ of £1.00?

2. What is $\frac{1}{2}$ of 50p?

3. What is $\frac{1}{4}$ of £1.00?

4. What is $\frac{3}{4}$ of £1.00?

5. What is $\frac{1}{3}$ of 90p?

6. What fraction of 50p is 25p?

7. What fraction of £1.00 is 75p?

8. What fraction of £1.00 is 10p?

9. What fraction of 20p is 10p?

10. What fraction of 60p is 20p?

Children continue to develop and refine written methods of addition and subtraction. The unit closes with some problem solving relating particularly to time. Children also learn to read the time from an analogue clock to the nearest minute and use am and pm notation.

LEARNING OBJECTIVES

	Topics	Starter	Main teaching activities
Lesson 1	Understanding addition and subtraction Mental calculation strategies (+ and –)	● **Use known number facts and place value to add or subtract mentally, including any pair of two-digit whole numbers, crossing the 10 (but not the 100) boundary.**	● Consolidate understanding of relationship between + and –. ● Find a small difference by counting up (for example: 5003 – 4996). ● Continue to use the relationship between + and –.
Lesson 2	Pencil and paper procedures (+ and –)	As for Lesson 1.	● **Develop and refine written methods for column subtraction of two whole numbers less than 1000.**
Lesson 3	Pencil and paper procedures (+ and –)	As for Lesson 1.	As for Lesson 2.
Lesson 4	Measures	● Derive quickly division facts corresponding to the 2, 3, 4, 5 and 10-times tables.	● Use, read and write the vocabulary related to time. ● Read the time from an analogue clock to the nearest minute, and from a 12-hour digital clock. ● Use am and pm and the notation 9:53.
Lesson 5	Problems involving 'real life', money and measures.	As for Lesson 4.	● Use all four operations to solve word problems involving time, using one or more steps.

Lesson overview

Learning objectives
Starter
● **Use known number facts and place value to add or subtract mentally, including any pair of two-digit whole numbers, crossing the 10 (but not the 100) boundary.**
Main teaching activities
● Consolidate understanding of relationship between + and –.
● Find a small difference by counting up (for example: 5003 – 4996).
● Continue to use the relationship between + and –.

Vocabulary
addition, add, plus, increase, subtraction, minus, subtract, take away, decrease, difference between, find the difference

You will need:

CD pages
'Blank number lines' (see General resources) for each child.

Equipment
Individual whiteboards and pens.

Lesson ①

Starter

Explain to the children that you will call out an addition sum and you want them to write the answers onto their whiteboards. Allow them five seconds to think about the question and write the answer, then ask them to hold up their whiteboards when you say: *Show me*. After each question, ask what strategies they used to work out the answer. Ask, for example: *24 + 35; 31 + 42; 29 + 32; 37 + 45…*

Main teaching activities

Whole class: Ask the children questions such as:
- *If you know that 24 + 35 = 59, what other addition and subtraction facts can you work out?*
- *How can you use addition to check a subtraction answer?*
- *How can you use subtraction to check an addition answer?*

Ask them to write down (on paper or on whiteboards) all the words they can think of that relate to addition (add, plus…). Repeat for words related to subtraction (subtract, minus, take away…). Write the words 'increase' and 'decrease' on the board to introduce this new vocabulary.

Now ask: *What does 'find the difference' mean? How can we find the difference between 9 and 16?* Explain that you could find the answer by subtraction, as in 16 – 9 = 7, but counting on is probably easier. Draw an empty number line on the board:
Show that you can count on 1 from 9 to 10, and then 6 from 10 to 16, so the difference is 7.

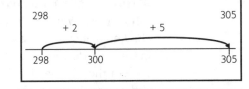

Ask the children if they can think of any other ways they might do it. Repeat this with other numbers that have a small difference (no more than 9), such as 18 – 14 or 54 – 38. Now extend this to differences for three-digit numbers, such as 305 – 298. Draw an empty number line on the board: Invite the children to suggest how to find the difference by counting up. Write:'298 + 2 = 300; 300 + 5 = 305; so 305 – 298 = 7'.

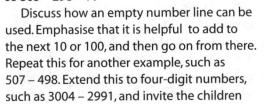

Discuss how an empty number line can be used. Emphasise that it is helpful to add to the next 10 or 100, and then go on from there. Repeat this for another example, such as 507 – 498. Extend this to four-digit numbers, such as 3004 – 2991, and invite the children to add on mentally: 9 + 4 = 13. Repeat this for other four-digit numbers.

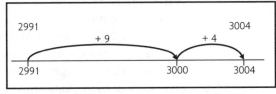

Group work: Ask the children to work in pairs. They take turns to write down any four-digit number that has zeros in the hundreds and tens places, such as 6003. Then they write down any four-digit number that has a thousands place 1 less, 9 in the hundreds and tens places, and any unit, such as 5994. They challenge their partner to find the difference between these two numbers. Provide copies of 'Blank number lines' as an aid. The children can write the numbers and draw arrows to help them to calculate. Ask the children to write ten difference sentences each.

Differentiation

Less able: Decide whether to ask the children to generate three-digit numbers in the same way.
More able: Challenge the children to work mentally, without the use of the blank number line.

Plenary & assessment

Invite children from each ability group to set one of their number sentences for the others to try. Check that they use the language of *What is the difference between…?* Ask questions such as: *How did you work that out? Who used a different method?*

Lessons   overview

Learning objectives

Starter
● **Use known number facts and place value to add or subtract mentally, including any pair of two-digit whole numbers, crossing the 10 (but not the 100) boundary.**

Main teaching activities
● **Develop and refine written methods for column subtraction of two whole numbers less than 1000.**

Vocabulary
addition, add, plus, subtraction, minus, subtract, find the difference

You will need:

Photocopiable pages
'Subtraction' (page 77) for each child.

CD pages
A set of 'Numeral cards 0–20' (seee General resources) for each pair; 'Subtraction', core, less able and more able versions.

Equipment
Individual whiteboards and pens.

Lesson

Starter
Repeat the Starter from Lesson 1, this time for subtraction, such as: *55 – 33; 87 – 43; 81 – 63; 51 – 24; 91 – 12…*

Main teaching activity

Whole class: Write on the board '745 – 76 = ☐', and explain to the children that one way of working out the answer is by counting up, as in Lesson 1. However, with bigger numbers and more 'jumps on' to keep track of, they will need a method of recording their work that also helps with the adding on at the end. Rewrite the subtraction in vertical format and demonstrate the steps to count up from 76 to 745 (right).

Repeat this for another example, such as 623 – 87. Ask the children to remind you of the steps to take to add on from 87 to 623. Now provide an example for the children to try in pairs, such as 521 – 78. Invite children from each ability group to explain each step.

745	
– 76	
4	to make 80
20	to make 100
600	to make 700
40	to make 740
5	to make 745
669	
So: 745 – 76 = 669	

Paired work: Provide each pair with a set of 0–9 numeral cards and some squared paper to assist in keeping numbers vertically aligned. Ask them to take turns to shuffle the numeral cards, then take the top five cards and make a three-digit and a two-digit number. They write a subtraction sentence with these numbers, and solve it using the vertical counting-up method.

Differentiation

Less able: Ask the children to work as a group and work together to make subtraction sentences to solve. Invite each child to help to solve a number sentence. When the children are confident, ask them to work in pairs to solve one for themselves.

More able: If the children are confident with this method, decide whether to introduce decomposition. (See the calculation units in Term 3.)

Plenary & assessment

Invite a pair of children from each group to write one of their number sentences onto the board for the others to solve. Ask the children who wrote up the problem to solve it for the class, and to explain each step. Listen to the language that they use and check that they understand that this method involves counting up to find the difference. Ask questions such as: *Why do you do that? Who can explain this?*

Lesson ③

Repeat the Starters from Lessons 1 and 2, including addition and subtraction questions. Review subtraction by counting on during the main teaching activity. Provide activity sheet 'Subtraction' for the children to use individually. This is available in differentiated form, with subtraction of two-digit numbers for the less able, who can use either the counting-on method or the empty number line method. For the more able, there are questions that ask for the differences between two three-digit numbers, then two four-digit numbers.

During the plenary, choose some questions from each sheet to review with the children. Invite children from each group to demonstrate how they solved the problem, writing on the board. Ask: *How did you work it out?*

Lessons ④ ⑤ overview

Preparation
Photocopy 'Time Pelmanism' and 'Clock face' onto thin card. Ask the children to cut out the clock faces and fit the hands to using a paper fastener.

Learning objectives
Starter
● Derive quickly division facts corresponding to 2-, 3-, 4-, 5- and 10-times tables.
Main teaching activities
● Use, read and write the vocabulary related to time.
● Read the time from an analogue clock to the nearest minute, and from a 12-hour digital clock.
● Use am and pm, and the notation 9:53.
● Use all four operations to solve word problems involving time, using one or more steps.

Vocabulary
day, week, month, year, hour, minute, second, today, am, pm

You will need:
Photocopiable pages
'Time problems' (page 78).

CD pages
'Time problems', core, less able and more able versions; 'Clock face' for each child and 'Time Pelmanism' for each pair (see General resources).

Equipment
Paper fasteners; digital clock; analogue clock; whiteboards.

Lesson ④

Starter
Explain that you will ask some division facts for the 2-, 3- and 4-times tables. Ask the children to write the answers on their whiteboards, and to hold up their boards when you say: *Show me*. Say, for example: *What is 14 divided by 2? Half of 20? Quarter of 24? How many 3s are there in 27?* Keep the pace sharp to encourage quick recall of division facts.

Main teaching activities
Whole class: Explain that you will say some times that you want the children to set on their clock faces. When you say: *Show me,* they hold up their clocks. Begin with times to the nearest five-minute interval, such as 8:15, 9:45, 7:05…

Next, use the teaching clock to explain that within each five-minute interval on the clock face, it is possible to set the clock to 1:01, 1:02, 1:03… Ask the children to look at their clock faces and note the one-minute intervals. They can count from, say, five past to ten past, in one-minute intervals. Ask the children to set their clocks as accurately as they can to the times that you give them. Say: *12:37, 18 minutes to 3, 13 minutes past 12, 5:28…* Check that the children understand, and are setting their clocks with reasonable accuracy. Make more able children aware of the way the hour hand moves on during each hour, too. At 3:28, for example, the minute hand will be just before the 6, and the hour hand about halfway between the 3 and the 4.

Remind the children that they have already learned how to read a digital clock to the nearest five minutes. Write on the board '11:55' and ask the children to set their clocks to this time. Then ask: *What will the digital clock read in 1 minute… 2 minutes… 5 minutes?* Each time, invite a child to write the time on the board. Check that the children understand that the hour changes to 12 five minutes after 11:55. Repeat this for other digital times in one-minute intervals, such as 5:08, 9:37…

Discuss when to use 'am' (from the Latin *ante meridiem* meaning 'before noon') and 'pm' (*post meridiem* meaning 'after noon'). Say: *It is 37 minutes past two in the afternoon. How would I write that?* Encourage a child to write on the board: '2:37pm'. Repeat this for other times, morning and afternoon.

Group work: Provide each pair with cards made from activity sheet 'Time Pelmanism'. They play Pelmanism with the cards. The children should match a digital to an analogue time. The winner is the child who collects more pairs of cards.

Differentiation

Less able: If the children are likely to struggle with the activity, suggest that they have their cards face up, and take turns to find matching pairs.

More able: When the children have played 'Time Pelmanism' two or three times, challenge them to take turns to say a time to their partner, using am or pm. Their partner sets their clock to the time, then says the time in as many ways as they can: '12:14', '14 minutes past 12', and so on.

Plenary & assessment

Set the teaching clock to different times. Invite children from each group to write the digital time on the board. Say whether it is morning or afternoon, and check that the children use am or pm appropriately. Ask questions such as: *If it is 11:45am, what time will it be in 20 minutes?*

Repeat the Starter from Lesson 4, including questions from the 5- and 10-times tables. Explain that the lesson is about time problems. On the board, show children how to use an empty number line to count on for the time, such as:

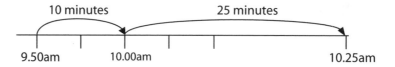

10 minutes   25 minutes

9.50am   10.00am   10.25am

Provide activity sheet 'Time problems', which is differentiated. Ask the children to work individually to solve the problems. Remind them that they can use clock faces or an empty time line to help them. During the plenary, review some of the questions from each sheet, and ask the children to explain how they worked out the answers. Check that they write the time in digital format, and use am and pm appropriately. Make sure they understand that digital time is not decimal: 11:55 plus 5 minutes is 12:00, not 11:60.

Name	Date

Subtraction

Find the answers to these subtraction problems.

Show your working.

1. Find the difference between 307 and 27.

5. What is 742 minus 87?

2. Find the difference between 434 and 149.

6. What is 666 take away 89?

3. Find the difference between 194 and 219.

7. Find the difference between 92 and 807.

4. What is 832 subtract 76?

8. Find the difference between 593 and 167.

Name	Date

Time problems

Write the answers to these time problems.

Show your working.

You may use a calculator to help with the last question.

1. Iqbal spent 35 minutes on his homework last night. He started it at 5.00pm and went to bed at 9.00pm. What time did he finish his homework?

2. Football matches often start at 3.00pm on Saturdays. The first half lasts 45 minutes. The match finishes at about 4.40pm. What time does the first half finish?

3. A joint of meat has to be cooked for half an hour for every 500g. It has to be cooked at gas mark 5. If a joint weighed 1500g, how long would it have to be cooked for?

4. A boy was trying to work out how many days he had left at school that term. His birthday was on 10 June. There were four weeks of the term left. How many days at school would that be?

5. Mrs Gallop was planning a trip around the world. She was 35 years old. She worked out that it would take about 2 years to travel all around the world. How many months would that be?

6. Bath time at 'Fido Dog's Home' is great fun. They have 100 dogs. They bathe each dog for 10 minutes. How many dogs can they bathe in an hour?

7. Mr Superfit ran one mile the other day in $4\frac{1}{2}$ minutes. He is 21 years old. How long would it take him if he ran two miles at the same speed?

8. It took Miss Climber exactly 2 hours and 10 minutes to climb Mount Snowdon. The mountain is over 3000 feet high. How many minutes did she take to get to the top? How many seconds would that be?

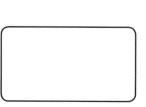

Handling data

Children make decisions about collecting, organising and representing data. They use tally charts, frequency tables, pictograms and bar charts for this purpose.

LEARNING OBJECTIVES

	Topics	Starter	Main teaching activities
Lesson **1**	Handling data	● **Use known number facts and place value to add or subtract mentally, including any pair of two-digit whole numbers**, crossing the 10 (but not the 100) boundary.	● Solve a problem by collecting quickly, organising, representing and interpreting data in tables, charts, graphs and diagrams, including those generated by a computer – tally charts, for example.
Lesson **2**	Handling data	As for Lesson 1.	As for Lesson 1.
Lesson **3**	Handling data	As for Lesson 1.	● Solve a problem by collecting quickly, organising, representing and interpreting data in tables, charts, graphs and diagrams, including those generated by a computer – frequency tables and pictograms (symbols representing 2, 5, 10 or 20 units), for example.
Lesson **4**	Handling data	● **Know by heart multiplication facts for 2-, 3-, 4-, 5- and 10-times tables.**	As for Lesson 3.
Lesson **5**	Handling data	As for Lesson 4.	● Solve a problem by collecting quickly, organising, representing and interpreting data in tables, charts, graphs and diagrams, including those generated by a computer – bar charts (with intervals labelled in 2s, 5s, 10s or 20s), for example.

Lesson   overview

Preparation
Photocopy 'Follow-me cards' onto thin card and cut out. (You can print the page 'complete' as a reference for the order and answers.) Enlarge 'Frequency table' and 'Pictogram' to model the children's work. Also enlarge 'Vegetables' and 'Bar chart' to A3 and pin to the board.

Learning objectives
Starter
● **Use known number facts and place value to add or subtract mentally, including any pair of two-digit whole numbers, crossing the 10 (but not the 100) boundary.**
● **Know by heart multiplication facts for 2-, 3-, 4-, 5- and 10-times tables.**
Main teaching activities
● Solve a problem by collecting quickly, organising, representing and interpreting data in tables, charts, graphs and diagrams, including those generated by a computer – for example, tally charts and frequency tables; pictograms (symbols representing 2, 5, 10 or 20 units); bar charts (intervals labelled in 2s, 5s, 10s or 20s).

Vocabulary
vote, survey, questionnaire, data, count, tally, sort, set, represent, table, list, graph, diagram, axes, label, title, most common or popular

You will need:
Photocopiable pages
'Reading tally chart' (page 83).

CD pages
Enough copies of 'Follow-me cards' for each class member to have a card (core, more able and less able sets provided); 'Reading tally charts', 'Bar chart' and 'Vegetables', one each for less able and more able child. Individual copies of 'Favourite colour survey', 'Frequency table' and 'Pictogram'.

Lesson ①

Starter

Give out the 'Follow-me' cards randomly – three differentiated sets are provided. Choose a child to start. They read out the calculation on their card, and another child will have the answer to that as the first part of the calculation on their card. They read it out and this carries on around the class. Ask questions such as: *How did you work that out?* If a child falters, say the answer in order to keep the pace of this activity.

Main teaching activities

Whole class: Ask the children questions such as:
- *If I wanted to find out your favourite colours, how could I do it?*
- *How could we present this information to other people?*
- *What is a tally mark?*

Write on the board 'PINK', 'BLUE', 'YELLOW', 'GREEN', 'PURPLE'. Ask the children to choose their favourite colour from this list. Give them time to discuss this for a few moments in groups, then select children to record the tallies for their group on the board. When they have finished, ask questions such as:
- *What is the most/least popular colour? How can you tell?*
- *Would the results be the same if we asked another class?*
- *What would the results be if you were allowed two votes for each colour?*

Explain that the class is going to split up into small groups to go around the school and find out the favourite colours of other classes. (Pre-warn other teachers of this impending event!)

Group work: Give each group a copy of 'Favourite colour survey' and agree which class they will visit to collect information. Set a clear time limit so that children go to do this quickly. When the children return, ask each group to think of five questions about their data, and to write these on the activity sheet.

While the children are working, collect the tally information onto one copy of the activity sheet, then write up the information on the board. Ask the children to answer these questions:
- *What is the most popular colour in our school?*
- *What is the least popular colour?*
- *How did you work out your answers?*

The children may need help with some of the calculations, depending on the results.

Differentiation

Less able: In the data collecting, you might send a group out with a classroom assistant. Alternatively, you might decide to have a mixed ability group. The children will need help with adding the whole-school scores, so have appropriate support material available (such as number lines or hundred squares).

More able: If you have a higher-ability group for the data collecting, they could record with numbers rather than a tally mark. When the children are recording the whole school, encourage the children to add up mentally.

Plenary & assessment

Invite the children to answer the three questions that you asked:
- *What is the most popular colour in our school?*
- *What is the least popular colour?*
- *How did you work out your answers?*

Ask the children what questions they wrote down. Invite one question from each of the groups and encourage the other children to try to answer it. Discuss whether or not it was a useful question to ask. A useful question might be 'Was red more popular than purple?', as this can be answered from the data. Questions that are not useful include those that cannot be answered from the data, such as 'What is Tom's mother's favourite colour?'

Lesson ②

Repeat the Starter from Lesson 1. Shuffle the cards so that each child gets a different card this time. Time the activity so that the children are motivated to keep the pace really sharp.

Review the work on tally charts undertaken in the previous lesson. Remind the children that they can use the data in the tally chart to help them to ask and answer questions. Provide a copy of activity sheet 'Reading tally charts' for each child. This is available in differentiated formats, with smaller numbers for the less able, and larger ones for the more able. Ask the children to use the tally charts to help them to answer the questions.

During the plenary, go through the questions on the sheet and discuss with the children how they found their answers. Discuss the titles for the chart that the children suggested, and invite them to say which they think is the most appropriate.

Ask the children what they would like to find out about in the next lesson by using a survey. These, typically, will be things like favourite pop group/TV programme/day of the week/sport. Choose six things and tell the children that you will let them choose which of the six survey groups they want to be in for the next lesson.

Lesson ③

Starter
Repeat the Starter from Lesson 1 again, but challenge the children to improve on the time that it took them in Lesson 2 to complete the activity.

Main teaching activities
Whole class: Choose one of the survey topics and write it as a title for the enlarged copy of 'Frequency table', pinned to the board. Ask the children to suggest what the headings should be for each of the rows in the table. For example, if they have suggested favourite pop groups, then each row may be headed with a pop group's name. When the chart on the board has row headings, ask the children to decide which of the pop groups is their favourite, then collect the data by show of hands for each heading. Write in the total for each pop group, as a number this time. Explain that this is another way of showing data that has been collected. Ask questions such: as *Which group is most/least popular? Which group has more votes than… fewer votes than…?*

Now explain that the data can be transferred to a pictogram. Pin up the enlarged 'Pictogram' and ask the children to help you to transfer the data from one chart to the other. Explain that the pictogram can have pictures to represent 1, 2, or more people. Decide how many people each of the pictures will represent and write in the relevant scale: 2s, 5s or 10s (using scales other than 1 provides an opportunity to use multiples of that number). Write the names of the pop groups onto the chart. Invite children to come out and glue the appropriate number of pictures for each pop group. When this is completed, ask questions about the data, and encourage the children to read how many there are. Check that they understand about the scale, and that each picture represents more than one person.

Group work: Ask the children to decide which survey they would like to carry out, and have groups of about four children. Provide activity sheets 'Frequency table' and 'Pictogram'. Give the children time to write the title and headings onto the frequency table. Asking one group at a time, they collect the data from the rest of the class (or a partner class, if you have two or more form entry). When all the information has been collected, ask the children to write five questions about their chart ready for the plenary. They should then construct a pictogram on the 'Pictogram' activity sheet.

Differentiation
Less able: The children will be working in mixed ability groups, so other children will no doubt help them. They will probably need support in writing the questions.
More able: Challenge the children to think of really difficult questions about their chart.

Plenary & assessment

Select children from each group to show the class their chart and ask their questions. Invite each group to explain how they transferred their data to the pictogram and how they chose their scale. Ask questions such as: *Was this a good scale to choose? Why/why not?* Check that the children can interrogate both the frequency table and the pictogram in order to ask and answer questions about the data.

Lesson ④

For the Starter, remind the children of inverses in the times tables. For example, 4 × 6 has the same answer as 6 × 4. Explain that you will say a table fact. Ask the children to put up their hands to respond with the answer, then with the other three related facts. Say, for example: *7 × 3*. The children should respond with '7 × 3 = 21'; '3 × 7 = 21'; '21 ÷ 3 = 7'; '21 ÷ 7 = 3'.

During the main teaching activity, review with the children what they learned about pictograms in the previous lesson. Discuss how they can use their table facts to help them to work out how many a series of pictures on a pictogram represents. For example: *If 1 picture represents 2, how many would 5 pictures represent? And if 1 picture represents 5, what would 3 pictures represent?* Provide copies of activity sheet 'Vegetables' and ask the children to work individually to answer the questions about the pictogram. This sheet is available in differentiated versions with simpler or harder counting. During the plenary, review the activity sheet that most of the class have worked on, using an A3 OHT version. Invite children from each group to suggest the answers. Discuss with the children what a suitable title for the chart would be, and why.

Lesson ⑤

Starter
Repeat the Starter from Lesson 4, this time using other facts from the 2-, 3- 4-, 5- or 10-times tables.

Main teaching activity

Whole class: Use the survey that was made into a pictogram again. Remind the children of the data collected by pinning this up on the board. Explain that another way of showing data is to produce a bar chart. Draw a bar chart outline on the board and discuss with the children what scale would be suitable, choosing from multiples of 2, 5, 10 or 20. Put the scale onto the y-axis of the chart, and write the headings along the x-axis. Invite children from each group to help with drawing in the appropriate size of bar. Ask: *Where will this bar come to?* When the chart is finished, invite the children to ask and answer questions, such as: *How many… are there? Are there more… or more…? How many more?*
Individual work: Ask the children to complete the 'Bar chart' activity sheet individually. This shows a bar chart, with a scale in 5s, for them to interrogate.

Differentiation

Less able: Decide whether to use the version of the activity sheet with a scale in 5s but with lower totals.
More able: Decide whether to use the version of the activity sheet with a scale in 10s.

Plenary & assessment

Review the 'Bar charts' sheets with all of the children, using A3 versions. Ask the children to answer the questions on the sheet. Choose children from each group to respond. Check that the children understand that a scale is used, and how to interpret the amount represented by a bar. Ask questions such as: *How many more/fewer… were there than…? How can you tell? Of which animal is there most/least?*

Name   Date

Reading tally charts

Answer the questions below about this tally chart.

Dog ЖН ЖН ЖН
Cat ЖН ЖН II
Hamster ЖН
Goldfish ЖН ЖН
Rabbit ЖН II

1. What do you think the chart shows? _____

_____

2. What was the most popular animal? _____

3. What was the least popular animal? _____

4. How many animals are in the chart altogether? _____

5. What do you think the title of the chart should be? _____

_____

Car ЖН ЖН ЖН ЖН I
Bus ЖН IIII
Train ЖН ЖН I
Bike ЖН
Aeroplane ЖН ЖН ЖН ЖН ЖН

Answer the questions below about the tally chart above.

1. What do you think the chart shows? _____

_____

2. What was the most popular transport? _____

3. What was the least popular transport? _____

4. How many things are in the chart altogether? _____

5. What do you think the title of the chart should be? _____

_____

EVERY DAY: Practise and develop oral and mental skills (counting, mental strategies, rapid recall of × and ÷ facts)
• Read and write whole numbers to at least 10 000 in figures and words, and know what each digit represents.
• Add/subtract 1, 10 or 100 to/from any integer.
• Count on or back in tens or hundreds from any whole number up to 10 000.
• Consolidate knowing by heart addition and subtraction facts for all numbers to 20.
• Derive quickly doubles of all whole numbers to 50, and the corresponding halves.
• Add 3 or 4 small numbers, finding pairs totalling 10, or 9 or 11.
• **Use known number facts and place value to add or subtract mentally, including any pair of two-digit whole numbers,** crossing the 10 (but not the 100) boundary.
• **Know by heart multiplication facts for 2-, 3-, 4-, 5- and 10-times tables.**
• **Derive quickly division facts corresponding to 2-, 3-, 4-, 5- and 10-times tables.**
• Multiply any integer up to 1000 by 10 and understand the effect.
• **Round any positive integer less than 1000 to the nearest 10 or 100.**

Units	Days	Topics	Objectives
1	3	Place value, ordering, rounding (whole numbers)	Multiply any integer up to 1000 by 10 (whole numbers) and understand the effect. Begin to multiply by 100. Read and write the vocabulary of comparing and ordering numbers. **Use symbols correctly, including less than (<), greater than (>), equals (=).** **Round any positive integer less than 1000 to nearest 10 or 100.** Give one or more numbers lying between two given numbers and order a set of whole numbers less than 1000. Read and write the vocabulary of estimation and approximation.
2	5	Understanding addition and subtraction	Understand the principles (not the names) of the commutative and associative laws as they apply, or not, to addition and subtraction. Add three or four small numbers, finding pairs totalling to 10.
		Mental calculation strategies for addition and subtraction	Partition into tens and units, adding tens first. Add three two-digit multiples of 10, such as 40 + 70 + 50. Add or subtract the nearest multiple of 10, then adjust. Use known number facts and place value to add or subtract mentally, including any pair of two-digit whole numbers (crossing 10 but not 100).
3	5	Written methods of addition and subtraction	Use informal pencil and paper methods to support, record or explain additions/subtractions. **Choose and use appropriate number operations and appropriate ways of calculating (mental, mental with jottings, paper and pencil) to solve problems.**
		Problem-solving	Develop and refine written methods for column addition of more than two whole numbers less than 1000.
		Making decisions	Develop and refine written methods for subtraction, building on mental methods.
		Problems involving 'real life' money or measures	Use addition/subtraction operations to solve problems involving numbers in 'real life', money and measures, using one step, then more than one step, including converting pounds to pence and metres to centimetres.
		Checking results	Check with equivalent calculations.
4	5	Measures	Estimate and check times using seconds, minutes, hours. **Know and use the relationships between familiar units of mass.**
		Shape and space	Suggest suitable units and equipment to estimate or measure mass. Know the equivalent of one half, one quarter, three quarters and one tenth of 1 kilogram in grams.
		Making decisions	Measure and calculate the area of rectangles and simple shapes, using counting methods and standard units (cm^2). **Record estimates to a suitable degree of accuracy.**
5	5	Problem-solving	**Choose and use appropriate number operations and appropriate ways of calculating (mental, mental with jottings, pencil and paper) to solve problems.**
		Making decisions	Check with equivalent calculations. Explain methods and reasoning about numbers orally and in writing.
		Reasoning about number and shapes	Solve mathematical problems or puzzles, recognise and explain patterns and relationships, generalise and predict. Suggest extensions by asking 'What if..?

EVERY DAY: Practise and develop oral and mental skills (eg counting, mental strategies, rapid recall of + and – facts)

- Read and write whole numbers up to at least 10 000 in figures and words, and know what each digit represents.
- Count on or back in tens, hundreds or thousands from any whole number up to 10 000.
- **Round any positive integer less than 1000 to the nearest 10 or 100.**
- Consolidate knowing by heart addition and subtraction facts for all numbers to 20.
- **Use known number facts and place value to add or subtract mentally, including any pair of two-digit whole numbers, crossing the 10 (but not the 100) boundary.**
- Know by heart multiplication facts for 2-, 3-, 4-, 5- and 10-times tables.
- **Derive quickly division facts corresponding to 2-, 3-, 4-, 5- and 10-times tables.**
- **Derive quickly doubles of all whole numbers to 50, and the corresponding halves.**
- Use known number facts and place value to multiply integers by 10.).

Units	Days	Topics	Objectives
6	3	Direction and angle	Use eight compass directions N, S, E, W, NE, NW, SE, SW. Make and measure clockwise and anticlockwise turns, for example, from SW to N. Begin to know that angles are measured in degrees and that one whole turn is 360 degrees or four right angles, a quarter turn is 90 degrees or one right angle, half a right angle is 45 degrees. Use of a clock face. Recognise positions and directions, for example, describe and find the position of a point on a grid of squares where the lines are numbered. Recognise simple examples of horizontal and vertical lines.
8	5	Properties of numbers	Recognise negative numbers in context. Recognise and extend number sequences formed by counting from any number in steps of constant size, extending beyond zero when counting back.
		Reasoning about numbers	Explain methods and reasoning orally and in writing. Make and investigate a general statement about familiar numbers by finding examples that satisfy it.
9	5	Mental calculation strategies for multiplication and division	Extending understanding of the operations of multiplication and division, and their relationship to each other and to addition and subtraction. Understand the principles (not the names) of the commutative, associative and distributive laws as they apply in multiplication.
		Understanding multiplication and division	**Find remainders after division.** Divide a whole number of pounds by 2, 4, 5 or 10 to give pounds and pence.
		Pencil and paper procedures	Use closely-related facts (for example, to multiply 9 or 11, multiply by 10 and adjust; develop the 6-times table from 4- and 2-times tables). Use the distributive law and partitioning to multiply TU by U.
10	5	Making decisions Problems involving 'real life', money and measures Checking results	**Use informal pencil and paper methods to support, record or explain divisions/multiplications. Choose and use appropriate number operations and ways of calculating (mental, mental with jottings, pencil and paper) to solve problems.** Approximate first. Use all four operations to solve word problems involving numbers in 'real life' money, using more than one step. Check with the inverse operation. Revise the vocabulary for time and estimate time durations.
11	5	Fractions and decimals	Use fraction notation. **Recognise simple fractions that are several parts of a whole**, such as 2/3 or 5/8, and mixed numbers such as 5 3/4. Identify two simple fractions with totals of one whole. **Recognise the equivalence of simple fractions.** Order simple fractions, for example, decide whether fractions such as 3/8 or 7/10 are greater than or less than 1/2. Understand decimal notation and place value for tenths and hundredths and use it in context, order amounts of money.
12	5	Handling data	Solve a problem by collecting quickly, organising, representing and interpreting data in tables, charts, graphs and diagrams. Using pictograms, bar charts, tally charts and frequency tables representing 2, 5 and 10 units. Using bar charts labelled in intervals in 2s, 5s, 10s or 20s. Using the computer. Using Venn diagrams. Using Carroll diagrams.

Ordering and rounding

Children learn to multiply any whole number by 10 and begin to understand the process of multiplying by 100. They practise using mathematical vocabulary to estimate, approximate, compare and order numbers and use 'greater than' and 'less than' symbols. They learn to round positive numbers less than one thousand to the nearest 10 or 100.

LEARNING OBJECTIVES

		Topics	Starter	Main teaching activities
Lesson	1	Place value, ordering, rounding (whole numbers)	● Count on and back in tens and hundreds from any two-digit or three-digit number.	● Multiply any integer up to 1000 by 10 (whole numbers) and understand the effect. ● Begin to multiply by 100.
Lesson	2	Place value, ordering, rounding (whole numbers)	● Read and write whole numbers to at least 10 000 in figures and words, and know what each digit represents.	● Read and write the vocabulary of comparing and ordering numbers. ● **Use symbols correctly, including less than (<), greater than (>), equals (=).**
Lesson	3	Place value, ordering, rounding (whole numbers)	● Use known facts and place value to multiply integers by 10 and 100.	● **Round any positive integer less than 1000 to nearest 10 or 100.** ● Give one or more numbers lying between two given numbers and order a set of whole numbers less than 1000. ● Read and write the vocabulary of estimation and approximation.

Lessons overview

Preparation
Prepare 'Place value grid' and 'Number ladder' as OHT's or enlarge to A3 and laminate to display on a whiteboard.

Learning objectives
Starter
● Count on and back in tens and hundreds from any two-digit or three-digit number.
● Read and write whole numbers to at least 10 000 in figure and words, and know what each digit represents.
● Use known facts and place value to multiply integers by 10 and 100.
Main teaching activities
● Multiply any integer (whole number) up to 100 by 10, and understand the effect.
● Begin to multiply by 100.
● Read and write the vocabulary of comparing and ordering numbers.
● **Use symbols correctly, including less than (<), greater than (>), equals (=).**
● **Round any positive integer less than 1000 to nearest 10 or 100.**
● Give one or more numbers lying between two given numbers, and order a set of whole numbers less than 1000.
● Read and write the vocabulary of estimation and approximation.

Vocabulary
units, tens, hundreds, thousands, zero, place value, place holder, greater than, less than, equal to, difference, round up, round down, round to nearest 100, round to nearest 1000

You will need:
Photocopiable pages
'Rounding up and rounding down' for each child (see page 89).

CD pages
'Ten times Bingo instructions' (see General resources) and 'Ten times Bingo questions' core, less able, more able and template versions; 'Place value grid' (see General resources); 'Rolling the dice' core, less able, more able and template versions; A3 copy of 'Number ladder' (see General resources); 'Rounding up and rounding down' core, less able, more able and template versions.

Equipment
Number fans; Post-it Notes; dice; Blu-tack; OHP (optional).

Lesson

Starter

Start from 10 and together count on in tens up to at least 200, then from 200 count back in tens. Next, start at 55 and count on in tens up to about 255, and then back again. Repeat with other starting points, eg 27, 66, 174, 821. Repeat the activity counting on and back in 100s from two-digit and three-digit starting points, eg 71, 126, 333.

Main teaching activities

Whole class: Provide each child with a number fan. Explain to the children that when you call out a single-digit number they should use their number fans to show you that number multiplied by 10. Repeat for several single-digit numbers and then move on to two-digit numbers. Ask: *How did you get the answer? What are you doing to multiply by 10?* Be sure that the children realise that the digit zero is being placed at the end of the number, and why this happens. *Could you multiply by 100?*

Now ask: *Give me the number that is ten times larger than…* (27, 270, for example). *Now give me the number that is ten times smaller than…* (500, 50, for example). Check responses.

Group work: Split the class into groups of four or five, by ability. Explain to the children that they will be playing 'Bingo'. In each group, one child should be the caller and should be given the set of 'Ten times Bingo instructions' and questions to read. Tell the children to call out if they get a line or a full house. Provide each child with a copy of the activity sheet 'Ten times Bingo questions' or prepare bingo cards with different sets of numbers.

Differentiation

Less able: Provide children with the version of 'Ten times Bingo questions' that uses a smaller grid and asks for multiples of 10.

More able: Provide children with the version of 'Ten times Bingo questions' that challenges the children to search for multiples of 10, 100 and 1000.

Plenary & assessment

Hold up number fans showing 27 and 270. Ask: *What is the relationship between these numbers?* Use the 'Place value grid' and ask various children to write in three- and four-digit numbers, including multiples of 10 and 100.

Write up the number 27 and ask a child to write up the answer to 27 multiplied by 10. Then ask: *What would happen if we divided 270 by 10?* Repeat with another two-digit number.

Lesson

Starter

Write '27' onto the enlarged 'Place value grid'. Ask the children: *What is the value of the 7?* (7 units) *What is the value of the 2?* (2 tens) *What would 27 multiplied by 10 be?* (270) Write '270' in the grid, emphasising the movement as you move each of the digits to the next column, and repeat the questions: *What is the value of the 7? What is the value of the 2?* Write in the grid progressively larger numbers, up to 10 000, continually referring to the headings at the top of each column. Check that the children realise that a digit written in the thousands column has a value ten times larger than the same digit written in the hundreds column, and so on.

Main teaching activities

Whole class: Give each pair a dice. Ask the children to roll their dice twice and record the numbers on the 'Rolling dice' activity sheet, for example, 2 and 6. Then ask who can make a two-digit number from their two numbers, for example, 26 or 62. Record the two numbers on the sheet. Ask: *Who has made the larger number? How do you know? What is the difference between your numbers?* Ask a pair to write their numbers on the board. Introduce 'greater than' and 'less than' and, if the two digits are the same, 'equal to' (26 < 62 and 62 > 26). Make the > and < into crocodiles: the crocodile always eats the larger fish!

Now repeat for three rolls of the dice. Ask: *How many three-digit numbers can be made?* Write an example of numbers, in order, on the board, for example, '123, 132, 213, 231, 312, 321'. Ask the children to do the same with their numbers.

Paired work: Provide fresh copies of the 'Rolling the dice' sheet. The core version requires the children to use four rolls of the dice to generate four-digit numbers and then to write their numbers in words. On the board, draw a number line from 1000 to 10 000. Ask the children to write their largest four-digit number on a sticky note and to attach it to the board in the approximate position. Discuss. For each number, use appropriate vocabulary: *Is it nearer to 1000 or 10 000? What number would be halfway between 1000 and 10 000? Is your number closer to 1000, 5000 or 10 000? Is your number greater than or less than 5000?* Invite individual children, using > and < signs drawn on sticky notes, to pick two four-digit numbers from the board and make a correct statement.

Differentiation

Less able: Use the version of 'Rolling the dice' activity sheet that focuses on rolling three-digit numbers.

More able: Provide copies of the extended version of the 'Rolling the dice' sheet on which children roll five-digit numbers.

Plenary & assessment

Invite children to pick two sticky notes from the board and describe a relationship, using a number sentence, for example, '2134 is less than 2341' or '1000 is ten times smaller than 10 000.' Write these on the board, using < or > signs. Ask: *How do you know which is the bigger number? Which digit /digits tell us? What is the value of the digit?*

Lesson

Starter

Ask individual children for a single-digit or two-digit number. Respond quickly with the number that is a hundred times larger, for example, 5 (500), 12 (1200).

Ask the children what you are doing to each number. Reverse roles by showing the children a single-digit or two-digit number and asking them to multiply the number by 100. Then ask the children to write on their whiteboards the number that is ten times smaller than the one shown to them, for example, 70 (7) and 130 (13).

Main teaching activities

Whole class: Display an A3 copy (or OHT) of the 'Number ladder' sheet on the board. Write in the numbers 320 and 330 at either end and 325 in the middle.

Ask: *Where would 327 go? Is 327 nearer to 320 or 330?* Repeat with other three-digit numbers.

Ask: *Which digit in the number helps us to decide whether to round up or down? What about numbers ending in 5? (They are rounded up.) What happens if we round to the nearest 100?* Write in the numbers 400, 450 and 500 on the number ladder or use a number line on the board. *What about numbers ending in 50? (They are rounded up.)*

Individual work: Provide a copy of the 'Rounding up and rounding down' sheet.

Main teaching activities

Less able: Work with these children. Write 'round up' and 'round down' on the number ladder and use as additional support. Decide whether to provide the version of the sheet with two-digit numbers to the nearest 10 and three-digit numbers to the nearest 100.

More able: Provide the version of the sheet with numbers up to 10 000.

Plenary & assessment

Write up 260–270 on the board and call out various numbers in this range, asking children to round to the nearest 10 and 100. Ask: *Why did you choose to round the number up/down? What number did you look at?* Write up 267 and ask: *Is 267 greater than, less than or equal to 270?* (Use >, =, <.) *Can you make a number sentence?* (For example, 270 > 267.)

Name	Date

Rounding up and rounding down

1. Put these numbers on the number line below.

141 144 149 145 147

140   150

Now round them to the nearest 10.

Number	Rounded to the nearest 10 (up or down)
141	
144	
149	
145	
147	

2. Put these numbers on the number line below.

670 650 660 630 610

600   700

Now round them to the nearest 100.

Number	Rounded to the nearest 100 (up or down)
670	
650	
660	
630	
610	

Spring term
Unit 2
Understanding addition and subtraction

Children develop their strategies for addition and subtraction mentally, to include any pair of two-digit whole numbers. They are introduced to the principles of the commutative and associative laws as they apply to addition, but not to subtraction. They explore different ways of finding pairs totalling 10, and multiples of 10. They practise partitioning into tens and units, and addition and subtraction to the nearest multiple of ten then adjusting.

LEARNING OBJECTIVES

		Topics	Starter	Main teaching activities
Lesson	1	Understanding addition and subtraction	● Say or write a subtraction statement to a corresponding addition statement.	● Understand the principles (not the names) of the commutative and associative laws as they apply or not to addition and subtraction.
Lesson	2	Understanding addition and subtraction	As Lesson 1.	● Add three or four small numbers, finding pairs totalling to 10. ● Partition into tens and units, adding tens first. ● Add three two-digit multiples of 10, such as 40 + 70 + 50.
Lesson	3	Understanding addition and subtraction Mental calculation strategies for addition and subtraction	● Consolidate knowing by heart addition and subtraction facts for all numbers to 20.	As Lesson 2.
Lesson	4	Understanding addition and subtraction	● Derive quickly all pairs of multiples of 50 with a total of 1000.	● Add or subtract the nearest multiple of 10, then adjust. ● Use known number facts and place value to add or subtract mentally including any pair of two-digit whole numbers (crossing 10 but not 100).
Lesson	5	Understanding addition and subtraction	As Lesson 4.	As Lesson 4.

Lessons overview

Learning objectives
Starter
● Say or write a subtraction statement for a corresponding addition statement.
● Consolidate knowing by heart addition and subtraction facts for all numbers to 20.

Main teaching activities
● Understand the principles (not the names) of the commutative and associative laws as they apply or not to addition and subtraction.
● Add three or four small numbers, finding pairs totalling to 10.
● Partition into tens and units, adding tens first.
● Add three two-digit multiples of 10, such as 40 + 70 + 50.

Vocabulary
addition, increase, sum, altogether, total, subtraction, difference, decrease, minus, take away, sentence, strategy

You will need:
Photocopiable pages
'Matching addition' (see page 95) for each child.

CD pages
'Spider diagrams' (see General resources); 'Matching addition', core, less able, more able and template versions; 'The Grid Game instructions' for each child and 'The Grid Game board' and 'The Grid Game Score sheet' (see General resources) for each pair.

Equipment
Whiteboards; Post-it Notes; colouring pencils; number fans; calculators.

Lesson

Starter

Write on the board the numbers 17, 3 and 20, and ask the children to write on their whiteboards two addition sentences using the three numbers (17 + 3 = 20, 3 + 17 = 20). Check responses and then ask: *Now can you write two subtraction sentences using the three numbers?* (20 – 17 = 3 and 20 – 3 = 17). Explain to the children that you will call out an addition sentence and would like them to write down a corresponding subtraction sentence. For example, call out: 3 + 12 = 15, and they can respond '15 – 12 = 3' or '15 – 3 = 12'. You may have to write the three numbers on the board to support the less confident children. Repeat this with several examples, highlighting the two different possible subtraction sentences.

Main teaching activities

Whole class: Explain that this is the first of five lessons on adding and subtracting mentally. In this lesson the children will be looking at patterns within addition and subtraction sentences that can help to add and subtract. On the board, write three numbers in a loop and ask individual children to draw 'arms' from the loop, each to show one number sentence that can be made with the three numbers.

Say that this is a spider diagram. Repeat with 123, 24 and 99. Say: *Look at the additions. Does it matter which way round we add the numbers?* (No. This is the commutative law of addition.) Ask: *Does it matter for subtraction?* (Yes.) Discuss and explain why, using examples such as 8 – 7 = 1 but 7 – 8 = –1.

Individual work: Ask the children to draw their own spider diagram with four legs to show four different number sentences that can be made by using three numbers. Use the numbers 24, 18 and 6, and then 29, 17 and 12, writing them on the board. Ask the children to check their calculations and to be systematic by working out the additions and then the subtractions.

Differentiation

Less able: Provide these children with three sticky notes on which they can write the numbers, so that they can move their numbers around in front of them to give the different combinations. A spider diagram template has also been provided to support them with this task.

More able: Set larger numbers with three or four digits, such as 278 or 1134.

Plenary & assessment

Ask individual children to show their completed spider diagrams. Ask: *What strategy did you use to find four number sentences? What strategies did you use to answer them?*

Lesson

Starter

Repeat the Starter from Lesson 1 but start with 23, 46 and 69. Ask the children to write the two possible addition sentences and the two possible subtraction sentences on their whiteboards.

Main teaching activities

Whole class: Write on the board: 70 + 4 + 30 = ☐ . Ask the children to work out the answer on their whiteboards. Ask: *How did you work this out?* Stress that the most straightforward way is to add together the 30 + 70 = 100 and then to add 4.

Write on the board: 70 + 4 + 30 + 6 = ☐. Ask the children to work out the answer on their whiteboards. Ask: *How did you work this out?* If the children did not pair the 70 + 30 and the 6 + 4 then highlight this method of pairing up numbers (the associative law of addition or partitioning).

Repeat with a few more examples such as $34 + 2 + 66 + 8 = \square$.

Stress that it does not matter how you pair the numbers. (For example, $66 + 34$ and $2 + 8$, or $34 + 2$ and $66 + 8$, or $30 + 60$, $4 + 6$ and $2 + 8$.) Discuss the various possibilities.

Individual work: Give the children the activity sheet 'Matching addition'. Explain that they will be practising more of these addition sentences. Ask the children to take two colouring pencils and to shade the pairs of numbers that they will be adding together first in the same colour. For Question 1, for example, children might decide to colour in the 12 and 8 in one colour (20) and the 13 and 7 in another colour (20).

Differentiation

Less able: Use the version of the activity sheet that has pairs of numbers partitioning to 10.
More able: Use the version of the activity sheet that includes three-digit numbers.

Plenary & assessment

Write on the board: $1 + 2 + 3 + 4 + 5 + 6 + 7 + 8 + 9 = \square$. Ask: *How could we work out this sentence?*
See if the children can partition the numbers ($1 + 9$, $2 + 8$, $3 + 7$, $4 + 6$) to get the answer.
Write on the board the numbers 12, 8, 7, 13 and ask individual children to give two pairs that make twenty (13, 7 and 12, 8). Ask: What is $90 + 40 + 10 + 30$? Check how the children worked this out.
Complete the session by drawing a spider diagram on the board with a three-digit target number (eg 180) and ask for different empty-box number sentences to make the target number, eg $30 + \square + \square = \square$.

Lesson

Starter

Explain to the children that you will give them a number and you want them to use their number fans to show you a number that they would add to your number to make twenty. (For example, 2 and 18.) Repeat with several more examples.

Main teaching activities

Whole class: Recap the plenary session from Lesson 2. Refer back to pairing numbers to make addition easier and, if appropriate, ask the children to explain how they joined pairs of numbers to make the additions on the 'Matching addition' sheet easier.

Paired work: Explain that the children are going to play a game, in pairs. Using activity sheets 'The Grid Game', 'The Grid Game instructions' and the 'Grid Game board' the children take turns to pick three numbers from the number grid that they think that they can add together. They must pick at least one two-digit number. The other player can use a calculator to check their response. If the number sentence is correct they get a point and cross the three numbers off the number grid; if they get an incorrect answer they do not get a point and it is the other player's turn. The winner is the person who has more points when all the numbers are crossed off the grid. Use the score sheet to keep a tally. Remind the children to use the method that they have been practising for the last few lessons and that it will get more difficult as the game progresses because they cannot pick their numbers so freely.

Differentiation

Less able: Children could play in mixed ability pairs or select just two numbers.
More able: Challenge the children to select four numbers to add together.

Plenary & assessment

Discuss efficient methods for winning the game.
Ask: *Were you always right?*
When did you get the answer wrong?
What did you need to do to get the correct answer?

Lessons   overview

Preparation
Before producing copies for the children, fill in questions on the template version of activity sheet 'Number line additions' to the appropriate levels for the children's abilities, if necessary.

Learning objectives

Starter
- Derive quickly all pairs of multiples of 50 with a total of 1000.

Main teaching activities
- Add or subtract the nearest multiple of 10, then adjust.
- Use known number facts and place value to add or subtract mentally, including any pair of two-digit whole numbers (crossing 10 but not 100).

Vocabulary
addition, increase, sum, altogether, total, subtraction, difference, decrease, minus, take away, sentence, strategy

You will need:

CD pages
'Number line additions', core, less able, more able and template versions; 'Number line subtractions', core, less able, more able and template versions.

Equipment
Interlocking cubes in columns of ten.

Lesson

Starter

On the board, write '1000' in a circle. Ask an individual child to tell you a sum of two multiples of 50 equal to 1000. Write this on an arm, as in the spider diagram in Lesson 1. Working with the children, systematically fill out the spider diagram, finding all the examples of pairs making 1000, using multiples of 50 (950 + 50, 900 + 100, 850 + 150, 800 + 200, 750 + 250, 700 + 300, 650 + 350, 600 + 400, 550 + 450, 500 + 500). As the children recognise a systematic approach, ask individual children for ideas for a pair, for example: *650 + what equals 1000?* When the spider diagram is complete, cover up one of the pairs and ask individual children to give the missing number.

Main teaching activities
Whole class: Remind children of the different methods of addition and subtraction they have been doing and prompt with some quick-fire questions involving multiples of 10, eg 90 – 20, 30 + 60, 50 + 60 + 40, 20 + 40 – 10 etc.

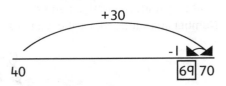

Ask: *What is 40 + 29? What if the calculation was 19 + 40? Discuss how children arrived at the answer and model it on the board using an empty number line*
Repeat with two or three examples, eg 39 + 39 (adjust by 2); 47 + 39 (adjust by 1).

Individual work: Provide copies of the 'Number line additions' sheet for each child.

Differentiation
Less able: Work with this group on the 'Number line additions' sheet. Support the children with the number line work. Decide whether to move the children to the version of the sheet that includes calculations that do not cross 100.

More able: Give each child a copy of 'Number line additions' that does not include a number line example and includes three-digit calculations.

Plenary
Write on the board:

77 + 9 = ☐
77 + 19 = ☐
77 + 29 = ☐

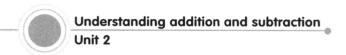
Ask the children for the answers and their methods. Discuss any patterns they have found. Ask individual children to extend the pattern using the empty number line on the board. Finish with one or two subtraction examples (eg 18 – 9, 28 – 9) to prepare the children for the next lesson.

Lesson ⑤

Starter

Call out a multiple of 50 and ask the children to hold up their number fans to show the number that you would have to add to make 1000, for example, 750 (250).

Main teaching activities

Whole class: Repeat the plenary from Lesson 4 (26 + 9 = ❑; 26 + 19 = ❑) and continue with 26 + 29 = ❑ and 26 + 39 = ❑.

Ask: *What do you notice? Is there a pattern?* Stress that the answer is increasing by ten each time. Ask: *Why do you think that is happening?* Point out the link between the increase in the number being added to 26 and the answer.

Ask quick-fire subtraction questions using multiples of 10, for example, 70 – 30 = ❑, 30 – 10 = ❑. Then ask: *How could you work out 70 – 29?* Discuss. Refine explanations by modelling them on empty number line (i.e. 70 – 30 + 1):

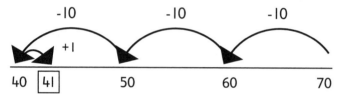

Repeat for other examples such as 50 – 18, 90 – 67. Establish that instead of several jumps on the number line, they need only one big jump to the nearest ten before adjusting.

Individual work: Provide copies of the 'Number line subtractions' sheet. Encourage the children to use one big jump rather than several smaller ones on their number lines.

Differentiation

Less able: Provide copies of the 'Number line subtractions' sheet that includes some single-digit calculations. Work with these pupils to check that they understand the method.

More able: Provide copies of the more able 'Number line subtractions' sheet and use the template version to provide some money problems.

Plenary & assessment

Write on the board:
86 – 9 = ❑
86 – 19 = ❑
86 – 29 = ❑

Extend the pattern and discuss how the children will answer these questions, using the empty number line if necessary. Highlight the link between the decrease in the answer and the increase in the amount being subtracted. Finish by asking one or two subtraction word problems, eg *Paul has 87p and spends 39p on sweets. How much does he have left?* Discuss answers and how the problem was solved.

Name   **Date**

Matching addition

You will need coloured pencils in two different colours.

You are going to add up these numbers. Making pairs will help.

Join each pair like this:

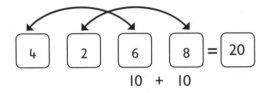

10 + 10

1. $12 + 8 + 13 + 7 = \boxed{}$

2. $14 + 5 + 6 + 15 = \boxed{}$

3. $17 + 7 + 13 + 3 = \boxed{}$

4. $15 + 3 + 5 + 17 = \boxed{}$

5. $30 + 20 + 10 + 80 = \boxed{}$

6. $40 + 40 + 20 + 10 = \boxed{}$

7. $30 + 20 + 50 + 70 = \boxed{}$

8. $20 + 60 + 40 + 80 = \boxed{}$

Make the target number.

$60 + \boxed{} + \boxed{} + \boxed{} \bigcirc 180 \bigcirc \boxed{} + \boxed{} + 40 +$

$\boxed{} + 90 + 20 + \boxed{} \qquad 110 + \boxed{} + \boxed{} + \boxed{} +$

Spring term
Unit 3
Written methods of addition and subtraction

Children continue to develop their skills for written methods of addition and subtraction. They develop informal pencil and paper methods to solve problems and they refine written methods for column addition of two whole numbers less than 1000. They practise these skills using 'real life' problems, developing their understanding of the vocabulary related to addition and subtraction and use of money.

LEARNING OBJECTIVES

	Topics	Starter	Main teaching activities
Lesson 1	Written methods of addition and subtraction Problem-solving	● Recognise the vocabulary used in addition and subtraction questions.	● Use informal pencil and paper methods to support, record or explain additions/subtractions. ● **Choose and use appropriate number operations and appropriate ways of calculating (mental, mental with jottings, paper and pencil) to solve problems.**
Lesson 2	Written methods of addition and subtraction	● Recognise the vocabulary used in addition, subtraction, multiplication and division questions.	● Develop and refine written methods for column addition of more than two whole numbers less than 1000.
Lesson 3	Written methods of addition and subtraction	● Add single-digit numbers to two-digit numbers, crossing the tens boundary.	● Develop and refine written methods for subtraction, building on mental methods.
Lesson 4	Written methods of addition and subtraction Making decisions	● **Use known number facts and place value to add or subtract mentally, including any pair of two-digit whole numbers (crossing 10 but not 100).**	● Develop and refine written methods for column subtraction of two whole numbers less than 1000. ● Use addition/subtraction operations to solve problems involving numbers in 'real life', money and measures, using more than one step, including converting pounds to pence and metres to centimetres.
Lesson 5	Problems involving 'real life' money or measures Making decisions Checking results	As Lesson 4.	● **Choose and use appropriate number operations and appropriate ways of calculating (mental, mental with jottings, paper and pencil) to solve problems.** ● Check with equivalent calculations.

Lessons   overview

Preparation
Copy, cut up and, if possible, laminate the cards from the activity sheet 'Operations cards'. Prepare several packs of number cards, 1–9. Prepare cards from 'Beat the brain cards', one set for each pair of children.

Learning objectives
Starter
● Recognise the vocabulary used in addition, subtraction, multiplication and division questions.
● Add single-digit numbers to two-digit numbers, crossing the tens boundary.
● **Use known number facts and place value to add or subtract mentally, including any pair of two-digit whole numbers (crossing 10 but not 100).**
Main teaching activities
● Use informal pencil and paper methods to support, record or explain additions/subtractions.
● **Choose and use appropriate number operations and appropriate ways of calculating (mental, mental with jottings, paper and pencil) to solve problems.**
● Develop and refine written methods for: column addition and subtraction of two whole numbers less than 1000 and addition of more than two such numbers.

Vocabulary
increase, decrease, equals, inverse, minus, difference, plus, more, total, altogether, sentences, digits, units

You will need:
Photocopiable pages
'Addition sums' (see page 101) for each child.

CD pages
'Operations cards' for each child (see General resources); 'Three-digit additions'; 'Number cards 0–9' (see General resources); 'Beat the Brain' cards, core, less able, more able and template versions.

Equipment
Three coloured pens for each pair; individual whiteboards.

Lesson ①

Starter

Give each child two pieces of paper, ask them to write 'add' on one and 'subtract' on the other, or use the activity sheet 'Operations cards' which includes cards showing 'add' and 'subtract'. Explain that you will ask the children different questions, tell them to listen carefully and then hold up the card for the operation, or type of 'number sentences', that they think they would use to answer the question. Ask individual children to answer questions such as: *Find the total of 13 and 14, What is the difference between 23 and 45? How many more than 15 is 78? How many fewer is 13 than 56? If I have 12p, 13p and 5p how many pence do I have altogether?*

Main teaching activities

Whole class: Write four single-digit numbers on the board, such as 1, 2, 3 and 4. Ask individual children to give addition sentences involving adding a two-digit number to another two-digit number, using all of the numbers on the board (12 + 34, 21 + 34, 12 + 43, 21 + 43, 13 + 42, 31 + 42, 13 + 24, 31 + 24, 14 + 32, 41 + 32, 14 + 23, 41 + 23). Be systematic in the way that you write the list. Explain to the children that it is important to have a logical way of finding all the possible additions.

Individual/Group work: Give individual children the activity sheet 'Addition sums'. The boxes at the top of the sheet have been left blank so that you can fill in numbers appropriate to the number of groups and ability levels, for example 1, 2, 3 and 0 (less able) or 2, 3, 4 and 5 or 6, 7, 8 and 9 (more able). Give pairs or groups copies with the same four numbers, so that they can work together later in the lesson. Ask the children to write down as many addition sentences as they can, using the four numbers at the top of the sheet. Check results. Ask: *How can you check to see if you have all of the possible sentences? How many should you have altogether?*

Now ask the children to work out the answers to their sentences. Explain that you will be asking them: *Which ones are easier to work out in your head? Which ones do you find it easier to write down?* Now ask the children to find others in the class who have the same numbers on their sheets. Ask the children to compare their findings. Ask: *Do you have the same answers? Did you work out the questions in the same way?* Go through all the different mental methods used to find the answers.

Differentiation

Less able: This group should have one of the units digits in their numbers as zero. This should allow them to work easily in multiples of ten.

More able: This group could work out subtractions as well as addition sentences. Encourage the children to be systematic and challenge them to be competitive about the number of sentences that they can make. You might also ask them to find the smallest total they can make!

Plenary & assessment

Write five numbers on the board, eg 78, 95, 121, 256, 87.

Ask individual children to choose two of the numbers and total them. Ask: *Which sentences did you want to write down? What could you use to help you find the answer?* (Some children might mention the empty number line method taught in the previous term or other informal jottings.) Explain that in tomorrow's lesson you will be showing them a written method to help you answer these more difficult questions.

Lesson ②

Starter

Repeat the Starter from Lesson 1 but this time children will need four pieces of paper (one to show multiplication and one to show division). Include questions such as: *What is £10 shared among ten people? How many sweets would I need if ten people each wanted 32 sweets? What is the product of 10 and 23?*

Main teaching activities

Whole class: Explain to the class that in today's lesson they will be looking at addition sentences and seeing what they can write down to help them work things out. Write on the board: 47 + 34 =❑. Ask: *How would you work this out? Put up your hand if you would work this out in your head.* Distribute pieces of scrap paper to those children who want to write things down. Ask the children to explain what they have done. Discuss mental strategies (rounding to the nearest 10, and partitioning).

```
   47
 + 34
 ─────
   70  (40 + 30)
   11  ( 7 + 4)
 ─────
   81
```

Now, using two colours, write down the example and explanation using the column method, looking at the units first (see left). Work through a couple of examples, such as 48 + 33, 46 + 35. Ask: *How do you think that this helps?*

Individual work: Ask the children to try a few examples of their own, using two colours, one for the tens and one for the units column. Check answers.

```
   123
 + 458
 ─────
   500  (100 + 400)
    70  (20 + 50)
    11  (3 + 8)
 ─────
   581
```

Whole class: Try an example with three digits, for example, 123 + 458. Use three colours (see left).

Paired work: Demonstrate using the number cards 1–9. Shuffle the cards, then pick six cards and make an addition sentence from them by selecting a pair of three-digit numbers. Ask the children to try a few examples of their own with one child selecting the cards and the other writing down the number sentences on the 'Three-digit additions' sheet and solving them. Ask them to solve three questions, then swap roles. Make sure that each pair has three coloured pencils so that they can use different colours for the hundreds, tens and units.

Differentiation

Less able: Give children in this group cards with numbers from 0–5 so that they can work with two- or three-digit numbers that will not require them to carry units or tens across, for example, 123 + 234 =❑. Consider dividing the class into mixed ability pairs and encourage the children to support each other when completing the 'Three-digit additions' sheet.

More able: Give these children cards with numbers from 3–9 so that they will be required to carry units or tens across.

Plenary & assessment

Write on the board: 333 + 419 =❑. Ask: *Is the answer going to be greater than 700? Is the answer going to be less than 800? Is the answer going to be less than 750? What would the answer be to the nearest 10? How could we work it out?* Generate one or two more pairs of three-digit calculations using the number cards and the written method, reminding the pupils to add the most significant digits first and to remember to line up the H, T and U under each other. Ask: *How would you decide whether to use a mental or written method?*

Lesson ③

Starter

Write 54 + 7 on the board. Ask: *How could you quickly work out the answer to this question?* Prompt for 50 + (4 + 7) = 50 + 11 = 61 or (54 + 6) + 1 = 61. Give further examples such as 77 + 6 or 58 + 5 and ask the children to write answers on their whiteboards. Ask individual children for their answers and methods of solving. Extend to HTU + U, eg 534 + 7. Write five additions of this type on the board for the children to answer in one minute.

Main teaching activities

Whole class: Explain to the class that in today's lesson they will be looking at subtraction sentences and seeing what they can write down to help them work things out. Write on the board: 47 – 34 =❑. Ask: *How would you work this out? Put up your hand if you would work this out in your head.* Distribute pieces of scrap paper to those who want to write things down. Ask the children to explain what they have done. Discuss mental strategies (rounding to the nearest 10 and partitioning). Now write on the board 94 – 26 =❑. Ask the same questions. *Would it help to write something down for this one? Why?*

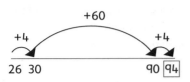

$$94 = 90 + 4 = \quad 80 + 14$$
$$-26 = 20 + 6 = \underline{-20 + \;-6}$$
Fig. 1 $\qquad\qquad 60 + 8 = 68$

Fig. 2

Remind the children of the method of decomposition used in Year 3 (Fig. 1), but also link to the method involving complementary addition used in previous units. Model this example on the board using an empty number line (Fig. 2).
Individual work: Ask the children to try a few HTU – TU examples of their own, using the method that they prefer.
Paired work: Explain to the children that they are going to play a game to see whether or not it is better to write down workings or to do calculations in your head. Give each pair a set of cards from the activity sheet 'Beat the brain cards'.
Explain that one person in the pair is the brain and must work everything out in their heads and the other person is the scribe, and must write down every single calculation that they do. The first person to get the correct answer wins the card.

Differentiation
Less able: Use the version of the activity sheet that has less complex addition and subtraction questions. Pair children according to ability and give extra support if possible.
More able: Provide the version of the sheet with more three-digit calculations.

Plenary & assessment
Discuss with the children: *Which cards could/did you work out mentally? Why? When was it useful to write something down? Is it always important to write something down? Which methods did you use?*

Lessons ④ ⑤ overview

Preparation
Copy, cut up and, if possible, laminate the cards from the activity sheet 'Operation follow-on'.

Learning objectives
Starter
● **Use known number facts and place value to add or subtract mentally, including any pair of two-digit whole numbers (crossing 10 but not 100).**
Main teaching activities
● Develop and refine written methods for column subtraction of two whole numbers less than 1000.
● Use addition/subtraction operations to solve problems involving numbers in 'real life', money and measures, using more than one step, including converting pounds to pence and metres to centimetres.
● **Choose and use appropriate number operations and appropriate ways of calculating (mental, mental with jottings, paper and pencil) to solve problems.**
● Check with equivalent calculations.

Vocabulary
difference, total, count on, pound, pence, inverse, measurement

You will need:
CD pages
'Operation follow-on'; 'Simply subtraction', core, less able and more able versions; (see General resources); 'Bargain hunter!' core, less able, more able and template versions.

Equipment
Individual whiteboards; pens.

Lesson ④

Starter
Shuffle the pack of 'Operation follow-on' cards and distribute all of them to the class. There are 35 cards in total, so some children may need to have two cards, depending on the size of the group. All the cards follow on from each other, for example, the answer (7) to '16 take away 9' will be found at the top of another card. Tell the children that they have to work out the calculation and then the child who has the card with that number at the top must stand up, say the answer and then read out the question on their own card. Note that you will need to remember the starting number (you can start anywhere in the loop) and that everyone should have a turn before play returns to the beginning of the loop.

57 – 6 = ☐
567 – 96 = ☐
567 – 396 = ☐

567
– 396
+4 → 400
+100 → 500
+67 → 567

100 + 67 + 4 = 171

Main teaching activities

Whole class: Remind the children of the subtraction methods used in the previous lesson. Write on the board (see left):
Ask children which questions they could work out mentally and which they would need to use a written method to answer. Ask for the answers and discuss methods used (eg mental strategies, decomposition, number line). Show a 'vertical' alternative to the number line method (see left):

Prompt for children's understanding that this method involves children counting up from the smaller to the larger number. The written method helps them to organise the stages involved in the calculation.

Individual work: Give each child a copy of the 'Simply subtraction' sheet. Ask the children to identify which questions they are able to answer mentally and which questions they need to work out using a written method. Space has been allowed on the sheet for them to show their workings out.

Differentiation

Less able: Provide these children with the version of the sheet with HTU–TU examples only.
More able: Provide these children with some four-digit subtractions. Challenge the children to think of a subtraction problem for others to solve. Warn them that they should know the answer before giving it to someone else!

Plenary & assessment

Discuss the questions on the sheet. Go through each question and ask for volunteers to explain their methods of answering each question. Collect alternatives and go over any mistakes. Explain that in the next lesson they will be reviewing all of the addition and subtraction methods and that you will be giving them examples of both types of question to answer.

Lesson ⑤

Starter

Divide the class into pairs. Write two TU + TU additions on the board, eg 54 + 45 = o, 66 + 23 = o. Give the pairs 15 seconds to answer each question on whiteboards. Continue with questions that cross the tens boundary, eg 26 + 35 = o and 47 + 26 = o. Next, include subtractions without crossing the tens boundary, eg 88 – 27 = ☐, 74 – 33 = ☐. Finally, extend to subtractions that cross the tens boundary, eg 76 – 38 = o, 94 – 45 = o. If necessary, reduce the time allowed to 10 seconds per question.

Main teaching activities

Paired work: Give each pair a copy of the 'Bargain hunter' sheet. Explain that you might like to buy a chair and a sofa and would like them to find the cheapest deal for you. You also need to know how much would be left to pay if you had to pay a deposit. Ask them to think about how they will go about this task. Tell them they can work out the totals mentally if they prefer, but then ask: *How could we check the answers?* (by using an equivalent calculation/counting up).

Differentiation

Less able: Work on this activity reminding the children of the method shown in the previous unit. If necessary, give them the version of the sheet in which the units digit does not cross ten.
More able: Provide the children with the version of the sheet that includes pairs of three-digit calculations.

Plenary & assessment

Establish that the answer is Easy Chairs. Ask children who answered correctly to show their methods of working. Make sure that all the children checked their answers by using an equivalent calculation or by counting up (for the subtraction). Go through the methods for each store.

Name	Date

Addition sums

Use these numbers.

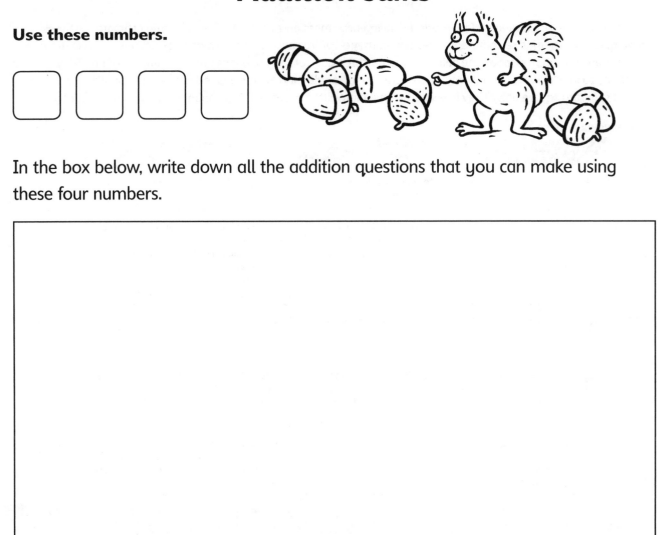

In the box below, write down all the addition questions that you can make using these four numbers.

Now work out the answers to your questions. What is the largest total that you can make?

If you work them out in your head write 'M' next to the sum. If you need to write anything down, use the space below.

Children learn to use a variety of measures involving time, mass, area and perimeter. Children estimate the times that it will take them to say different times tables. They are introduced to the relationships between familiar units of mass and the equivalent of one half, one quarter, three quarters and one tenth of 1 kilogram in grams. They continue to look at ways of finding the perimeters of rectangles and are introduced to the concept of area and the use of standard square units. They investigate how many different shapes they can make with an area of 12 cm².

LEARNING OBJECTIVES

	Topics	Starter	Main teaching activities
Lesson 1	Measures	● **Count in steps of five minutes from given starting points.**	● Estimate and check times using seconds, minutes, hours.
Lesson 2	Measures	● **Know by heart multiplication facts for 2-, 3-, 4-, 5- and 10-times tables.**	● **Know and use the relationships between familiar units of mass.** ● Suggest suitable units and equipment to estimate or measure mass. ● Know the equivalent of one half, one quarter, three quarters and one tenth of 1 kilogram in grams.
Lesson 3	Measures	● Derive quickly doubles of multiples of 10 to 500 and corresponding halves (emphasis on 1000).	As Lesson 2.
Lesson 4	Measure Shape and space	● **Round any positive integer less than 1000 to the nearest 10.** ● Know and use the relationship between familiar units of mass.	● Measure and calculate the area of rectangles and simple shapes, using counting methods and standard units (cm²).
Lesson 5	Measures Making decisions	As Lesson 4.	● **Record estimates to a suitable degree of accuracy.** ● Measure and calculate the area of rectangles and simple shapes, using counting methods and standard units (cm²).

Lessons   overview

Preparation
Enlarge activity sheet 'Weighing in' and cut into cards, each showing one image.

Learning objectives
Starter
● **Count in steps of five minutes from given starting points.**
● **Know by heart multiplication facts for 2-, 3-, 4-, 5- and 10-times tables.**
● Derive quickly doubles of multiples of 10 to 500 and corresponding halves (emphasis on 1000).
Main teaching activities
● Estimate and check times using seconds, minutes, hours.
● **Know and use the relationships between familiar units of mass.**
● Suggest suitable units and equipment to estimate or measure mass.
● Know the equivalent of one half, one quarter, three quarters and one tenth of 1 kilogram in grams.

Vocabulary
hour, minute, second, mass, big, bigger, small, smaller, weight, heavy, light, lighter, heavier, lightest, heaviest, kilogram, gram, balances, scales

You will need:
Photocopiable pages
'Estimating mass' for each pair of children (see page 107).

CD pages
A copy of 'Times table times' for each pair of children; copes of 'Show me' and 'Weighing in' (see General resources); a copy of 'Estimating mass' for each child; a copy of 'Comparing mass 1 & 2' for each child.

Equipment
Whiteboards; pens; stop watches; Post-it Notes; bathroom scales; Plasticine (about 500 grams); some everyday household objects such as an apple; a can of beans or a pencil, and a dial balance to weigh them.

Lesson  ①

Starter

Remind children that 60 minutes is 1 hour. Ask children to count in five minute intervals from 2.00 p.m. to 2.55 p.m. Repeat for 2.40 to 3.10. Ask: *What happened when you got to 2.55? What time comes next?* Repeat for different starting and finishing times.

Main teaching activities

Whole class: Explain to the children that today they will be measuring time. Ask: *How can we measure time? What units of measurement can we use for time?* Write on the board 'minutes', 'hours', 'seconds', '>', '<', '='. Invite children to make up statements, using two of the words (1 minute < 1 hour, 1 minute > 1 second, 1 minute = 60 seconds, 60 minutes = 1 hour).

Paired work: As an introduction, ask the children to estimate how long it will take the class to get into order of height. Ask: *Will it take longer/less than a minute?* Now time the children getting into order of height and compare times. Ask them to get into their pairs.

Give each pair a copy of the activity sheet 'Times table times'. Ask the children to estimate how long it will take them to say two of the times tables on their sheet. Note that the sheet has 2-, 3-, 4-, 5- and 10-times tables so you will need to indicate which tables you would like each pair to use. Explain that they must speak clearly, say the whole sum (2 multiplied by 4 is 8) and if they get one wrong they need to start again at the beginning. Now, using stop watches, the pairs take it in turns to time and check each other's answers. They record the results onto their activity sheets.

Whole class: Ask: *Who was the fastest? What was your time? Who took over a minute?* Write on the board '69 seconds' and explain that this is one minute and nine seconds.

Repeat the activity, with children either using the same times tables and beating their previous time, choosing two different times tables or listing them backwards, for example, starting with $12 \times 2 = 24$. Make sure the children estimate how long it will take before completing each of the times tables. Ask: *Do your estimates improve?*

Differentiation

Less able: These children should use just the 2-, 5- or 10-times table.

More able: These children may choose the 3- or 4-times table or estimate how long it would take to say the times table they have chosen. They can discuss ways of refining estimates by timing any times table and using that information to help estimate times for other times tables.

Plenary & assessment

Write on the board '69 minutes'. Ask: *Who can tell me what this would be in hours and minutes?* Repeat with 129 minutes. Ask children to think of something that could take this long. (A film or a play.) Ask: *How many times tables do you estimate that you could say in one hour? What else could you do in one hour?*

Lesson ②

Starter

Call out quick-fire multiplication questions and ask the children to write their answers on their whiteboards. Discuss strategies to help them remember their tables, for example, numbers in the 2-times table always end in 2, 4, 6, 8 or 0. Numbers in the 4-times table are double those in the 2-times table. Numbers in the 5-times table always end in 0 or 5. Multiples of 10 always end in 0. Now tell the children that you are going to play a game: you will ask multiplication questions within the 2-, 3-, 4-, 5- and 10-times tables. The last child to hold up the correct answer to each question will be out of the game. The winner will be the last child left playing.

Main teaching activities

Whole class: Explain to the children that today's lesson is about mass. *When you weigh yourself, you find your mass.* Ask: *What units of measurement can we use to measure mass?* (kilograms, grams, milligrams, tonnes, ounces, pounds, stones, tons). Explain that today they are going to learn about kilograms, grams, milligrams and tonnes (write them on the board) and that although there are other measurements that also measure mass, these are the most common measurements used. Write on the board the symbols '>', '<' and '='. Ask the children to make up some statements using the symbols and two words (kilogram > gram; gram > milligram; milligram < kilogram; 1000 kilograms = 1 tonne; 1000 grams = 1 kilogram, 1000 milligrams = 1 gram).

Now give each of the children four pieces of scrap paper and ask them to write on them the four measurements or use the 'Show me' cards from the General resources (tonnes, kilograms, grams, milligrams). Explain that you are going to say the name of an object, hold up an object or a picture of an object, and ask them to hold up the units in which they think the mass should be measured. Show the children a range of objects with a variety of masses to use all measurements. For larger objects, such as an elephant or a car (tonnes), use images from the general resource sheet 'Weighing in'. Sort the objects in order of mass and discuss how to write their masses. Now weigh the smaller items, attaching a Post-it Note to each item, with its mass and the unit of measurement on it. Draw a number line on the board.

0 kg ———————————————————————————— 1 kg

Ask a child to come and mark the halfway point. Ask: *How could we label this?* (half a kilogram, 0.5 kilogram) Ask: *How many grams in a kilogram?* (1000 grams) Ask: *What is half of 1000 grams?* (500 grams) Mark this on the number line. Now ask: *Where could I put 250 grams?* (Halfway between 0 kg and 500 grams.) Repeat for 750 grams.

Individual work: Give the children activity sheet 'Estimating mass' and ask them to estimate where the measurements would go on the number line.

Differentiation

Less able: These children may need extra help to plot the measurements on the number lines.
More able: Ask: *Could you draw a number line from 0 grams to 1 gram?* Ask them to fill in various measurements in milligrams, such as 500mg, 700mg, 750mg.

Plenary & assessment

Ask the children to place the Post-it Notes from your items onto a number line, each time asking: *Is its mass greater than one kilogram? Is it less than one kilogram?* If its mass is less than one kilogram, then it will go onto the number line, for example; the elephant would not go onto the number line. Ask: *Is its mass less than 500 grams? Is it more than 500 grams?*

Lesson ③

Starter

Write on the board the words 'double' and 'half'. Explain to the children that when you call out a number and point to either 'double' or 'half', they have to give the answer. Call out various simple examples that end with zero, such as 1000 (500), 500 (250), 250 (500), 500 (1000).

Main teaching activities

Group work: Split the children into groups of four or five. Explain to the children that you are going to continue to look at mass. Set up five stations around the classroom and explain to the children that they will visit all five stations. You will time them and they will have to move to the next station as soon as you tell them to. By the end of the lesson they should complete the activity sheets 1 and 2 'Comparing mass'. The stations are as follows.

Lesson ①

Starter

Remind children that 60 minutes is 1 hour. Ask children to count in five minute intervals from 2.00 p.m. to 2.55 p.m. Repeat for 2.40 to 3.10. Ask: *What happened when you got to 2.55? What time comes next?* Repeat for different starting and finishing times.

Main teaching activities

Whole class: Explain to the children that today they will be measuring time. Ask: *How can we measure time? What units of measurement can we use for time?* Write on the board 'minutes', 'hours', 'seconds', '>', '<', '='. Invite children to make up statements, using two of the words (1 minute < 1 hour, 1 minute > 1 second, 1 minute = 60 seconds, 60 minutes = 1 hour).

Paired work: As an introduction, ask the children to estimate how long it will take the class to get into order of height. Ask: *Will it take longer/less than a minute?* Now time the children getting into order of height and compare times. Ask them to get into their pairs.

Give each pair a copy of the activity sheet 'Times table times'. Ask the children to estimate how long it will take them to say two of the times tables on their sheet. Note that the sheet has 2-, 3-, 4-, 5- and 10-times tables so you will need to indicate which tables you would like each pair to use. Explain that they must speak clearly, say the whole sum (2 multiplied by 4 is 8) and if they get one wrong they need to start again at the beginning. Now, using stop watches, the pairs take it in turns to time and check each other's answers. They record the results onto their activity sheets.

Whole class: Ask: *Who was the fastest? What was your time? Who took over a minute?* Write on the board '69 seconds' and explain that this is one minute and nine seconds.

Repeat the activity, with children either using the same times tables and beating their previous time, choosing two different times tables or listing them backwards, for example, starting with $12 \times 2 = 24$. Make sure the children estimate how long it will take before completing each of the times tables. Ask: *Do your estimates improve?*

Differentiation

Less able: These children should use just the 2-, 5- or 10-times table.

More able: These children may choose the 3- or 4-times table or estimate how long it would take to say the times table they have chosen. They can discuss ways of refining estimates by timing any times table and using that information to help estimate times for other times tables.

Plenary & assessment

Write on the board '69 minutes'. Ask: *Who can tell me what this would be in hours and minutes?* Repeat with 129 minutes. Ask children to think of something that could take this long. (A film or a play.) Ask: *How many times tables do you estimate that you could say in one hour? What else could you do in one hour?*

Lesson ②

Starter

Call out quick-fire multiplication questions and ask the children to write their answers on their whiteboards. Discuss strategies to help them remember their tables, for example, numbers in the 2-times table always end in 2, 4, 6, 8 or 0. Numbers in the 4-times table are double those in the 2-times table. Numbers in the 5-times table always end in 0 or 5. Multiples of 10 always end in 0. Now tell the children that you are going to play a game: you will ask multiplication questions within the 2-,3-,4-,5- and 10-times tables. The last child to hold up the correct answer to each question will be out of the game. The winner will be the last child left playing.

Main teaching activities

Whole class: Explain to the children that today's lesson is about mass. *When you weigh yourself, you find your mass.* Ask: *What units of measurement can we use to measure mass?* (kilograms, grams, milligrams, tonnes, ounces, pounds, stones, tons). Explain that today they are going to learn about kilograms, grams, milligrams and tonnes (write them on the board) and that although there are other measurements that also measure mass, these are the most common measurements used. Write on the board the symbols '>', '<' and '='. Ask the children to make up some statements using the symbols and two words (kilogram > gram; gram > milligram; milligram < kilogram; 1000 kilograms = 1 tonne; 1000 grams = 1 kilogram, 1000 milligrams = 1 gram).

Now give each of the children four pieces of scrap paper and ask them to write on them the four measurements or use the 'Show me' cards from the General resources (tonnes, kilograms, grams, milligrams). Explain that you are going to say the name of an object, hold up an object or a picture of an object, and ask them to hold up the units in which they think the mass should be measured. Show the children a range of objects with a variety of masses to use all measurements. For larger objects, such as an elephant or a car (tonnes), use images from the general resource sheet 'Weighing in'. Sort the objects in order of mass and discuss how to write their masses. Now weigh the smaller items, attaching a Post-it Note to each item, with its mass and the unit of measurement on it. Draw a number line on the board.

0 kg ———————————————————————— 1 kg

Ask a child to come and mark the halfway point. Ask: *How could we label this?* (half a kilogram, 0.5 kilogram) Ask: *How many grams in a kilogram?* (1000 grams) Ask: *What is half of 1000 grams?* (500 grams) Mark this on the number line. Now ask: *Where could I put 250 grams?* (Halfway between 0 kg and 500 grams.) Repeat for 750 grams.

Individual work: Give the children activity sheet 'Estimating mass' and ask them to estimate where the measurements would go on the number line.

Differentiation

Less able: These children may need extra help to plot the measurements on the number lines.
More able: Ask: *Could you draw a number line from 0 grams to 1 gram?* Ask them to fill in various measurements in milligrams, such as 500mg, 700mg, 750mg.

Plenary & assessment

Ask the children to place the Post-it Notes from your items onto a number line, each time asking: *Is its mass greater than one kilogram? Is it less than one kilogram?* If its mass is less than one kilogram, then it will go onto the number line, for example; the elephant would not go onto the number line. Ask: *Is its mass less than 500 grams? Is it more than 500 grams?*

Lesson

Starter

Write on the board the words 'double' and 'half'. Explain to the children that when you call out a number and point to either 'double' or 'half', they have to give the answer. Call out various simple examples that end with zero, such as 1000 (500), 500 (250), 250 (500), 500 (1000).

Main teaching activities

Group work: Split the children into groups of four or five. Explain to the children that you are going to continue to look at mass. Set up five stations around the classroom and explain to the children that they will visit all five stations. You will time them and they will have to move to the next station as soon as you tell them to. By the end of the lesson they should complete the activity sheets 1 and 2 'Comparing mass'. The stations are as follows.

● At Station 1, a set of bathroom scales where they can estimate their own mass, then weigh themselves. They calculate the difference between their measured mass and their estimate.
● At Station 2 they will make a ball of Plasticine with an estimated mass of 100 grams. They weigh their ball to see how close they were and record its mass.
● At Station 3 they will complete the >, < and = boxes on the activity sheet.
● At Station 4 they will write down the masses of various objects, using the scales provided (either balance with weights or dial balances). Then answer the question: *What is the difference in mass between the heaviest and lightest object?*
● At Station 5 they will fill in the suitable measurements in the boxes on the activity sheet and ask them to identify the difference between the lightest and heaviest.

Differentiation

Less able: These children may need more assistance or practical experience of weighing objects.
More able: Challenge the children to estimate the measurements at Stations 4 and 5.

Plenary & assessment

Ask: *Did anyone make a ball of exactly 100 grams at Station 2? Who made a ball that weighed less than 100 grams? Whose ball weighed more than 500 grams? How much did it weigh?* Talk through the answers for Stations 3 and 5. Focus in particular on the fractional equivalences, eg 500g = 1/2 kg.

Lessons overview

Preparation
Cut the rectangles from activity sheet 'Rectangles'. Copy activity sheet 'Rectangles continued' onto an OHT and cut out centimetre squares for the demonstration.

Learning objectives
Starter
● **Round any positive integers less than 1000 to the nearest10.**
● Know and use the relationship between familiar units of mass.

Main teaching activities
● Measure and calculate the area of rectangles and simple shapes, using counting methods and standard units (cm²).
● **Record estimates to a suitable degree of accuracy.**

Vocabulary
area, squared centimetre, regular, irregular, rectangle, square, perimeter, length, width

You will need:
CD pages
A copy of 'Rectangles' for each child; a demonstration copy of 'Rectangles continued' (see General resources); a copy of 'Introducing area' (see General resources.)

Equipment
Centimetre cubes; peg boards and elastic bands.

Lesson

Starter
Explain to the children that you will be asking them to round masses between 1kg and 2kg to the nearest kilogram. The children should touch the floor if a mass rounds down to 1kg, and stand up if it is nearer 2kg. Draw a number line and call out several masses, eg 1¼kg, 1350g, 1½kg.

Main teaching activities
Whole class: Give each child one rectangle cut from 'Rectangles' (see General resources). Ask: *How can we find the area of this rectangle?* Agree with the children that the area is the space inside the rectangle and discuss how you could measure it. Ask: *Which units of measurement could we use?* Now explain to the children that you would like each of them to find the area of their rectangle by folding carefully. Demonstrate with an enlarged rectangle, cut from the 'Rectangles' continued

sheet. Fold it parallel to its shorter side, in half, in half again and then in half for the third time, splitting the shape into eighths, and then unfold and count together.

Then turn the rectangle and fold it this time parallel to its longer side, in half and in half again splitting the shape into quarters and unfold. The rectangle should now have 32 squares for the children to count. Ask the children to use a ruler and measure the length, width and the size of the squares. Agree that the rectangle is 4cm by 8cm, that each of the small squares is 1cm by 1cm and that there are 32 of them. Agree that if we folded the shape very accurately all of the squares would be of the same size. Explain that the rectangle has an area of 32 square centimetres (cm^2). Ask: *Can anyone see how we could have made 32 cm^2 another way? (*Refer to 4×8 or 8×4 from the board.)

Explain that if you multiply a number by itself, for example, 2×2, this is a squared number, therefore an area of 1 cm by 1 cm will be one square centimetre, and can be written as $1cm^2$.
Individual work: Give each child 36 centimetre cubes and challenge them to make as many different rectangles as they can. They should record each rectangle on squared paper and write its dimension and area.

Differentiation
Less able: Provide each child with only 24 cubes and ask another adult to support the children with this activity.
More able: Provide each child with 48 cubes and challenge them to find all the possible rectangles.

Plenary & assessment
Discuss the children's rectangles. Ask: *How many rectangles did you find? What units did you use to measure their areas?* (cm^2) *What strategies did you use to find the area of each rectangle?* (counting squares) *What is meant by the word 'area'?* (Try to establish that the 'area' of the rectangle is the length × breadth or the amount of surface it covers).

Lesson

Starter
Repeat the Starter from Lesson 4, but this time with a scale of 0kg to 10kg, and then 0kg to 100kg.

Main teaching activities
Whole class: Distribute squared paper and display a square grid (see 'Introducing area' General resources) on an overhead projector. Ask: *Can you draw me a shape that has an area of 12 cm^2?* Ask individual children to draw their responses on the grid on the OHT. Illustrate that you can count the squares and explain that the area is the space inside the shape.
Individual work: Ask the children to investigate how many different shapes they can make with an area of $12cm^2$. You may want to state a rule that rotating a shape does not give a different shape.

Differentiation
Less able: Limit the work to rectangles. Provide each child with a peg board and elastic bands in different colours, so they can form the outlines easily without spending lots of time redrawing.
More able: These children could try working with shapes other than rectangles. Ask: *Can you make a triangle with an area of $18cm^2$?* They will have to count half-squares. *Is there a shape that will have the same perimeter and area?* (Yes, a 4×4 square.)

Plenary & assessment
Ask: *What if we had an irregular shape like your hand? How could we work out the area?* Draw on squared paper and count the squares. Show an example on the OHT, counting up half-squares to make a whole. Make sure that the children realise that this is approximate, like an estimate. Establish that squares are useful for measuring area and so that is why area is measured in square centimetres (cm^2).

Name   Date

Estimating mass

On the number line below, write in 250 grams, 500 grams and 750 grams in the boxes provided.

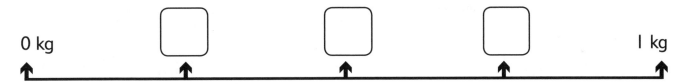

0 kg ⬆   ⬆   ⬆   ⬆   ⬆ 1 kg

Now estimate where the measurements below would go. Write in your measurements in the correct places beneath the line.

1.   100 grams
2.   300 grams
3.   700 grams
4.   800 grams
5.   900 grams
6.   10 grams

On the number line below, write 100g, 200g, 300g, 400g, 500g, 600g, 700g, 800g and 900g, as accurately as possible above the number line.

0 kg   1 kg

⬆   ⬆   ⬆   ⬆   ⬆

Now estimate where the measurements below would go. Write in your measurements in the correct places beneath the line.

7.	150 grams	10.	50 grams.
8.	850 grams	11.	750 grams
9.	250 grams	12.	450 grams

Children continue to choose and use appropriate number operations and appropriate ways of calculating (mental, mental with jottings, pencil and paper) to solve problems. They practise using the different vocabulary related to addition, subtraction, multiplication and division and begin to identify which calculations can be tackled mentally and which would be aided by some jottings or written calculations. Children are encouraged to think of different ways to tackle the same problem and how to check answers.

LEARNING OBJECTIVES

		Topics	Starter	Main teaching activities
Lesson	1	Problem-solving Making decisions	● Begin to know multiplication facts for 9-times table.	● **Choose and use appropriate number operations and appropriate ways of calculating (mental, mental with jottings, pencil and paper) to solve problems.** ● Check with equivalent calculations.
Lesson	2	Problem-solving Making decisions	● Begin to know multiplication facts for 6- and 8-times tables.	As Lesson 1.
Lesson	3	Problem-solving Making decisions	● Begin to know multiplication facts for 6-, 8- and 9-times tables.	● **Choose and use appropriate number operations and appropriate ways of calculating (mental, mental with jottings, pencil and paper) to solve problems.** ● Explain methods and reasoning about numbers orally and in writing.
Lesson	4	Problem-solving Making decisions	● Begin to know multiplication facts for 7-times table.	As Lesson 3.
Lesson	5	Problem-solving Reasoning about number and shapes	● Begin to know multiplication facts for 6-, 7-, 8- and 9-times tables.	● Solve mathematical problems or puzzles, recognise and explain patterns and relationships, generalise and predict. ● Suggest extensions by asking 'What if..?' ● Explain reasoning and methods about numbers orally and in writing.

Lessons overview

Preparation
Copy 'Questions on cards' and cut up, making a set for each group.

Learning objectives
Starter
● Begin to know multiplication facts for 6-, 7-, 8- and 9-times tables.
Main teaching activities
● **Choose and use appropriate number operations and appropriate ways of calculating (mental, mental with jottings, pencil and paper) to solve problems.**
● Check with equivalent calculations.
● Explain methods and reasoning about numbers orally and in writing.
● Solve mathematical problems or puzzles, recognise and explain patterns and relationships, generalise and predict.
● Suggest extensions by asking 'What if..?

Vocabulary
total, difference, minus, multiply, divide, together, product, share, double, halve

You will need:
Photocopiable pages
'Mrs Shopper's shopping problem' (see page 113) for each group.

CD pages:
'What's the method?' core, less able, more able and template versions; 'Questions on cards' (see General resources); 'Mrs Shopper's shopping problem', core, less able, more able and template versions; 'How many different ways?', core, less able, more able and template versions.

Equipment
Whiteboards; pens; five different newspapers; dial balance.

Lesson ①

Starter

Stand in front of the class and say the 9-times table. As you are saying it, hold up your hands in front of you. As you say '1 × 9' hold down the smallest finger on your right hand, then lift it up. As you say '2 × 9' hold down the next finger along, then lift it up and continue to do this with each finger in turn until you say '10 × 9' and have your little finger on your left hand down. Ask: *Can anyone see what I am doing to help me remember my 9-times table?* Now repeat this, asking the children to join in and follow your actions with their hands. Now ask the children a few questions from the 9-times table, such as 3 × 9, 8 × 9. Ask: *What do you notice about all the answers in the 9-times table? What would happen if you added the digits of the answers together each time?* (They add up to 9.)

Main teaching activities

Whole class work: Write an addition sentence on the board, eg 63 + 58 = ❑. Ask the children to work out the answer using mental methods or by writing on their whiteboards. Ask: *How did you work it out?* Discuss and record the methods used, eg

Mental method: 63 + 58 = 63 + 60 − 2 = 123 − 2 = 121

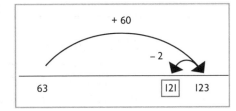

Number line method (see right).

Repeat with a pair of three-digit numbers such as 658 + 137 = ❑. Again, record methods and discuss strategies, eg adding the most significant digits first (column addition).

Group or independent work: Provide the children with 'What's the method?' which includes questions involving all four operations. The children have to decide and identify the method to use to answer each question. Tell them that it is alright to use written methods if they help them. However, before deciding the method they should look at the numbers involved and decide first whether they can answer the question in their heads. The questions have been provided on cards. They can therefore be answered on the sheet or cut out and divided among groups for more discussion on strategies used. The groups could then be asked to divide the questions into those that could be calculated mentally and those that needed written methods.

Differentiation

Less able: Provide the version of 'What's the method?' for less-able children.
More able: Provide the version of 'What's the method?' for more-able children.

Plenary & assessment

Ask the children to explain and model examples of their calculations on the board. Ask: *Which calculations could you not do mentally? Why?* Ask if any of the pupils used checking strategies to make sure that their answers were correct. Again, ask for the methods used.

Lesson ②

Starter

Ask the children to help you write up the 3- and 4-times tables in columns on the board. Leave a column next to each times table. Now say the 6-times table and write it in the column next to the 3-times table as you go. Ask: *What do you notice about the numbers in the 6-times table?* (They are double those in the 3-times table.) Ask: *What do you think you will notice about the numbers in the 8-times table?* (They will be double the numbers in the 4-times table.) Ask individual children to help you write down different facts from the 8-times table, using whiteboards to help them. Call out a sample of questions from the 6- and 8-times tables, each time relating the answer back to the 3- and 4-times table, such as 3 × 8 (6 × 4), 3 × 4 (6 × 2), 5 × 8 (10 × 4).

Main teaching activities

Group work: Split the children into groups of four or five. Give each group four sheets of paper. Explain that they are going to be learning about words in problems that give clues about the operation involved. Ask: *What are the four operations?* (+, −, × and ÷) Ask the children to draw the signs, one in the middle of each piece of paper. Give out shuffled cards from the activity sheet 'Questions on cards' to each group. Ask the children to sort the cards into four piles on top of the pieces of paper, depending on what type of number sentence they think it is. Now explain that they have five minutes to write down, around the sign on each sheet, as many words as they can think of that are connected with that sign. Ask each group to share ideas with the rest of the class and record collective ideas on the board. Add any extra from the lists below.

Now ask the children to work out the questions in each pile, using mental or written methods.

Add or addition	Subtract	Multiply	Divide
total	minus	product	share
altogether/together	take away	double	equal groups of
increase	difference	lots of	half
sum	decrease	groups of	
more	left/left over	times	
plus			

Differentiation

Less able: These children should focus on addition and subtraction questions before tackling multiplication and division.

More able: Ask the children in this group to make up some extra questions of their own for each pile and let others in the group work out the answers.

Plenary & assessment

Ask: *Which questions did you work out in your head? For which did you need to write something down? What did you write down?* Look at examples and ask individuals to go through the answers to the questions. Share methods and ideas. Finally, read through the list of vocabulary for each operation.

Lesson ③

Starter

Using vocabulary such as 'multiply', 'product', 'double', 'lots of' and 'groups of', give quick-fire questions testing 9-, 8- and 6-times tables and let the children write their answers on their whiteboards. Check responses and relate back to the Starters in Lessons 1 and 2. Write any questions that are still unfamiliar in the corner of the board to come back to later.

Main teaching activities

Whole class work: Remind the class how they used key words in problems to identify which operation they needed to answer the question.

Provide a problem based on those in 'Mrs Shopper's shopping problem' sheet such as:
Mrs Shopper buys 3 packets of biscuits. Each packet weighs 300 grams and costs 35 pence. What is the total weight of Mrs Shopper's biscuits? How much did the biscuits cost altogether?

Ask children to discuss in their groups which operation(s) are needed to answer the questions and to consider appropriate ways to work out the answers (eg mental or mental with jottings).

Group work: Split the children into groups of three or four. Each group will need a piece of paper and a pencil, and a set of clue cards from the activity sheet 'Mrs Shopper's shopping problem'. When the children are given the clue cards they should shuffle them and deal them equally among the group, but they must not look at them. Explain that once the children have their own sets of cards they can look at them but they cannot show them to anyone else in the group. Write these two questions on the board:
How much does the shopping in Mrs Shopper's basket cost?

How much does the shopping in Mrs Shopper's basket weigh?

Suggest that they might find it useful to organise the information in some way, for example a table, to help them answer the questions.

Now explain that they can talk about the information on the cards with the other members of their group but they must not show the others their cards or they will be out of the game. The winning group is the group that answers the two questions correctly first.

Differentiation

Less able: Use the version of the sheet that has a table on it. If necessary this group could lay their cards down and look at them together.

More able: Use the version of the sheet that has a few 'red herrings' included in the clues.

Plenary & assessment

Discuss the methods of solving 'Mrs Shopper's shopping problem'. Identify whether the children used a table or some other method of organising the data such as a list. Ask: *What operations did you use when calculating the answers? Which calculations did you need to write down? What is 4040 grams in kilograms?*

Finish the lesson with one or two multiplication and division 'shopping problems'. Children should write the answers on their whiteboards: Ask: *How much would two dozen eggs weigh? How did you work this out? Did anyone work it out a different way?* Resolve any outstanding queries that were raised earlier.

Lesson

Starter

On the board, write as a starting number '2' and ask the children to count up together, from it, in sevens. Then write '0' and, with the children, say the 7-times table together twice. Then ask questions of the class who can show their answers on number fans. Write any problem statements, such as '8 × 7 = 56', in the corner of the board.

Main teaching activities

Whole class: Explain to the children that today they will be thinking about different ways to solve problems. Ask the children to think back to Mrs Shopper's eggs. Ask: *What does one dozen mean?* (12) Now write on the board '3 eggs cost 15 pence.' Ask: *How much does a dozen eggs cost?* (60 pence) Ask: *How did you work that out?* (Find that one egg costs 5 pence then multiply 5 by 12, or multiply 15 by 4 to give the cost of 12 eggs.) Explain that there is often more than one way to work out the answer to a question.

Write on the board: *Mrs Shopper has 1kg of sugar. She wants to bake some cakes. Each cake requires 150g of sugar. How many cakes can she bake? How much sugar would be left over?* Ask: *Can you think of two ways to work out the answer to this question?* Provide children with paper if necessary. (Estimate through knowledge of multiples of 10 and 100; use jottings to divide by 100, then divide by multiples of ten.)

Individual work: Distribute activity sheet 'How many different ways?', which gives several number problems. Ask the children to think of different ways to solve the problems. If they choose to work out the problem mentally, ask them to write down what they did to answer the question. For example, for Question 1, mentally they could double 25 four times to give 25 × 8 or they could multiply by ten and then subtract 50 grams (2 × 25 grams).

Differentiation

Less able: These children should concentrate on answering all six questions before coming back to think of other ways to solve them. Provide the version of the sheet in which the number operations are more obvious.

More able: Use the version of the activity sheet that has questions involving more difficult numbers and asks: *Can you think up another problem that can be answered in different ways?*

Plenary & assessment

Discuss each question and ask the children to explain their methods (mental, mental with jottings, written methods). Ask: *Did anyone do it a different way?*

Model a selection of answers. Finish by asking individual children to challenge the class with their own number problems that might be answered in different ways. Make sure each child knows the answer and at least one method of solving it before asking the rest of the class.

Lesson ⑤

Starter

Call out numbers from the 6-,7-,8- and 9-times tables. If the number is in the 6-times table, children should put their hands on their heads. If it is in the 7-times table, they put up one hand. If it is in the 8-times table, they put their hands in the air and if it is in the 9-times table they hold their hands up in front of them, using the finger trick they learned in the Starter for Lesson 1 if they wish. Call out several numbers. This can be played as a game of elimination, with the last person with the correct answer standing to one side.

Main teaching activities

Whole class work: Write the digits 1, 2, 3 and 4 and the four operations symbols ($+$, $-$, $\times$ and $\div$) on the board. Tell the children that it is possible to make 6 by using each of the digits 1, 2, 3 and 4 once, and any operation: for example

$6 = (4 + 3) - (2 - 1)$

Ask if they can think of other ways to do this. Prompt for different methods, eg $6 = (21 + 3) \div 4$. Explain that the calculations in the brackets are always done first.

Paired work: In pairs, challenge the children to use each of the digits 1, 2, 3 and 4 and any of the four operations to make each number from 1 to 20. For example:

$$1 = \frac{4+1}{3+2} \; ; \; 2 = (4+2) - (3+1); \; 3 = (4+2) - \frac{3}{1} \; ; \; 4 = \frac{4+3+1}{2} \; ; \; 5 = (4 \times 2) - \frac{3}{1} \; ;$$

$$6 = (4+3) - (2-1) \; ; \; 7 = \frac{3+4}{(2-1)} \; ; \; 8 = \left(\frac{24}{3}\right) \div 1 \; ; \; 9 = \frac{4+3+2}{1} \; ; \; 10 = 4 + 3 + 2 + 1$$

Differentiation

Less able: Children might be limited to the numbers 1 to 10. If necessary, ask another adult to work with the children to model some of the number statements and to consolidate understanding of the use of the brackets.

More able: Challenge the children to go further (to 40 or 50). Ask: *How far can you go? Can you make all multiples of 10 to 100?*

Plenary & assessment

Ask: *Were there any numbers that you could not make?* Prompt for difficult numbers and ask children to explain how they made them. Also, identify how each pair tackled the problem (did they work systematically? did they break each number down? etc) Ask: *Did anyone notice any patterns?* (For example, if you combined an addition statement with a subtraction statement you could leave a number unchanged).

Name	Date

Mrs Shopper's shopping problem

Questions

How much does the shopping in Mrs Shopper's shopping basket cost? _____

How much does the food in the basket weigh? _____

Mrs Shopper buys two bags of sugar.	Sugar weighs 1 kilogram per bag.	She buys a dozen eggs.	Half a dozen eggs weigh 320 grams.
Twelve eggs cost £1.00.	A dozen is 12.	1 kilogram is 1000 grams.	Sugar costs 55 pence a bag.
She buys a jar of salt.	Salt costs £1.65 per jar.	The salt jar weighs 200 grams.	She buys a loaf of bread.
The bread costs 60 pence.	The bread weighs 800 grams.	She buys four onions.	Five onions weigh 50 grams.
The onions cost 40 pence.	She buys a packet of biscuits.	The biscuits cost 90 pence.	The biscuits weigh 300 grams.

Direction and angle

Children make decisions about positioning, direction and angle. They use the eight points of the compass, turning and measuring angles in clockwise and anticlockwise directions. They begin to know that angles are measured in degrees, that a whole turn is 360 degrees or four right angles. The children develop this by using a clock face. They also look at how a point is positioned on a grid, using horizontal and vertical numbered lines.

LEARNING OBJECTIVES

	Topics	Starter	Main teaching activities
Lesson 1	Direction and angle	● Use doubling and halving starting from known facts.	● Use eight compass directions N, S, E, W, NE, NW, SE, SW. ● Make and measure clockwise and anticlockwise turns, for example, from SW to N. ● Begin to know that angles are measured in degrees and that one whole turn is 360° or four right angles.
Lesson 2	Direction and angle	● Use doubling and halving starting from known facts.	● Begin to know that angles are measured in degrees and that one whole turn is 360 degrees or four right angles, a quarter turn is 90 degrees or one right angle, half a right angle is 45 degrees. ● Use of a clock face.
Lesson 3	Direction and angle	● Start to order a set of angles less than 180 degrees.	● Recognise positions and directions, for example, describe and find the position of a point on a grid of squares where the lines are numbered. ● Recognise simple examples of horizontal and vertical lines.

Lessons   overview

Preparation
Copy 'Eight compass point labels' onto A3 cards and have them ready, with Blu-Tack. Copy 'Co-ordinates grid' onto an OHT.

Learning objectives
Starter
● Start to order a set of angles less than 180 degrees.
● Use doubling and halving starting from known facts.
Main teaching activities
● Use eight compass directions N, S, E, W, NE, NW, SE, SW.
● Make and measure clockwise and anticlockwise turns; for example from SW to N.
● Begin to know that angles are measured in degrees and that one whole turn is 360 degrees or four right angles, a quarter turn is 90 degrees or one right angle, half a right angle is 45 degrees.
● Use of a clock face.
● Recognise positions and directions, for example, describe and find the position of a point on a grid of squares where the lines are numbered.
● Recognise simple examples of horizontal and vertical lines.

Vocabulary
north-east, north-west, south-east, south-west, clockwise, anticlockwise, rotate, whole turn, half turn, quarter turn, angle, right angle

You will need:
CD pages
'Eight compass points' and 'Eight compass point labels' (see 'General resources'); 'Points of the compass' core and more able versions; 'Clock face' (see General resources); 'Round the clock' core, less able and more able versions; 'Co-ordinates grid' (see General resources).

Equipment
Number fans; Blu-Tack; OHP protractor; geo-rods; paper fasteners (to join geo-rods), a clock face with movable hands; whiteboards.

Lesson 1

Starter

Say an even number from 2 to 500. Ask the children to use their number fans to show you half that number. Include 360, 180 and 90. Repeat, asking the children to show you doubles. Write on the board the numbers 360, 180, 90 and 45 and note they are all halves of the previous number.

Main teaching activities

Whole class: Explain to the children that they will be looking at directions. Find north in the class room and stick up the 'North' sign from the General resource sheet 'Eight compass point labels', using Blu-Tack. Say: *Stand up and face north.* Children should face north. Now say: *Face south.* When all the children have turned correctly to face south, stick up the 'South' sign. Repeat for the 'East' and 'West' signs. Now say: *What if I want to face in a direction that is in between north and east?* Ask the children to face the appropriate corner and put up the sign 'North-east' Repeat for 'North-west', 'South-west' and 'South-east'. Ask: *How could we abbreviate the names for north, south, east and west?* (N, S, E and W.) Repeat for north-east (NE), north-west (NW), south-west (SW) and south-east (SE). Explain to the class that they will now play a game. Explain that you will call out a direction and you would like the children to start by facing north, then to turn clockwise to face the requested direction, for example, from north to south. Repeat, this time asking the children to turn anticlockwise. Each time ask: *How much did you turn? Did you turn more than half a turn?*

Now ask: *How do we measure a turn?* (Degrees) *How many degrees in a full turn? (*360) Show the children a protractor, preferably on an overhead projector. Now ask: *Starting from north, turn 360 degrees.* All children should end up facing north. Repeat with another starting point. Ask: *If 360 degrees is a full turn, how many degrees in a half-turn?* (180) Now, starting from north, children turn through 180 degrees. All children should be facing south. Repeat with a few more examples based around the compass directions.

Now ask: *If 180 degrees is a half-turn, how many degrees are there in a quarter-turn?* (90) *What other name is there for a 90-degree turn?* (Right angle) *Now, starting at north, turn 90 degrees.* All children should be facing east or west. Ask: *Does it matter if you turn clockwise or anticlockwise? Why?* Repeat with a few more examples, giving directions based around the compass directions.

Now say: *Write down an instruction that would turn you through 45 degrees.* (For example, north to north-west.) Ask individuals for examples. Draw out that 45 degrees is half of a right angle.
Individual work: Give each child a copy of 'Points of the compass' sheet and ask them to add the unmarked directions to reinforce their understanding of compass directions.

Differentiation

Less able: Children may find it useful to have in front of them the version of 'Points of the compass' that shows the eight compass points for the whole class work. They can then trace around the points with their fingers.
More able: Ask: *How many different directions could you give that would make us turn 90 degrees?* Remember anticlockwise and clockwise. (16)

Plenary & assessment

Using the activity sheet activity sheet 'Points of the compass', call out directions such as 'south to north' and ask the children to call out the number of degrees they would need to turn. They can trace around the compass points with their fingers. Repeat with several examples.

Lesson ②

Starter

Repeat the Starter from Lesson 1, this time starting with 360. Use rapid-fire questions.

Main teaching activities

Whole class: Remind children of the work in the last lesson. Ask the children to stand up and turn through one whole turn. Ask: *How many degrees in one whole turn?* (360) *How many right angles did you turn?* (4) How many right angles in half a turn? (2) How many degrees in half a turn? (180° – or half of 360°). Display a large empty clock face (use activity sheet 'Clock face') and say: *Imagine you are standing in the centre of a clock and pointing at the number 12. If you turn from 12 to 3, how much of a turn is this?* (Quarter turn). *How many degrees is this?* (90)

Use two large rulers to demonstrate the right angle between the 12 and 3. Demonstrate some angles greater than 90° and less than 90° on the clock.

Individual work: Give the children activity sheet 'Round the clock', which asks them to use a clock face to give different directions. Ask the children to complete the activity sheet. In the second section of the sheet, children investigate the number of ways that they can turn 180 degrees on the clock face. Work through the first example with them, using the clock face diagram at the top of the sheet.

Differentiation

Less able: Use the version of the activity sheet that does not have the second section. These children will find it helpful to work with a clock face with hands that they can move.

More able: Use the version of the activity sheet in which the children have to find different ways to make 90° on the clock face. Those who finish quickly could investigate how many degrees there are in half a right angle, and how this could be shown on a clock face.

Plenary & assessment

Use a clock face. Move the hand from 12 to 3 and ask: *How many degrees have I turned clockwise?* (90°, or one right angle.) Then move the hand from 12 to 3 anticlockwise and ask: *How many degrees have I turned now?* Agree that it is three right angles. Write down 90 + 90 + 90 = ☐ Ask: *How could you work this out?* (300 – 30, or 9 × 3 then multiply by 10.) Establish that 90° (or other angles) can be measured from any point on the clock!

Lesson ③

Starter

Use two connected geo-rods to make an acute angle. Ask: *Is this angle more than 90 degrees?* Make a larger angle and ask: *Is this angle more than 90 degrees?* Repeat with several more examples. Now say that you will make an angle. If it is less than 90 degrees, the children touch the floor. If it is more than 90 degrees, they stand up. Give several examples. For the last few examples use different sets of geo-rod angles, using Blu-Tack to attach them to the board. Finally, put the angles in order by comparing sizes.

Main teaching activities

Whole class: Set 36 chairs out in the middle of the class room, in six rows of six. Ask the children to stand around the edge of the chairs. Stand near to one corner (indicated by A and marked with a circle in the bottom left-hand corner in the diagram). Ask: *Who can describe where I am standing?* If no child suggests it, introduce the idea of coordinates by saying that you are at (1, 1), one chair across and one up from the corner. Then say to a child: *You will be (0, 0).* Give this child a whiteboard to hold, with (0, 0) written on it, and ask them to stand by the chair marked B in the diagram (in the position marked by the triangle). Repeat with a few more examples: C(2, 2), D(5, 5), E(2, 4) and so on. Now say sets of coordinates and ask individual children to stand by the correct seats. Say, for example: *Can you stand in the position (1, 1)?* Explain that the chairs are like a grid, each row has a number and each column has a number. Ask all children to stand so they are along the *x*-axis (in front of the board). Now ask five children to stand at the coordinates (2, 0), (2, 1), (2, 2), (2, 3), (2, 4) and (2, 5). As they get into position say, for example, *Two across and one up,* (2, 1) to describe the numbers in the coordinates. At this point you may want to use whiteboards labelled 0–5 to label the *x*-axis and *y*-axis. Now ask: *Can anyone describe that line?* (Vertical) Now ask: *Can anyone give me five coordinates that would make another vertical line?* (For example, (5, 0), (5, 1), (5, 2), (5, 3), (5, 4) and (5, 5).) Ask children to stand in the appropriate positions. Repeat with another example. Then repeat for horizontal lines, for example, (0, 2), (1, 2), (2, 2), (3, 2), (4, 2) and (5, 2).

Differentiation
Less able: Give these children examples involving same-digit coordinates such as (1, 1) or (4, 4).
More able: Ask: *Could we make a diagonal line with the coordinates? What would the coordinates be?* (0, 0), (1, 1), (2, 2), (3, 3), (4, 4) and (5, 5) or (0, 5), (1, 4), (2, 3), (3, 2), (4, 1) and (5, 0). Ask: *Where would point (0.5, 4.5) be?*

Plenary & assessment
Display the OHT version of the General resources sheet 'Coordinates grid', which is a grid labelled from 0 to 5 on both axes. Ask individual children to come and mark coordinates onto the grid. Ask: *Who can tell me how many coordinates making horizontal lines we could draw on this grid? How many vertical lines could we draw?*

Properties of numbers

The children explore number patterns. They learn to recognise negative numbers in context and extend number sequences formed by counting forward and backwards from any number in steps of a constant size. They extend this by investigating a number pattern. They investigate statements about odd and even numbers. Children develop their understanding of multiplication by 10 by looking at number patterns in which the next term is the previous term multiplied by 10.

LEARNING OBJECTIVES

	Topics	Starter	Main teaching activities
Lesson 1	Properties of numbers	Read and write whole numbers to 10 000 in figures and in words, and know what each figure represents.	Recognise negative numbers in context.
Lesson 2	Properties of numbers	Count from any number in steps of a constant size, extending beyond zero.	Recognise and extend number sequences formed by counting from any number in steps of constant size, extending beyond zero when counting back. Explain methods and reasoning orally and in writing.
Lesson 3	Reasoning about numbers	Round three digit numbers to the nearest 10 or 100.	Make and investigate a general statement about familiar numbers by finding examples that satisfy it.
Lesson 4	Reasoning about numbers	Derive quickly doubles of multiples of 10 to 500, and corresponding halves.	Make and investigate a general statement about familiar numbers by finding examples that satisfy it. Recognise and extend number sequences.
Lesson 5	Reasoning about numbers	Use known number facts and place value to multiply integers and divide integers.	Make and investigate a general statement about familiar numbers by finding examples that satisfy it.

Lessons   overview

Learning objectives

Starter

● Read and write whole numbers to 10 000 in figures and in words, and know what each figure represents.

● Count from any number in steps of a constant size, extending beyond zero.

● Round three digit numbers to the nearest 10 or 100.

● Derive quickly doubles of multiples of 10 to 500, and corresponding halves.

● Use known number facts and place value to multiply integers and divide integers.

Main teaching activities

● Recognise negative numbers in context.

● Recognise and extend number sequences formed by counting from any number in steps of constant size, extending beyond zero when counting back.

● Explain methods and reasoning orally and in writing.

● Make and investigate a general statement about familiar numbers by finding examples that satisfy it.

Vocabulary

positive, negative, above and below, zero, minus, total, next, consecutive, sequence, general statement, multiples, sort, predict, continue, relationship, rule, example, pattern

You will need:

Photocopiable pages

'Negative numbers' (page 123) and 'Number rules' (page 124) for each child.

CD pages

'Negative numbers', 'Number rules', 'Investigating statements' core, less able, more able and template versions; 3 × 3 grids (see General resources); 'Pencil squares' (for less able only).

Equipment

Whiteboards; Post-it Notes; interlocking cubes; hundred squares; coloured pencils; headless matches or straws; Blu-Tack; thermometer.

Lesson

Starter

Call out a number, for example, 9412. Ask the children to write the number, in digits, on their whiteboards. Then ask: *What is the value of the 2? The 9?* Repeat with several examples.

Main teaching activities

Whole class work: Ask: *Where would you see negative numbers?* Discuss examples such as bank accounts, temperature, floors in a building (lifts that go below ground level), divers descending to the bottom of the sea, etc. Show the children a thermometer and explain that the thermometer tells the temperature in degrees Celsius (°C). Record some temperatures around the school, eg near central heating, in a fridge, etc. Compare climates and discuss times of the year or parts of the world where temperatures will be below zero.

In the classroom, draw a vertical number line on the board. Mark and label the positions +5, 0 and –5, then ask individual children to add the missing numbers on Post-It Notes. When the line is completed ask the whole class to count back and forward from –5 to 5, then place the Post-Its randomly around the board. Pick –2 and –4 and ask: *Which is the smaller number? Which would be the lower temperature?* Invite two children to pick two Post-It Notes and use them to make a number sentence with < or >, for example –4 <–2.

Individual work: Give each child a copy of the 'Negative numbers' sheet to complete.

Differentiation

Less able: Give each child the version of the sheet with extra support and an additional number line activity.

More able: Give each child the sheet with a wider range of numbers (–20 to 20). Ask the children to write some number sentences using negative numbers in the format ❑ > ❑.

Plenary & assessment

Attach the sticky notes to the board. Ask the children to close their eyes and then remove a number. Ask: *Which number is missing?* Remove three or four numbers in the same way, then ask: *Can you put these numbers in order of size? Which is the largest number? Which is the smallest number?* Repeat and to extend this ask: *Can you give me four numbers that are less than 4? Less than 2? Less than, –1? …*

Lesson

Starter

Start at 20 and count up in units, asking the children to join in when they spot the pattern. Stop when all of them have joined in. Now repeat, starting at 10 and count back in units, and continuing past zero to –10. Start at 50 and count up in tens, then back down in tens, continuing to –50. Repeat, starting at 50 and counting in jumps of 5 up to 100 and then back past zero to –20. Then start at 20, counting in jumps of 2, up to 40 and back. Each time ask: *Can you describe what I am doing in this sequence? What happens when we get to zero?*

Main teaching activities

Whole class: Explain that you will be looking at number sequences. Ask: *What are number sequences? Can anyone give me an example of a number sequence? What would its rule be? What would the next number in the sequence be?*

 Write '20' on the board, saying that this is the starting number in a sequence. Now write the rule: 'add three'. Ask: *What will the second, third, fourth number in the sequence be? Will 22 be in the sequence?* Write each term clearly on the board showing an arrow marked + 3 after each term. Change the rule to 'add 25', then 'subtract five', add 'two' and finally 'multiply by two'.

Individual work: Give the children activity sheet 'Number rules', which has various sequences for the children to generate, given a starting number and a rule each time. The children are asked to decide which sequences will contain the number 40. Then the sheet lists five sequences for which the children need to describe the rule.

Differentiation

Less able: Provide each child with a version of 'Number rules' focusing on multiples of 2, 5 and 10.
More able: Provide each child with a version of the 'Number rules' sheet, which includes negative numbers and steps of 25 to 1000.

Plenary & assessment

Ask: *What general statements can you make about the number 40?* (multiples of 2, 4, 5 and 10 all make 40; or 40 has factors of 2, 4, 5 and 10). *How did you work these out? Did you write anything down to help you?* Ask each child to offer a number sequence and then make a general statement about it.

Lesson

Starter

Write a set of 3-digit numbers on the board, eg 247, 369, 411, 385, 564. Ask children to round each number to the nearest 10, then the nearest 100. Next, write a set of 3-digit multiples of 10, eg 260, 340, 450, 510, 670. Point to each number in turn and ask the children to hold up their whiteboards when they have a number that when rounded to the nearest 10 would give the number on the board. Repeat for 3-digit multiples of 100, with the children giving numbers that would make each number when rounded to the nearest 100. Ask: *How many possible numbers are there?*

Main teaching activities

Whole class: Explain that today you are going to be investigating odd and even numbers. Ask: *Who can give me an example of an odd number? An even number? Who can tell me the rule for the even numbers, starting from 0? What is being added each time?* Repeat with odd numbers. *Can anyone think of any other statements or rules about odd and even numbers?* Write down the children's suggestions on the board and ask for any examples to satisfy each statement.
Individual work: Give the children the activity sheet 'Investigating statements', which has some general statements about odd and even numbers. Ask them to investigate the statements by working out some examples. The children will need to decide whether each statement is true or false. Go through the first example with the class. Write on the board 'Every even number ends in 0, 2, 4, 6 or 8.' Try several different examples and establish that this rule is correct.

Differentiation

Less able: Provide the version of the activity sheet with easier statements to investigate.
More able: Provide the version of the activity sheet which includes questions in which the children will need to find the difference between odd and even numbers.

Plenary & assessment

Write on the board 'odd', 'odd', 'even', 'even'. Point to two of the words and say: *Add.* Children who think that the answer will be even stand up and children who think that the answer will be odd touch the floor. Repeat, changing the question between 'odd' and 'even'. Give an example each time, such as 34 + 22 = 56. Ask: *How can we tell that 56 is even?* (It ends in a 0, 2, 4, 6 or 8.) Write the results of the investigation onto the board.
O + O = E (the odd 'ones' pair up each time so the answer is always even, for example 7 + 7 = 14)
E + E = E
E + O = O
O + E = O

Lesson ④

Starter

Write a number on the board. Ask the children to write the number that is double on their whiteboards and hold it up, for example, show 50 (100), 40 (80). Repeat, with the children writing on their whiteboards the number that is half that on the board.

Main teaching activities

Whole class: Draw a 3 × 3 grid on the board or display the '3 × 3 grids' sheet using an OHP or whiteboard. Write in the numbers 1–9 as shown:

1	2	3
4	5	6
7	8	9

Point out that these numbers are consecutive numbers and discuss how they have been arranged on the grid.

Challenge the pupils to make some statements about the numbers on the grid. Write down and agree any statements that they make, eg 'All the corner numbers are odd'. 'The middle row, the middle column and both diagonals equal 15'. Establish if all the children agree with this statement.

Paired work: Give each pair a copy of the '3 × 3 grids' sheet. Write on the board: 'When nine consecutive numbers are arranged on a 3 × 3 grid, the middle row, middle column and both diagonals will have the same total.' Ask each pair to investigate this statement using the '3 × 3 grids' sheet. If time is available, suggest another statement, eg 'The sum of three odd numbers is odd'. Ask them to test this statement using the 3 × 3 grid.

Differentiation

Less able: Focus children on the first of these two statements and limit the range of consecutive numbers they use to investigate the statement.

More able: Give the children an additional challenge: 'Arrange the numbers 1–9 in the grid so that each side of the square totals 12.'

Plenary & assessment

Ask the class: *Is the statement I made about consecutive numbers true or false? Why?* (Ask the children for examples that match.) Discuss children's understanding of the properties of consecutive numbers. Ask individual children to add two, then three consecutive numbers together, eg *1 + 2 + 3 = 6; 4 + 5 + 6 = 15. Is there a pattern in the totals? Can you describe it?* (Multiples of 3).

Lesson ⑤

Starter

Say the numbers in a sequence: 1, 10, 100, 1000, 10 000. Ask the children to join in when they can. Ask: *What is the rule?* (Multiply by 10.) Repeat with 2, 20, 200, 2000, 20 000, then with 5, 50, 500, 5000, 50 000. Now work backwards, with 40 000, 4000, 400, 40, 4 and then 60 000, 6000, 600, 60 and 6. Ask: *What is the rule?* (Divide by 10.)

Main teaching activities

Paired work: Give each pair a pile of coloured pencils of equal length, headless matchsticks or straws. Ask the children to use four of these rods to make a square.

Now ask: *How many squares do you have?* (1) *How many sticks have you used?* (4) *How could you record these results?* Give the children paper and ask them to draw a table.

Number of squares	Number of sticks used

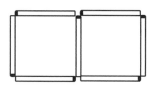

Give each pair three more sticks and ask them to make two squares.

Ask them to write the information in their tables. Repeat for three, four and five squares.

Now set the challenge: *How many sticks are you adding each time?* (3) *How many sticks would you need to make 10 squares?* (31) *20 squares?* (61) *30 squares?* (91) ...

Ask: *How many more sticks will you need to make 11 squares from that first square?* Point out that you add on 30. (3 × 10)

Differentiation

Less able: Let these children record their results on activity sheet 'Pencil squares', which has a grid to help them identify what is happening.

1 square	2 squares	3 squares	4 squares	5 squares	6 squares	7 squares	8 squares	9 squares	10 squares
4	7	10	13	16	19	22	25	28	31

11 squares	12 squares	13 squares	14 squares						
34	37	40	43						

More able: Ask these children to try to describe, in words, the relationship between the number of sticks and the number of squares. They should find that: the number of sticks = the number of squares multiplied by 3, then add 1.

For example, (12 × 3) + 1 = 36 + 1 = 37 or (100 × 3) + 1 = 300 + 1 = 301.

Ask: *Can you use your statement to find out how many sticks you would need to make 100 squares?*

Plenary & assessment

Use new or equal-length coloured pencils and Blu-Tack. Choose a red pencil and stick it vertically to the board, then pick three blue pencils and add them, to make a square. Ask: *How many squares do I have? How many coloured pencils have I used altogether? How many blue? How many red?* Now add on another three blue pencils and repeat. Repeat for three squares. Ask: *How many coloured pencils do I add on each time? If I have nine blue pencils for three squares, can anyone spot a pattern?* (3 × 3 = 9) *Then how many other pencils do I have?* (One red pencil) *Can you describe the relationship between the number of squares and the number of pencils?* (Number of squares × 3 + 1)

Name   Date

Negative numbers

Write the correct temperatures in the boxes below.

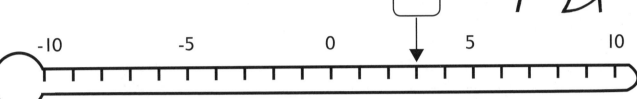

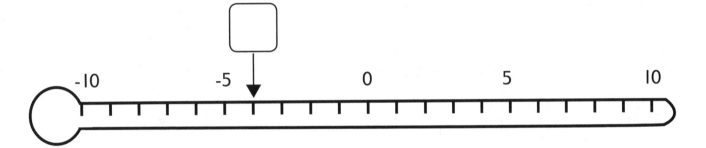

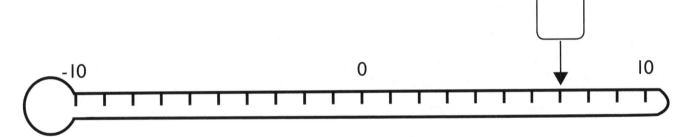

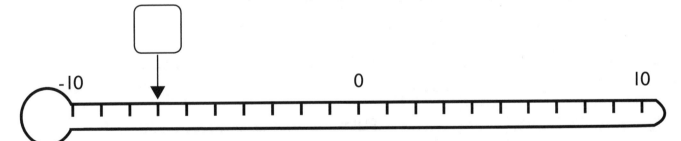

Complete this number line.

☐ > -2   -3 > ☐

0 < ☐   ☐ < ☐

Name   Date

Number rules

Continue each of the sequences below by filling in the boxes.

1.   Starting number: 5   Rule: add 5

[5] [10] [ ] [ ] [ ]

2.   Starting number: 30   Rule: take away 3

[30] [ ] [ ] [ ] [ ]

3.   Starting number: 56   Rule: subtract 4

[56] [ ] [ ] [ ] [ ]

4.   Starting number: 10   Rule: multiply by 2

[10] [ ] [ ] [ ] [ ]

5.   Starting number: 15   Rule: add 15

[15] [ ] [ ] [ ] [ ]

Now look at the sequences above. If you carried on, which sequences would have 40 in them?
Show your working or reasoning. _____

Now look at these sequences. What is the rule for each?
Write the next number in each of these sequences.

6.   34, 37, 40, 43, 46, 49, [ ]   Rule: _____

7.   3, 6, 12, 24, 48, [ ]   Rule: _____

8.   67, 62, 57, 52, 47, 42, [ ]   Rule: _____

9.   2, 4, 6, 8, 10, 12, 14, [ ]   Rule: _____

10. −2, −4, −6, −8, −10, [ ]   Rule: _____

Understanding multiplication and division

Children extend their understanding of multiplication and division and the relationship of these operations to each other and to addition and subtraction. They develop their understanding of the distributive law, that is that $4 \times 5 = 5 \times 4$ or $2 \times 2 \times 5$, and how this can help with mentally solving multiplication calculations. They investigate finding remainders by sharing different amounts of money among two, four, five or ten people. Children use closely-related facts to multiply by 9 or 11, by multiplying by 10 and adjusting and partitioning, for example, $12 \times 4 = (10 \times 4) + (2 \times 4)$, in order to develop their mental strategies.

LEARNING OBJECTIVES

		Topics	Starter	Main teaching activities
Lesson	1	Understanding multiplication and division	● **Use known facts and place value to add and subtract mentally, including any pair of two-digit whole numbers.**	● Extending understanding of the operations of multiplication and division, and their relationship to each other and to addition and subtraction.
Lesson	2	Understanding multiplication and division Pencil and paper procedures	● **Know by heart multiplication facts for 2-, 3-, 4-, 5- and 10-times tables.**	● **Find remainders after division.** Divide a whole number of pounds by 2, 4, 5 and 10 to give pounds and pence.
Lesson	3	Understanding multiplication and division Pencil and paper procedures	● **Derive quickly division facts corresponding to 2- 3-, 4-, 5- and 10-times tables.**	● Understand the principles (not the names) of the commutative and associative laws as they apply to multiplication.
Lesson	4	Mental calculation strategies for multiplication and division	● **As Lesson 3.**	● Use closely-related facts (eg to multiply by 9 or 11, multiply by 10 and adjust; develop the 6-times table from 4- and 2-times tables).
Lesson	5	Understanding multiplication and division	● Derive multiplication facts in x6 table and begin to recall them.	● Use the distributive law and partitioning to multiply TU by U.

Lessons   overview

Preparation
Photocopy 'Operation follow-on' (see Unit 3) and cut into cards. Photocopy 'Money cards' and cut into cards.

Learning objectives
Starter
● **Use known facts and place value to add and subtract mentally, including any pair of two-digit whole numbers.**
● **Know by heart multiplication facts for 2-, 3-, 4-, 5-and 10-times tables.**
● **Derive quickly division facts corresponding to 2-, 3-, 4-, 5- and 10-times tables.**
● Derive multiplication facts in × 6 table and begin to recall them.
Main teaching activities
● Extending understanding of the operations of multiplication and division, and their relationship to each other and to addition and subtraction.
● **Find remainders after division.**
● Divide a whole number of pounds by 2, 4, 5 or 10 to give an answer in pounds and pence.
● Understand the principles (not the names) of the commutative and associative laws as they apply in multiplication.
● Use closely-related facts (eg to multiply by 9 or 11, multiply by 10 and adjust; develop the 6-times table from 4- and 2-times tables).
● Partition, for example, $23 \times 4 = (20 \times 4) + (3 \times 4)$.

Vocabulary
times, multiply, multiplied by, product, multiple, inverse, x, divided by, repeated subtraction, repeated addition

You will need:

CD pages
'Arrays' core, less able and more able versions; 'Money cards' (see General resources), 'Money station' (see General resources); 'Rearrange it' and 'Let's calculate!' core, less able, more able and template versions.

Equipment
Interlocking cubes; dice; a £5 note; plastic or real coins; a mixed amount of money for each of five tables.

Lesson ①

Starter

Use the 'Operation follow-on' cards to give the children practice in their addition and subtraction skills. Distribute all the cards to the children. As there are 35 cards in total, some children may have two cards. The cards follow on from each other, with the number at the top of the card being the answer to an instruction written under the number on a different card. See the Starter for Unit 3, Lesson 3 of this term.

Main teaching activities

Whole class: Explain that children will be looking at the links between multiplication and division. Place 12 counters on an OHT in a 3 × 4 arrangement or demonstrate using interlocking circles (see left). Ask: *What number sentences can we make from this?*

Demonstrate how the arrangement could be seen as 3 columns of 4, or 4 rows of 3 counters. Establish that the children are also aware of the link here between repeated addition and multiplication (3 + 3 + 3 + 3 is the same as 4 × 3).

Ask: *How many 3s are there in 12?* (4) *How else can we write this?* (12 ÷ 3 = 4). Make sure children understand the link with written subtraction, perhaps by modelling the answer using a number line pointing to each 'step' of four. Ask the children to think of all of the possible number sentences for the above array using all four operations. As well as the examples above these should include the following: 12 – 3 – 3 –3 – 3 = 0; 12 ÷ 4 = 3; 12 ÷ 3 = 4; 3 + 3 +3 + 3 = 12; 4 + 4 + 4 = 12; 3 × 4 = 12; 4 × 3 = 12.

Paired work: Give each pair a copy of the 'Arrays' activity sheet. Ask: *What +, -, × and ÷ sentences can you make about each array?* Each pair discusses all the possible number sentences and records these on the sheet.

Differentiation

Less able: Give these children interlocking cubes to model each number sentence. You might also supply the version of the sheet with some partially completed sentences.

More able: Provide the version of the sheet that challenges the children to devise at least two more arrays with all the possible number sentences associated with each one.

Plenary & assessment

Collect responses to the 'Arrays' activity. Ask: *Have you found all the possible combinations? Did you use repeated addition? Repeated subtraction? Multiplication? Division?* Check that all that children understand the links between them by asking them to model their answers on a number line.

Lesson ②

Starter

Tell the children that you are thinking of a number. Invite them to ask you questions about the number, explaining that you will only answer 'Yes' or 'No'. Write on the board some vocabulary ideas to help.

- Is it greater than/less than…?
- Is it in the 2-, 3-, 4-, 5- or 10-times table?
- Is it a one-, two- or three-digit number?

Explain that their aim is to ask as few questions as possible so it is better not just to guess the number straight away but to limit the possibilities. As the children are guessing, remind them of some basic rules, for example, if it is in the 2-, 4- or 10-times table the number will be even (ending with 0, 2, 4, 6 or 8), if it is in the 5-times table it will end in 0 or 5, if it is in the 10-times table it will end in zero. Repeat with another example or ask a child to think of a number and you can join with the rest of the class in trying to guess.

Main teaching activities

Whole class: Review the Starter activity. Remind the children that dividing by 2 is halving and dividing by 4 is halving and halving again. Dividing by 5 is the same as dividing by 10 and doubling. Write on the board 12 ÷ 3 = ❑. Ask: *What is the answer?* (4) Leave a gap and write below it '15 ÷ 3 = ❑. Ask: *What is the answer?* (5) Now, under 12 ÷ 3 =❑, write 13 ÷ 3 = ❑. Ask: *If I had 13 sweets and divided them among three people, how many sweets would each person have? Would I have any left over? How many would I have left over?* (1) Now, underneath, write 14 ÷ 3 = ❑ and repeat the previous questions, modified appropriately. (There will be two left over.) Ask: *When we divide by three would we ever have three or more left over? Why is that?*

Show the children a £5 note and ask: *If I were to share this with ...* (pick a child's name), *how much would we both get?* If appropriate, change the £5 note for four £1 coins and two 50 pence pieces. Establish with the children that the answer is £2.50. Repeat, this time sharing among four people and making the link that the result would be £2.50 divided by 2. Repeat, by sharing among 10 people. (50p)

Group work: Split the class into groups of five or six. Explain that there are five stations around the room and every group will visit each station. At each station, the children divide the amount of money among two, four, five or ten people. Provide the children with the 'Money station' sheets and ask them to record their results in some way. Tell them they can use the plastic or real coins to help them. Place a card cut from activity sheet 'Money cards', with the corresponding amount of money, on each table.

Differentiation

Less able: Limit these groups to the first two money stations and the first 'Money station' sheet. Give assistance as required, using the plastic money to model the different amounts.
More able: Refer this group to the General resource sheet 'Money cards'. Ask: *Which of these amounts can be divided easily by 3? By 6? By 9? Challenge these groups to record all the answers as division sentences eg £25 ÷ 4 = £6.25.*

Plenary & assessment

Work through the process of dividing £34.00 among two, four, five or ten people together, then invite each group to discuss their earlier results with the rest of the class. Ask: *How did you work out the pounds and pence? Can anyone else think of another way of working out the amounts? How did you record your results?* Discuss division by other numbers and strategies for working out answers.

Lesson ③

Starter

Say a multiplication sentence, for example: *Three multiplied by four equals 12.* Ask the children to write on their whiteboards a division sentence using the same numbers. Discuss the fact that there are two possible division sentences (12 ÷ 3 = 4 and 12 ÷ 4 = 3) and they will both be correct. Give several more examples covering facts from 2-, 3-, 4-, 5- and 10-times tables, each time discussing the two possibilities.

Main teaching activities

Group work: Write on the board: 5 × 6 = ❑ and 6 × 5 = ❑.

Ask: *Do these sums have the same answer?* Remind the children of work completed in Lesson 1 by modelling the array on the board (see left).
Ask: *How many dots are there?* Check that the children's understand that it does not matter if we count six lots of five or five lots of six – the answer is the same. Explain that we can use this fact when we multiply as we can change the order of the numbers to make a multiplication easier.

Write on the board: 2 × 6 × 5 = ❑. Ask: *How would you work this out? Can you rearrange the numbers to make it easier?* Prompt the following if necessary: *Cover the 6 so that you are left with 2 × 5. Using the answer 10, write 10 × 6. What is 10 × 6?*

Repeat the above with $4 \times 6 \times 5$. Demonstrate that $4 \times 5 = 20$ as is 2×10, so we could also represent the question as $2 \times 10 \times 6$ or 2×60.

Explain that multiplying can be made easier by rearranging the numbers or using known number facts eg $8 \times 16 = 8 \times (4 \times 4) = (8 \times 4) \times 4 = (8 \times 4) \times (2 \times 2) = 32 \times (2 \times 2) = 64 \times 2 = 128$.

Highlight the use of the brackets to make the stages of the multiplication easier.

Individual work: Give each child a copy of the 'Rearrange it' sheet to complete. Ask them to use the methods shown to make the multiplications easier. Make sure that they show their working out!

Differentiation

Less able: Give children the version of the sheet that includes examples requiring understanding of the commutative law only (ie that addition can be done in any order).

More able: Give children the version of the sheet that extends understanding of the associative and commutative laws including some multiplication problems to solve.

Plenary & assessment

Discuss the children's work, asking for different methods of rearranging the multiplications. Identify and correct any misunderstandings. Write the numbers 2, 3, 4 and 5 in one box on the board and the numbers 20, 25, 30 and 35 in another box. Challenge individual children to choose one number from each box (or two single-digit and one two-digit number) and to multiply them together using the modelled methods. Repeat as time allows.

Lesson ④

Starter

Repeat the Starter from Lesson 3 but ask the children to write both of the possible division sentences on their whiteboards.

Main teaching activities

Whole class: Write on the board $6 \times 10 = \square$. Ask: *What is the answer?* Now ask: *What would happen if I added 6 onto this answer?* Illustrate with six sticks of ten interlocking cubes, adding on another six cubes to give sticks of eleven cubes. Write $6 \times \square = 66$. Write in '11'. Repeat with $4 \times 10 = 40$, then add 4 to give 44 (4×11) Ask: *Will this always work?*

Paired work: Ask the children to think about the two examples. Ask: *Will this always work? Can you give me another example?* After five minutes ask some of the pairs to explain their examples. Write on the board $5 \times 10 = 50'$ Now ask: *What would I find if I took away 5?* (5×9) *Can you find another example of this?* Let the pairs think about this, then illustrate with interlocking cubes. Discuss. Establish that, for example, $3 \times 11 = (3 \times 10) + (3 \times 1)$ and $3 \times 9 = (3 \times 10) - (3 \times 1)$. Each time, use the sticks of interlocking cubes to show how it works. Challenge the children to work out the 11-times table up to 20×11.

Ask: *Could we use this method to find any other times tables?* Give some interlocking cubes to each pair. Ask: *Can you make six columns, each seven cubes high? What multiplication sentence would this be? What would the answer be?* (42) *What if we split it up, which tables do you know well?* (2-, 4-times tables) Split up your columns so that you have four columns and then two columns. Write on the board '$(7 \times 4) + (7 \times 2) = \square$'. Establish with the children that it also gives the answer 42. Ask: *Will this always work? Can you work out another example using the 6-times table in your pairs?* Discuss more examples such as $3 \times 6 = (3 \times 4) + (3 \times 2)$.

Differentiation

Less able: Make up columns of interlocking cubes for these children in advance, so that they can easily manipulate the rods. It may be useful to place stickers on the rods to remind the children how many cubes there are in the column. Limit the pairs to work out the 11-times table up to 10×11.

More able: Challenge these children to extend the idea for the 6-times table, to develop a method for finding the 12-times table. (For example, $(4 \times 10) + (4 \times 2)$ or $4 \times 6 \times 2$.)

Plenary & assessment

Ask: *What are the main skills that you have learned today?* Write on the board:

$4 \times 11 = \square$ $7 \times 9 = \square$ $9 \times 6 = \square$

Collect answers and ask: *How can you work these out? What are the main points that you want to remember?* (How to partition into pairs of easier multiplication sentences to manage the numbers.) Ask the whole class: *How can we extend this work to the 12-times table? Partition into $10 \times \square + 2 \times \square$ or $\square \times 6 \times 2$).* Encourage the children to explain these methods.

Lesson

Starter

Remind the children that the 6-times table can be made by doubling the 3-times table. Ask the children to use whiteboards to answer a series of mental maths questions involving the 6-times table. Each time ask: *How did you work out the answer?* Remind children of work done on the 7- and 8-times tables. Emphasise that by knowing the 2- and 3-times tables we can derive the 4-, 5-, 6-, 7- and 8-times tables. Ask for suggested strategies for these times tables from the children.

Main teaching activities

Whole class: Write on the board $4 \times 11 = (4 \times \square) + (4 \times \square)$. Invite a child to fill in the numbers represented by blank boxes. Now underneath write $4 \times 12 = (4 \times 10) + (4 \times \square)$. Invite a child to fill in 2 for the blank box. Mark and discuss another example. Now ask: *How could you work out 4×13?* ($(4 \times 10) + (4 \times 3)$). Demonstrate how this can be recorded in a different way using a grid:

x	10	3	
4	40	12	= 52

Individual work: Give each child a copy of 'Let's calculate!' which contains a range of calculations in the 13-, 14- and 15-times tables.

Differentiation

Less able: Provide the version of the sheet which includes some modelled answers. Work together with this group to ensure that they understand both methods of calculation (distributive law and partitioning into TU by U).

More able: Provide the version of the sheet which sets some questions in a problem-solving context and which extends the range of questions to multiplications in the 17- and 18-times tables.

Plenary & assessment

Invite the children to explain how they worked out answers on the sheets and prompt for alternative methods (multiplying in any order, using known facts, partitioning etc.). Pose a problem from the more able sheet, discuss the questions and use children's responses to assess understanding.

Review all of the strategies for multiplication taught this week and take feedback from children on their preferred methods of calculation.

Calculations and problem-solving

Children use appropriate number operations and ways of calculating to solve problems. They develop the use of partitioning, writing it more formally in a grid. They discuss approximating answers and checking calculations and investigate various methods. They begin to look at multi-step operations and how to use inverse operations to check them. They split the day up into time periods and calculate time durations.

LEARNING OBJECTIVES

	Topics	Starter	Main teaching activities
Lesson 1	Pencil and paper procedures ($\times$ and $\div$)	● Derive quickly all number pairs that total 100.	● **Use informal pencil and paper methods to support, record or explain multiplications.** ● Approximate first.
Lesson 2	Making decisions	● Derive quickly all number pairs of multiples of 50 that total 1000.	● **Choose and use appropriate number operations and ways of calculating (mental, mental with jottings, pencil and paper) to solve problems.** ● Approximate first.
Lesson 3	Problems involving 'real life', money and measures Checking results	● Multiply any integer up to 1000 by 10 and understand the effect.	● **Use informal pencil and paper methods to support, record or explain divisions.** ● Approximate first. ● Check with the inverse operation.
Lesson 4	Problems involving 'real life', money and measures Checking results	● Divide any integer up to 1000 by 10 and understand the effect.	● Use all four operations to solve word problems involving numbers in 'real life' time, using more than one step. ● Check with the inverse operation.
Lesson 5	Problems involving 'real life', money and measures Checking results	● Read the time from an analogue clock to the nearest minute and from a 12-hour digital clock. Count in steps of half an hour.	● Revise the vocabulary for time and estimate time durations. ● Use all four operations to solve word problems involving numbers in 'real life' measures, using more than one step (time). ● Check with the inverse operation.

Lessons   overview

Preparation
Copy 'Practising the grid method' onto an OHT.

Learning objectives
Starter
● Derive quickly all number pairs that total 100.
● Derive quickly all number pairs of multiples of 50 that total 1000.
Main teaching activities
● **Use informal pencil and paper methods to support , record or explain multiplications.**
● **Choose and use appropriate number operations and ways of calculating (mental, mental with jottings, pencil and paper) to solve problems.**
● Approximate first.

Vocabulary
total, inverse, half, double, pair, find the difference, estimate, factors, approximate, multiply, division, remainder

You will need:
Photocopiable pages
A copy of 'Practising the grid method' for each child (see page 135).

CD pages
'Practising the grid method' core, less able, more able and template versions; 'Multiplication challenge' (see General resources).

Equipment
Whiteboards; number fans.

Lesson

Starter

Hold up a number, for example, 45 and say the number aloud. Ask the children to write on their whiteboards the number that is the pair to your number, to total 100 (55). Tell them not to hold up their whiteboards until you say: *Now*. Then repeat your number (45) and they say their number (55) aloud. Then put their number (55) onto your fan and ask the children to find the corresponding number pair (45). Repeat with several examples ending in 5 and then finish with an example such as 63 (37).

Main teaching activities

Whole class: Write on the board $13 \times 4 = \square$ and ask: *Who can remember how we worked this out before?* Recap $13 \times 4 = (10 \times 4) + (3 \times 4)$.

Now ask: *What could you write down to help you do this calculation? Could you write this in another way?* Draw out the grid, showing carefully where each number will go. Remind the children of their use of the grid method in the autumn term.

Now write on the board $23 \times 4 = \square$. Ask the children to estimate what the answer would be. Ask: *Will it be greater than 52? How do you know that?* Write some of the children's estimates on the board then ask: *How could you work it out?*

×	20	3	
4	80	12	= 92

Individual work: Use the OHT version of 'Practising the grid method' to check that the children can put the numbers in the correct boxes. Work out the answer together (see left) and compare the answer to the estimates. Ask: *How did you estimate your answer?* Repeat with some different examples, such as 16×4, 26×4, 27×5, 28×5 and 31×6, estimating the answers each time. Let the children work through the activity sheet.

Differentiation

Less able: Let these children use the version of the activity sheet that restricts them to multiplication of a single-digit number by a number less than 20.

More able: Provide the version of the sheet which includes multiplication of a single-digit by two-digit numbers over 50 as well as a challenge similar to the one set out in the plenary in which the children have to identify the original number sentence from a partially completed grid. Ask these children to estimate their answers first and to find the difference between their estimates and their answer for each calculation. Encourage these children to use a mental strategy such as partitioning to find more accurate estimates.

×	?	?	
?	360	18	= 378

Plenary & assessment

Draw on the board this grid (see left) : Ask: *What could the question marks stand for?* Now write on the board $42 \times 9 = \square$. Ask the children to estimate the answer (400). Discuss and compare approaches to finding the estimates ($4 \times 9 \times 10$) or (40×10). Then discuss how to work out the calculation: ($4 \times 10 \times 9$) + (2×9) or (40×10) + (2×10) − 42 (378).

Lesson

Starter

Say that you will be looking at number pairs that make 1000. Say a number and ask the class to say the number that you would add to it to make 1000. Keep a rhythm going. Start with 50 (950), then 100 (900) and work up to 950 (50). Then work down again before randomly picking some numbers that are divisible by 50.

Main teaching activities

Paired work: Explain that the children will be looking at methods of multiplying and estimating answers. They will play two different games, in pairs. Draw a blank grid on the board, or display the OHT of 'Practising the grid method' (template version). Talk through one example, such as 27×8.

×	?	?	
?	40	4	= 44

Remind the children which numbers go in each box. Now each child uses the template version of the activity sheet 'Practising the grid method' to help them work out a multiplication question of their choice, keeping the answer to themselves. Draw a blank grid on the board and explain that you have thought up a multiplication. Fill in the two total boxes and the answer and explain to the children that they have to fill in the other boxes correctly in as few guesses as possible (see left). The minimum number of goes will be three.

Ask individual children to fill in the numbers represented by question marks. Each time a correct response is guessed, fill in the box. If a guess is incorrect make a tally at the side and count up the tallies at the end. They are now going to use the multiplications they made up earlier, with their grids, to play against each other. Let them play the first round and then check with you. As you go around, ask: *How are you working out the missing numbers? What information can you use to help you?*

Now ask the children to count up the tallies and explain that they will be going on to round two. Ask the children to work out four multiplication questions on the General resource sheet 'Multiplication challenge', again keeping the answers to themselves. Demonstrate the game on the board by thinking of a multiplication question, for example, 23 × 4 = ❑ (92). Invite a child to estimate the answer and ask: *How did you work that out?* Suggest that they could double and then double again or work out 20 × 4. Explain how they will score points. If their partner's estimate is within 20 of the actual answer, then the child setting the question gets no points. Otherwise, they find the difference between their partner's estimate and the actual answer and this is the number of points awarded to the child who set the question. The aim is to find a way of giving a good estimate, so that the other child does not gain points. Ask the children to take turns working out estimates, and discuss how they worked them out.

Differentiation

Less able: Limit these children to choosing less complex calculations, limiting their two-digit numbers to those less than 20.

More able: Challenge these children to choose more complex numbers in their calculations and suggest more than one way of estimating answers.

Plenary & assessment

Ask: *In which round did you lose the most points? Who had the most effective method of estimation? What did you do? Did anyone else find a different way? What was the most effective approach to round one?* Emphasise the benefit of thinking through all the factors that give a particular number, for example, with 40 (1 × 40, 2 × 20, 4 × 10 or 5 × 8). Play the game several times with the class.

Lessons   overview

Preparation

Make sets of cards (enough for one between two) from the top part of 'Time after time cards' plus extension set for more able pupils. Copy 'Word problems question' onto acetate (see General resources).

Learning objectives

Starter
● Multiply or divide any integer up to 1000 by 10 and understand the effect.
● Read the time from an analogue clock to the nearest minute and from a 12-hour digital clock. Count in steps of half an hour.

Main teaching activities
● **Use informal pencil and paper methods to support, record or explain divisions.**
● Approximate first.
● Use all four operations to solve word problems involving numbers in 'real life' money, using more than one step.
● Check with the inverse operation.
● Revise the vocabulary for time and estimate time durations.

Vocabulary

total, inverse, half double, pair, find the difference, estimate, factors, approximate

You will need:

Photocopiable pages
A copy of 'Word problems' (page 136) for each child.

CD pages

'Check it!' core, less able, more able and template versions, 1 for each pair of children; 'Word problems' core, less able, more able and template versions for each pair; 'Word problem question' for OHP (see General resources); 'Time after time cards' for each pair; 'Going to school' (see General resources) .

Equipment

Number fans; clock faces; OHP.

Lesson 3

Starter
Remind children that when they multiply by 10 the whole number moves one position to the left and a zero is placed in the units column. Call out a number, the children multiply this by 10 and show their answer on a whiteboard. Repeat for other numbers, eg 56, 60, 75 etc. Ask the children to explain the effect of multiplying by 10 after each answer.

Main teaching activities
Remind children of the work in the previous two lessons. Discuss the children's methods for approximating the answers to the multiplication questions (eg using known number facts, using factors etc.). Write $57 \div 3$ on the board. Ask: *How can we approximate this answer?*
Discuss suggestions, and if necessary remind the children that multiplication is the *inverse* of division and can be used to approximate or check answers, eg 'We know that *15 × 3 = 45* and *20 × 3 = 60*, so the answer is between 15 and 20'.

```
   57
 - 45     (15 × 3)
   12
 - 12     ( 4 × 3)
    0
Answer: 19
```

Demonstrate how to find the answer by 'chunking' multiples of the divisor 3, '15 threes makes 45, that leaves 12'. Ask: *How many 3s make 12?* (4). 'There are 15 threes and four threes in 57 – that makes 19 threes altogether'. Show this 'chunking' method on the board (see left): Discuss methods for checking that the answer is correct. Prompt if necessary for using the inverse operation: $57 \div 3 = 19$ should mean that $57 = 19 \times 3$. (Encourage the children to use the grid method or partitioning to work out the multiplication.)
Paired work: Give each pair a copy of 'Check it!' Ask one child to approximate the answer to each division question. They should then work together to solve it using the 'chunking' method described above. Finally, the second child should check the answer using the inverse operation.

Differentiation
Less able: Provide the version of the sheet with the 'chunking' method of calculation already defined.
More able: Provide the version of the sheet, which includes answers with remainders. Work with this group on these questions setting them in a problem-solving context if necessary (eg 'Paul has 95p which he has to share equally with his two sisters. How much will each child get?').

Plenary & assessment
Focus on the 'chunking' method and use the children's answers to the 'Check it!' questions to assess their understanding of the method and to correct any misconceptions. Complete one problem together using the chunking method: 'Mrs Smith has made 96 cakes for the school fete, which she sells in packs of 8. How many packs of cakes will she be able to make?'.

Lesson 4

Starter
On the board write some two-digit and three-digit numbers, eg 50, 90, 150, 240, 570. Ask: *What is 50 ÷ 10?* Establish the answer is 5 and check by multiplying 5 by 10. Establish that the digits move one place to the right. Emphasise the inverse relationship here between multiplication and division and how this can be used as a checking strategy. Go through the other numbers on the board dividing by 10 each time.

Main teaching activities
Whole class: Review the multiplication and division methods and approximation and checking strategies introduced in this unit using examples such as (see left).

```
66 ÷ 6 = ☐
37 × 4 = ☐
and so on.
```

Write a word problem on the board such as the following: '88 counters are shared between 8 children. How many counters does each child get?' Ask: *Which words tell us what type of calculation to do?* (Shared) *What other information does this problem give us?* Highlight the numbers and key words in the problem. Ask the children to write the calculation on the board (88 ÷8 = ❏). Again, ask all of the children to approximate the answer then use the 'chunking' method to solve it. Discuss answers and any alternative methods.

Paired work: Provide each pair with a copy of 'Word problems'. Explain that some of the questions include more than one step and that the children should discuss with their partners which operations are required (+, –, × or ÷) before solving each problem.

Differentiation

Less able: Provide the version of the sheet with a mixture of single-step and multi-step operations.
More able: Provide the version of the sheet with more complex multi-step problems.

Plenary & assessment

Use the OHT of 'Word problems question' (see General resources). Work through the problem together, covering up each line on the OHT, then revealing it. Ask: *What could you write to help you answer this question?* Then work backwards, asking: *What is the opposite of add 1? What is the inverse? What is the opposite of × 2? What is the inverse?* Say: *Therefore the number Henry thought of was 61.* Emphasise the use of inverses as a checking strategy. Repeat the use of inverses with another example.

Lesson ⑤

Starter

Show a clock face to the children. Set a time, eg 1:15 and ask the children: *How can we say this time?* Continue with a selection of times (half past, quarter to etc.) and ask the children to write the times on their whiteboards. Extend to writing using digital times. Say a time and ask the children to count up in steps of half an hour from that time, each time you point at them, until you say: *Stop.* Start with 4 o'clock (half past four, five o'clock…). Then start again with quarter past four (quarter to five…), then 5:15 (5:45, 6:15…). Then repeat with 4:05 (4:35…).

Main teaching activities

Whole class: Tell the children that they will be looking at problems involving time. Go through the problem on the 'Going to school' sheet. Now write on the board two times: 4:05 and 5:45. Ask: *How can you work out how long it is from 4:05pm to 5:45pm?* Draw arrows and discuss each step. Suggest that the children work up to the hour and then past (see left). Ask: *How could you check this? How many hours and minutes is this?* (1 hour and 40 minutes).

4:05 ⟶ 5:00 ⟶ 5:45 55 + 45 = 100 minutes

55 minutes   45 minutes

Paired work: Give each pair of children some paper and a set of 'Time after time' cards. Ask them to shuffle the cards and then the first player takes two cards. They must put the earlier time on the left-hand side of the paper and the later time on the right-hand side of the paper, in a line. Now they need to write any workings on the paper, to work out the interval between the two times on the cards. The second player watches and must be convinced of the method. When they have agreed on the time interval, they replace the cards, shuffle them and the second player has a turn. When the activity is completed, ask the children to make up a problem involving two of the times.

Differentiation

Less able: Let these children start with only the cards showing times from 1am to 2am and work in hour, quarter and three-quarter hour steps.
More able: Let these children use the cards on the activity sheet that are labelled 'Extension set', which has some extra later times printed.

Plenary & assessment

Discuss the children's work on time. Pick two cards and copy the times onto the board. Ask: *How could you work out the time between these two times?* Ask individual children to demonstrate their methods, using arrows. Ask: *How could you check the answer is correct? Check on a clock face or work backwards.*

Name   Date

Practising the grid method

Use the grids below to help you set out and answer these multiplication questions.

1.   8 × 26

2.   7 × 18

3.   5 × 24

4.   9 × 32

5.   42 × 3

6.   28 × 4

7.   41 × 7

8.   6 × 33

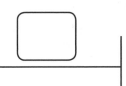

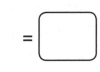

Name	Date

Word problems

Work out each problem in the space below it, showing your workings carefully.

1. There are 34 children in Class 1 and 35 children in Class 2. Altogether, there are 30 boys in Classes 1 and 2. How many children in Classes 1 and 2 are girls?	
2. There are 56 chairs for the audience and 23 chairs on the stage. If I take away five chairs, how many chairs are left altogether?	
3. Henry thought of a number. He doubled it and then added twenty-one and his answer was 143. What was the number that Henry thought of?	
4. At Footgreat School there are 115 pupils that play football. There are four teams at the school and every pupil is in only one team. The first team has 24 pupils, the second team has 30 pupils and the third team has 12 pupils. How many pupils are in the fourth team?	
5. Annie spent £3.50 on apples and £4.00 on bananas. How much change did she receive if she paid with a £10 note?	
6. Tins of baked beans come in packs of four. I buy four packs and it costs me £1.60. How much have I paid for each can of beans?	

Fractions and decimals

The children look at using fraction notation, recognising simple fractions and identifying two fractions with totals of a whole. They start to look at equivalent fractions and ordering fractions, deciding whether they are less than or greater than one half. They use money to understand decimal notation and place value for tenths and hundredths. They start to look at fractions and decimals greater than one.

LEARNING OBJECTIVES

		Topics	Starter	Main teaching activities
Lesson	1	Fractions and decimals	● Count on or back in steps of 1/2, 1/4, 1/3.	● Use fraction notation. ● **Recognise simple fractions that are several parts of a whole**, such as 2/3 or 5/8 and mixed numbers such as 53/4. ● Identify two simple fractions with totals of 1 whole.
Lesson	2	Fractions and decimals	● Identify two simple fractions with totals of 1 whole.	● Use fraction notation. ● **Recognise simple fractions that are several parts of a whole**, such as 2/3 or 5/8 and mixed numbers such as 53/4. ● **Recognise the equivalence of simple fractions.**
Lesson	3	Fractions and decimals	As Lesson 2.	● Order simple fractions, for example, decide whether fractions such as 3/8 or 7/10 are greater than or less than 1/2.
Lesson	4	Fractions and decimals	● Order simple fractions, for example, decide whether fractions such as 3/8 or 7/10 are greater than or less than 1/2.	● Understand decimal notation and place value for tenths and hundredths and use it in context.
Lesson	5	Fractions and decimals	● Understand decimal notation for tenths.	● Understand decimal notation and place value for tenths and hundredths and use it in context, order amounts of money.

Lessons   overview

Preparation
Cut out and prepare cards from 'Less than Snap'. Copy 'Fraction stories' onto OHT.

Learning objectives
Starter
● Count on or back in steps of 1/2, 1/4, 1/3.
● Identify two simple fractions with totals of 1 whole.
Main teaching activities
● Use fraction notation.
● **Recognise simple fractions that are several parts of a whole**, such as 2/3 or 5/8, and mixed numbers such as 53/4.
● Identify two simple fractions with totals of 1 whole.
● **Recognise the equivalence of simple fractions.**
● Order simple fractions, for example, decide whether fractions such as 3/8 or 7/10 are greater than or less than 1/2.

Vocabulary
fraction, decimal, whole number, greater than, less than, half, halves, third, quarter, sixth, fifth, eighth, tenth, twentieth, equal parts, zero

You will need:
CD pages
A copy of 'Fraction stories' core, less able, more able and template versions; 'Whole fractions' (see General resources); 'Fraction strips' core, less able, more able and template versions; 'Less than Snap' and 'Less than Snap instructions' (see General resources) .

Equipment
Whiteboards; a 1 kilogram bag of pasta; a suitable set of scales.

Lesson ①

Starter

Draw a number line on the board and add the numbers 0 to 10 along it. Ask the children to count in steps of 1/2 from zero (eg one half, two halves, three halves). Point to the markers on the board, eg point to 1 for 'two halves' etc. Next, ask the children if there is another way of saying this. Establish that two halves is the same as 1, three halves is 1 1/2 etc. Ask the children to repeat the count this time saying half, one, one and a half etc. Fill in the gaps on the number line. Extend the count to quarters and thirds if time is available.

Main teaching activities

Whole class: Show the example question from 'Fraction stories' on an OHT or copy onto the board. Ask: *How many whole rectangles do we have?* Agree that there is a whole rectangle divided into six equal parts. Cover up the shaded part (5/6 are left), then the rest of the shape (leaving one sixth). Write on the board: 1/6 + 5/6 = 6/6 = 1 whole.

Establish that children understand that one whole is equivalent to two halves and six sixths etc. Shade in other squares and repeat for 2/6, 3/6 and 4/6. (You might also prepare an OHT using the 'Whole fractions' general resource sheet for this purpose.)

Individual work: Provide each child with a copy of 'Fraction stories' to complete. Remind the children to look in particular for fractions that equal one whole.

Differentiation

Less able: Provide the version of the sheet that includes only simple fractions such as 3/4 and 2/3.
More able: Provide the version of the sheet in which the children also have to recognise equivalent fractions. Work with this group to highlight equivalences if necessary.

Plenary & assessment

Review the children's 'Fraction stories' sheets. Draw some rectangles divided into sixths and eighths on the board or use the 'Whole fractions' sheet. Ask the children to shade squares and then write the fraction story underneath. If any equivalent fractions are given ask the class: *Can you give me another story for the same picture?* Use this method to introduce the idea of equivalent fractions.

Lesson ②

Starter

Draw five dots onto the board. Cover up some of the dots and say the fraction you have covered. Ask the class to say the fraction of dots that are left, for example, 4/5 and 1/5. Repeat with six dots and then with eight dots. Ask: *What does 7/8 + 1/8 make?* (1 whole). Now say a fraction and ask the children to give you the other part of the fraction pair that makes 1 whole, for example, 5/6 (1/6) or 3/4 (1/4). Repeat with several more examples.

Main teaching activities

Review the 'Fraction stories' work from the previous lesson. Display an OHT of the 'Whole fractions' general resource sheet and focus on the tenths. Cover various parts of the rectangle and ask: *What fraction can we see?* Shade five of the squares.

Ask: *What fraction of the shape can you see?* Prompt for 5/10 but agree and show the children that this is equivalent to 1/2. Repeat for the other rectangles on the 'Whole fractions' sheet. Extend to twelfths by drawing a rectangle divided into 12 equal parts on the board. Set the class the challenge of writing as many fractions that are equivalent to one half as they can in five minutes. Discuss their answers and write them up on the board.

Paired work: Give each pair a copy of 'Fraction strips'. Explain that the strips show fractions of one whole. Challenge the children to mark on all of the divisions of each strip and to highlight any equivalent fractions at the bottom of the sheet. You might provide the pairs with strips of paper to check their answers. You might complete one example, eg '1/2 is in the same position as 2/4'.

Differentiation

Less able: Give each pair the partly completed version of 'Fraction strips'. Work with these pairs to establish which are the equivalent fractions using strips of paper to check.

More able: Give each pair the version of the sheet which includes twelfths. Encourage the children to use paper strips to demonstrate the equivalences.

Plenary & assessment

Use the children's completed sheets to establish their understanding of equivalences. Model some of the answers on the board drawing strips or number lines of the same size. Draw strips of the same size with divisions for twelfths and twentieths. Point to divisions and ask children to name the fractions and determine equivalent fractions.

Lesson ③

Starter

Repeat the Starter for Lesson 2. Say a fraction and ask the children to give you the other fraction in the pair that makes 1 whole. Repeat with several examples.

Main teaching activities

```
0      1/4     1/2    3/4      1
```

Whole class: Write on the board:

Now ask: *Is three quarters less than half? Is a quarter less than half?* Ask individual children to use the symbols '>' and '<' to write some appropriate number sentences on the board.

Review the 'Fraction strips' sheets completed in Lesson 2. Using an OHT of this sheet, point to different divisions and ask for the fraction. Focus on the halfway marks on the halves, quarters, sixths and eighths and ask children for the equivalent fractions. Remind the children that each of these fractions represents part of one whole. Draw a number line with 0 at one end and 1 at the other. Now refer back to the number line drawn earlier and ask: *Where would I put one third on my number line?* Write '1/3' onto a sticky note and ask the children to estimate where it would go. Ask: *Is it more than or less than half?* Establish that it needs to be between a quarter and half. Repeat with two thirds. Explain that these are estimates. Now use a ruler to draw a line 80cm long on the board.

$$\frac{4}{8} \div 4 = \frac{1}{2}$$

$$\frac{2}{8} \div 2 = \frac{1}{4}$$

Mark it equally into eighths. Label 0 and 1. Ask: *Where would half go?* (4/8) *Where would quarter go?* (2/8) Mark on three quarters (6/8) and mark 8/8 in the same way. Show that these fractions in eighths are equivalent to the quarters and halves drawn earlier by dividing the numerator (top number) and denominator (bottom number) by the same amount each time, for example (see left).

Now say that you will play a game. You will call out a fraction and if it is equivalent to a half then the children sit on their chairs, if it is less than a half they are to touch the floor and if it is greater than a half they are to stand up. Start slowly, each time showing the equivalent fraction and relating it back to the number line. For example, three eighths will be less than one half as four eighths is equivalent to one half (3/8 < 4/8).

Paired work: Children use the cards and rules from General resource sheets 'Less than Snap' and 'Less than Snap instructions' to play a game of Snap, placing the fraction cards on the correct pile to make a correct 'less than' expression, or shouting 'equal' if the cards are equivalent.

Differentiation

Less able: For these children, limit the cards to denominators of 2 and 4 before introducing eighths.

More able: Pair these children accordingly and encourage good use of mathematical language. Use template versions to add cards to the game from 1/12 to 12/12.

Plenary & assessment

Pick up a pile of all the cards from activity sheet 'Less than Snap' say that you want to put them, in order, on a number line. Discuss equivalent fractions and ask individual children to put different cards up with Blu-Tack, each time saying, for example, 'A quarter is less than a half,' or 'Five eighths is greater than a half.' Ask another child to check that the fractions are in order.

Lessons overview

Learning objectives

Starter
● Order simple fractions, for example, decide whether fractions such as 3/8 or 7/10 are greater than or less than 1/2.

Main teaching activities
● Understand decimal notation and place value for tenths and hundredths and use it in context, order amounts of money.

Vocabulary

tenths, hundredths, decimal point, decimal place

You will need:

CD pages
'Number lines' (see Summer term General resources); 'Dotty decimals' core, less able, more able and template versions.

Equipment
£1 coin and a mixed bag of coins so that the £1 can be split into change to share.

Lesson

Starter

Write a set of rules as follows: the children must sit on the chairs for a fraction equivalent to a half, stand up if it is greater than a half and touch the floor if it is less than a half. Use examples such as the following: 2/4, 1/3, 5/6, 7/7, 6/10, 3/6, 2/5 etc. Put the three headings on the board and write each fraction under the appropriate headings after each one is agreed.

Main teaching activities

Fraction	Decimal
$\frac{1}{10}$	0.1
$\frac{2}{10}$	0.2
$\frac{3}{10}$	
$\frac{4}{10}$	
$\frac{5}{10}$	
$\frac{6}{10}$	
$\frac{7}{10}$	
$\frac{8}{10}$	
$\frac{9}{10}$	
$\frac{10}{10}$	

Whole class: Take a £1 coin and say: *I would like to share this among 10 of you. How could I do it? How much should I give each person?* (Exchange for smaller coins and give each person 10 pence.) *So what is 10 pence as a fraction of £1?* (1/10) *How would you write 10 pence in pounds?* (£0.10) So in decimals, one tenth is 0.1. ('zero point one'). Write this on the board. Ask: *How could I write 2 divided by 10?* Explain that £2 /10 = 20 pence which is £0.20 so is 0.2 of a pound ('zero point 2'). Discuss the fact that with money it is important to include the zero, for example, £0.30, but it is not necessary in decimal notation: you can just write 0.3. Write 2/10 = 0.2 onto the board and draw up a table (see left). Complete the table with the children, recognising and highlighting equivalences such as 2/10 = 1/5, 4/10 = 2/5, 5/10 = 1/2, 6/10 = 3/5 and 8/10 = 4/5. Draw a number line on the board with 0 at one end and 1 at the other. Prompt the children to complete the number line in tenths using decimal notation. When it has been completed count with the class from 0 to 1 in fractions (1/10, 2/10…) then in decimals (0.1, 0.2, 0.3). Emphasise that the point separates the whole number from the tenths (N.B. watch in particular for any child saying 'zero point ten' for one whole). Ask: *What happens when we count past 1?*

Discuss suggestions and write on the board 10/10 + 1/10 = 11/10. Establish that the count continues to 12/10, 13/10 etc. Ask: *What is this the same as?* Continue the count on the board, recording values on the number line….1.1, 1.2, 1.3 etc. Compare the two fraction forms and ask questions about them, eg *What is 15/10 in decimals?* Record these in your table to 20/10 or 2.0.

Individual work: Give each child a copy of the individual 'Number lines' and ask them to record from 0 to 1, 1 to 2 and 2 to 3 using decimal and improper fraction notation.

Differentiaition

Less able: Work with the groups focusing on 0 to 1. Highlight the position of the decimal point and how this separates the whole number from the tenths.

More able: Challenge the children to write their own start and finish number – perhaps using two-digit whole numbers.

Plenary & assessment

Write on the board: 23.4. Ask: *What is the value of the 2? The 3? The 4?* Discuss and put the headings T, U and t above the number, eg

T	U	.	t
2	3	.	4

Write some numbers underneath the headings and challenge individual children to read the numbers emphasising the decimal point. For each number ask a child: *What is the value representing…?* etc. Repeat for other numbers including some three-digit numbers, eg 127.9.

Lesson ⑤

Starter

Repeat the Starter for Lesson 4 but add in a few simple decimals, for example, 0.1 and 0.5.

Main teaching activities

Whole class: Ask: *How do we write one penny in pounds?* (£0.01) Repeat the activity for Lesson 4 dividing £1 by 100 and write 1/100 = 0.01 (zero point zero one), 2/100 = 0.02 etc. Ask: *What would seven hundredths be as a decimal? What would ten hundredths be? Is this the same as one tenth?* Write some amounts on the board such as £3.24. Ask: *What is the 3 worth? What is the 2 worth? What is the 4 worth?* Emphasise that the 3 is 3 whole pounds and that the other digits represent parts of £1.

Repeat the above for measures such as 4.50 kg and 4.05 kg. Ask: *Which is the heavier? Why?*

Individual work: Give each child a copy of the 'Dotty decimals' sheet and let them practise ordering whole number and decimal amounts. Discuss ways of converting from pounds to pence and metres to centimetres.

Differentiaition

Less able: Use the version of the sheet that includes mainly whole numbers and tenths.

More able: Use the version of the sheet that includes two-digit and three-digit whole numbers to order as well as a final challenge to make up a question for a partner. Remind the children that they will need to know how to order the numbers before setting the challenge.

Plenary & assessment

Write on the board: 123.45. Ask: *What is the value of the 1? The 2? The 3?* and so on. Discuss and put the headings H, T, U, . , t and h above the number, for example

H	T	U	.	t	h
1	2	3	.	4	5

Write four more numbers underneath the headings and challenge individual children to read the numbers emphasising the decimal point. For each number ask another child: *What is the value representing…?* etc. Challenge the children to order the five numbers at the end of the session. Collect answers and discuss strategies for ordering the numbers.

Handling data

Children make decisions about how to sort objects, using pictograms, tally charts, frequency diagrams and bar charts labelled in intervals of 2s, 5s, 10s or 20s. They are encouraged to use computers to show ways of displaying data quickly. Children sort shapes and numbers by properties into Venn diagrams and Carroll diagrams.

LEARNING OBJECTIVES

	Topics	Starter	Main teaching activities
Lesson 1	Handling data	● **Know by heart multiplication facts for 2-, 3-, 4-, 5- and 10-times tables.** ● Begin to know multiplication facts for 6-, 7-, 8- and 9-times tables.	● Solve a problem by collecting quickly, organising, representing and interpreting data in tables, charts, graphs and diagrams. ● Using pictograms, bar charts, tally charts and frequency tables representing 2, 5 and 10 units. ● Using bar charts, labels in intervals of 2s, 5s 10s, or 20s.
Lesson 2	Handling data	● **Derive quickly division facts corresponding to 2-, 3-, 4-, 5- and 10-times tables.**	● Solve a problem by collecting quickly, organising, representing and interpreting data in tables, charts, graphs and diagrams. ● Using bar charts labelled in intervals of 2s, 5s, 10s or 20s.
Lesson 3	Handling data	● **Use known number facts and place value to add or subtract mentally, including any pair of two-digit whole numbers.**	● Solve a problem by collecting quickly, organising, representing and interpreting data in tables, charts, graphs and diagrams. ● Using a computer.
Lesson 4	Handling data	As Lesson 3.	● Solve a problem by collecting quickly, organising, representing and interpreting data in tables, charts, graphs and diagrams. ● Using Venn diagrams.
Lesson 5	Handling data	● Recognise and extend number sequences formed by counting from any number in steps of constant size.	● Solve a problem by collecting quickly, organising, representing and interpreting data in tables, charts, graphs and diagrams. ● Using Carroll diagrams.

Lessons   overview

Preparation
Prepare the cards from 'Operation follow-on' (or use those prepared for Unit 3, Lesson 3). Copy 'Tally charts' (2 sheets) onto OHTs. Look carefully at the data-handling program on your computer that you intend to demonstrate to the class.

Learning objectives
Starter
● **Know by heart multiplication facts for 2-, 3-, 4-, 5- and 10-times tables.**
● Begin to know multiplication facts for 6-, 8-, 7- and 9-times tables.
● **Derive quickly division facts corresponding to 2-, 3-, 4-, 5- and 10-times tables.**
● **Use known number facts and place value to add or subtract mentally, including any pair of two-digit whole numbers.**
Main teaching activities
● Solve a problem by collecting quickly, organising, representing and interpreting data in tables, charts, graphs and diagrams.
● Using pictograms, bar charts, tally charts and frequency tables representing 2, 5 and 10 units.
● Using a computer.
● Using bar charts labelled in intervals of 2s, 5s, 10s or 20s.

Vocabulary
tally, sort, pictogram, graph, group, set, bar chart, tally chart, frequency table, Venn diagram, and Carroll diagram

You will need:
CD pages
A copy of 'Operation follow-on'; (see Unit 3); 'Post-it Notes charts' (see General resources); 'Key charts'; 'Tally charts' (2 sheets) and 'Bar chart' (see General resources) for the teacher and for each child.

Equipment
Whiteboards; Post-it Notes; a pile of newspapers or magazines (up to five for each child); a database or suitable data handling package.

Lesson

Starter

Ask the children quick-fire multiplication tables questions, within 2-, 3-, 4-, 5- and 10-times tables, such as 6 × 3, 7 × 4, 8 × 5 and 9 × 4 and let them write their answers on their whiteboards. Write any common mistakes in the corner of the board to recap later in the lesson. Ask: *How did you work out the answer? Did you know the fact or did you use another fact to help you? If so, what did you use to help you?*

Main teaching activities

Whole class: In this lesson children will revise their data-handling work from previous years and the autumn term of Year 4. Use the 'Post-it Note charts' as a support tool in this activity. Ask each child to draw a quick sketch of their favourite animal on a Post-it Note and stick it on the board when they have finished. Ask: *What was the most popular animal? How many people like cats the best?* The children will find it difficult to use the information as it is on the board. Ask: *How can we rearrange the information to make it easier for us to read?* Ask for suggestions and see if the children place the sticky notes into rows or columns to make a pictogram, or add a key (1 sticky note = 1 animal), as on 'Post-it Note charts' sheet. Then use the same sticky notes to make a simple bar chart. Ask: *Does this make it easier to read the information? How many children in the class like dogs the most? What was the most popular animal? How can we make this clearer?* (By labelling the type of animal and the number of animals on the two axes.) Now ask again: *What was the most popular animal? Is this easier to see? How else could we arrange this information to make it clearer?*

Group work: Challenge the children, in groups of two or three, to use a different key or scale, such as 1 sticky note = 2 animals, 4 animals, 5 animals, 10 animals. Explain that each sticky note represents a different number of votes now, not just the one that it did before. With a key of one sticky note representing two votes (or animals) then three sticky notes would represent six votes. Give groups one of the keys above and ask them to construct bar charts to answer the questions on activity sheet 'Key charts'. Encourage the groups not to reveal the keys they have chosen. Then, as the group reads out their results for the four statements on the sheet, they can challenge the other groups to guess their key. Compare and discuss results.

Differentiation

Less able: Give this group a key of one Post-it Note to two votes.
More able: Challenge the group to display the information in a number of different ways and think about a wider variety of scales.

Plenary & assessment

Take a vote to decide which group has the clearest results. Ask: *What made the information clearer to read? How many more children prefer cats to dogs? If you were asked the question, 'Are dogs more popular than cats?' how would you answer, given this information? Do you think that will always be the case? Discuss.* Discuss the children's bar charts and ask questions such as *What is the scale of your vertical axis? What did you put along the horizontal axis?* etc. Ask: *Do you think that bar charts or pictograms are easier to read?* Highlight the importance of labels in bar charts. Recap any multiplication facts from the Starter.

Lesson

Starter

Repeat the Starter from Lesson 1 but ask division facts (from the 2-, 3-, 4-, 5- and 10-times tables) rapidly. For example, '35 ÷ 5 = ☐'. (7)

Quantity of advertisements	Number of pages
No advertisements on the page	
Less than (<) half the pages contains advertisements	
More than (>) or equal to half the page contains advertisements	
Whole page of advertisements	

Main teaching activities

Whole class: Remind children of work completed in the autumn term on tally charts and frequency charts and bar charts. Ask: *When would you use a frequency chart* (as a quick way to collect and order small amounts of data). Explain that the children will be investigating the statement 'Half of the pages in magazines and newspapers are made up of adverts.' Ask: *Do you think that this is true?*

Group work: Split the children into five groups of four or five. Give each group a pile of newspapers or magazines. Ask the children for ideas on how to test the statement. Agree on the approach, collecting the data into a tally chart (see left). Give each group the first page of pupil sheet 'Tally charts', (see General resources) which provides the chart to complete for each magazine. If each child counts three to five magazines, this will give a significant sample (about 100).

Ask: *How could we check the information?* (Count the number of pages and total the tallies.)

Whole class: Ask the different groups to summarise their findings, using the frequency chart. Compare results and ask: *Do you think that the original statement is true?* Then, on an OHT of 'Tally chart', collect all of the information to make a combined frequency table.

Now ask: *How could we show this information on a bar chart?* Use an OHT of the blank graph from the sheet 'Bar chart' (see General resources) to draw up the information on the axes. The vertical column has been left blank to enable you to explore the different intervals 2, 5 or 10 on the scales. Ask: *What would be the best way to fit the numbers onto this axis? Do I need to put in every number?*

Differentiation

Less able: Ask this group to select from fewer magazines/newspapers and to focus on a bar chart with a scale of no more than 5 units.

More able: Challenge this group to use a wider selection of magazines/newspapers and select their own scales/vertical axes for the bar charts.

Plenary & assessment

Ask: *Who thinks that the statement about advertising in newspapers and magazines is correct? Why? Who disagrees? What could we do to investigate further? How else could we have recorded the results? Which do you think is the best way? Why do you think that?*

Lesson

Starter

Use cards prepared from 'Operation follow-on' (see Lesson 3 of Unit 3) to revise addition and subtraction. The cards follow on from each other, with the number at the top being the answer to a question on another card. Complete a loop of the cards once slowly, each time asking: *How did you work that out? What did you do to help you?* Then speed up and time the children for one loop.

Main teaching activities

(Ideally, work in the school computer room.)

Whole class: Say to the children that computers can help us with data handling. Show some examples of charts and graphs cut from newspapers and explain that many companies use computers to help them draw charts. Set up a computer so that the children can see the screen; one with a link to a whiteboard is ideal. Use a data-handling package to input some simple data such as eye colours for the class. Complete a quick count as you sit at the computer and process the information. Demonstrate how the computer can illustrate the information in a number of ways, such as bar charts and line graphs, using various scales.

In lessons:	5 1/2 hours
Playtime:	2 hours
Eating:	2 1/2 hours
Watching TV:	2 1/2 hours
Reading and homework:	1 1/2 hours
Sleeping:	9 hours
Travelling to school:	1 hour

Paired/Individual work: If possible, use the computer to display information gathered from the children. Ask them to take a typical school day, spilt it into 24 hours and work out how long they spend doing different things in the day, (see left).

Ask the children to present their findings as a bar chart, choosing a suitable non-unitary scale, for example, in half hours. If computers are not available this can be done by hand. If a database is used, then work with the children to establish how many and what type of fields they will require (one text field and one number field).

Differentiation

Less able: This group should work with a teaching assistant to pool their data. Let the children enter any data they can. Ask the children to round their activities up to the nearest hour and check that they add up to 24 before they draw anything.

More able: These children could start to think about splitting their day into 10-minute or 20-minute periods.

Plenary & assessment

Ask the children to present their bar charts to the rest of the class. Discuss interval scales and ask: *Is the information clear? How could it be clearer?* Compare results, asking: *Who spends the most time watching television, reading, playing, eating?* Encourage the children to make some statements of their own about their bar charts.

Lessons   overview

Preparation
Prepare the cards from 'Operation follow-on' as for Unit 3, Lesson 3. Copy the 'Carroll diagram' and 'Venn diagram' sheets onto OHTs and prepare enlarged (A3) copies of the 'Carroll diagram' for group work.

Learning objectives
Starter
● **Use known number facts and place value to add or subtract mentally, including any pair of two-digit whole numbers.**
● Recognise and extend number sequences formed by counting from any number in steps of constant size.
Main teaching activities
● Solve a problem by collecting quickly, organising, representing and interpreting data in tables, charts, graphs and diagrams.
● Sorting information into Venn diagrams and Carroll diagrams.

Vocabulary
square, rectangle, triangle, equilateral triangle, isosceles triangle, quadrilateral, pentagon, hexagon, heptagon, octagon, Carroll diagram, Venn diagram, right diagram

You will need:
CD pages
'Operation follow-on' cards (see Unit 3); 'Carroll diagram'; 'Venn diagrams' (see General resources).

Equipment
Post-it Notes; two hoops (large enough to make Venn diagrams with the geo-rods) for each group of two or three children; enough geo-rods per group to make several shapes; fasteners for geo-rods.

Lesson

Starter
Repeat the Starter from Lesson 3 but start by timing the children for one loop and compare their time to yesterday.

Main teaching activities
Now ask the children to make a quadrilateral (four-sided shape) from the geo-rods. Explain that you expect the groups to work together and that the group should show you the shape only when

you ask. As the groups show you a new shape ask them to make a pile to one side so that they can sort the shapes later in the lesson. Run through the characteristics of a square; ask: *How many right angles does it have? How many lines of symmetry?* Repeat for a rectangle and then compare a square to a rectangle.

Whole class: Draw a Carroll diagram on the board or copy the 'Carroll diagram' sheet onto an OHT. Ask: *What is a quadrilateral? What is a right angle?* Pull out a 2-D shape made from geo rods and ask the class to decide where to put it on the 'Carroll diagram'. Continue with one or two more examples.

Group work: Give each group an enlarged copy of the 'Carroll diagram' sheet. Explain to the groups that they have to make and then sort a number of 2-D shapes onto the grid. Challenge the groups to make a range of quadrilaterals and other shapes. Work with the groups on this sorting task. If time is available, encourage the children to prepare a second Carroll diagram. Ask them to think about the type of criteria that they could use to sort triangles for example.

Differentiation

Less able: Limit the range of shapes used by these children to triangles and simple quadrilaterals.
More able: Let these children work with a range of polygons and encourage them to complete a second Carroll diagram on the grid, this time thinking of their own criteria for sorting the shapes.

Plenary & assessment

Establish that each shape in the activity either satisfies each criterion or it does not – ie it either is or is not a quadrilateral! It should therefore be possible to place any 2-D shape onto this grid.

	Hot dog	No hot dog
Popcorn	3	4
No popcorn	6	5

Ask: *What else could we use Carroll diagrams for?* Take ideas and develop one on the board. Here is a suggested alternative if required (see left). Ask: *what could this be about?* (eg items bought in a cinema). *How many people had a hot dog, but no popcorn?* (6) *How many people had neither?* (5)

Lesson

Starter

Split the class into six groups. Start a sequence of numbers, for example 12, 15, 18, 21, 24… and then point to a group to take over. When you want that group to stop and the next group you point to to take over, say: *Change.* Continue until all groups have had a turn and then repeat with several other sequences. Changing groups frequently will keep the children alert.

Main teaching activities

Group work: Explain to the children that they will be looking at shapes and sorting them. Split the children into groups of two or three and give each group two hoops and a number of geo-rods and clips. Explain that you will start by asking the groups to make shapes, using the geo-rods, and then you will sort the shapes. Challenge the groups to show you a triangle, quadrilateral, pentagon, hexagon, heptagon, octagon and discuss the characteristics of each shape. Highlight numbers of sides and angles.

Challenge the group to make three different sorts of triangle. Compare results and discuss equilateral (all sides equal and all angles equal), isosceles (two angles equal and two sides the same) and scalene (all angles different and all sides different, although the children need not know the name until Year 5). The children may make a right-angled triangle, in which case discuss this too.

Ask each group to use the two hoops independently and sort the shapes into 'all sides equal' in one hoop and 'right angles' in the other. Ask: *Is there a shape that could go into both hoops?* (square) Show them how to place the hoops so that they overlap, and place the square in the intersection of the loops.

Now ask each group to sort the shapes. Explain that each hoop must have a label. Challenge the children to look at the other groups' hoops and make a guess at what the labels could be. Discuss and compare results.

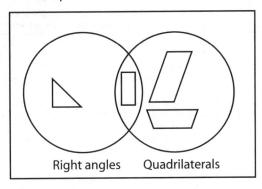

Right angles   Quadrilaterals

Now overlap the two hoops and place shapes in the hoops as shown in the diagram.

Repeat as before and ask: *What could the labels be?* Discuss and stress that the overlap must contain shapes that have right angles and are quadrilaterals. Then ask the children to pick a few shapes and use their hoops to sort them into a two-region Venn diagram. Challenge the other groups to guess the labels for the sets and discuss/compare.

Differentiation

Less able: Limit the range of shapes used by these children to triangles and simple quadrilaterals.
More able: Let these children work with a range of polygons including triangles, quadrilaterals, pentagons, hexagons and octagons. They could also use regular and irregular shapes. Discuss how they choose to label their Venn diagrams. As an extra challenge, you could ask this group to design their own Venn diagram with some questions about it.

Plenary & Assessment

Copy the 'Venn diagram' sheet onto an OHT and display it to the whole class. Ask: *How have I sorted these shapes? What are the names of the shapes? How many lines of symmetry does a rectangle have? How many right angles does a rectangle have? How many sides are the same in an isosceles triangle? How many sides are the same in a rectangle? What can you say about all the angles of an equilateral triangle and all the angles in a rectangle? What do the positions of the shapes in the Venn diagram tell us? How could I label this Venn diagram?* Establish that the children understand that Venn diagrams can be used to classify objects or statements with different criteria, as well as classify objects/statements that satisfy both criteria.

EVERY DAY: Practise and develop oral and mental skills (for example, counting, mental strategies, rapid recall of × and ÷ facts)

- Read and write whole numbers to at least 10 000 in figures and words, and know what each digit represents.
- Add/subtract 1, 10 or 100 to/from any integer.
- Count on or back in tens and hundreds or thousands, from any whole number up to 10 000.
- Consolidate knowing by heart addition and subtraction facts for all numbers to 20.
- Derive quickly doubles of all whole numbers to 50, and the corresponding halves.
- Add 3 or 4 small numbers, finding pairs totalling 10, or 9 or 11.
- **Use known number facts and place value to add or subtract mentally, including any pair of two-digit whole numbers, crossing the 10 (but not the 100) boundary.**
- **Know by heart multiplication facts for 2-, 3-, 4-, 5- and 10-times tables.**

- **Derive quickly division facts corresponding to 2-, 3-, 4-, 5- and 10-times tables.**
- Multiply any integer up to 1000 by 10 and understand the effect.
- **Round any positive integer less than 1000 to the nearest 10 or 100.**
- Choose and use appropriate number operations and appropriate ways of calculating (mental, mental with jottings, pencil and paper) to solve problems.
- Consolidate understanding of 1/2, 1/3, 1/4, and 3/4.
- Derive quickly doubles of multiples of 100 to 5000.
- Derive quickly all number pairs that total 100.
- Recall addition and subtraction facts for all numbers to 20.
- Add or subtract a pair of two-digit numbers (crossing the 10s but not the 100s boundary).

Unit	Days	Topics	Objectives
1	3	Place value	Order a set of whole numbers less than 10 000. **Use symbols correctly, including less than (<), greater than (>) and equals (=).** Read and write the vocabulary of comparing and ordering numbers. Partition numbers into thousands, hundreds, tens and units. Give one or more numbers lying between two given numbers. **Round any positive integer less than 1000 to the nearest 10 or 100.** Multiply and divide any integer up to 1000 by 10 (whole number answers), and understand the effect. Begin to multiply whole numbers by 100.
2	5	Understanding addition and subtraction Mental calculation strategies for addition and subtraction	Understand the principles (not the name) of the associative law as it applies to addition. Add or subtract the nearest multiple of 10, then adjust. Use known facts and place value to add or subtract mentally, including any pair of two-digit whole numbers. Develop written methods for column addition of two or more whole numbers less than 1000. Give a number lying between two given numbers and order a set of whole numbers less than 10 000.
3	5	Understanding addition and subtraction.	**Develop and refine written methods for column subtraction of two whole numbers less than 1000.** Money calculations (for example, £7.85 +/– £3.49). Use addition and subtraction to solve word problems involving numbers in real life and money using one or more steps, including converting from pounds to pence. Use all four operations to solve word problems involving numbers in real life, and money using one or more steps, including converting from pounds to pence. Use knowledge of sums or differences of odd and even numbers.
4	5	Capacity Problem-solving	**Suggest suitable units and measuring equipment to estimate or measure capacity.** Use, read and write standard metric units (l, ml) and imperial (pints). Begin to recognise the equivalent of one half, one quarter, three quarters and one tenth of of 1 litre in millilitres. Convert up to 1000ml to litres and vice versa. **Write the equivalent of one half, one quarter, three quarters and one tenth of 1 litre in millilitres.** **Record measures using decimal notation and mixed numbers.** **Know and use relationships between familiar units of capacity.** Record readings from scales. Use all four operations to solve measurement word problems.
5	5	Reasoning about shape	Identify lines of symmetry in 2-D shapes. Understand and use the associated vocabulary. **Classify polygons using criteria such as number of right angles, whether or not they are regular, symmetry properties.** Classify 2-D shapes according to lines of symmetry. Make shapes: for example, construct polygons by paper folding. Describe and visualise 3-D and 2-D shapes, including the tetrahedron and heptagon. Sketch the reflection of a simple shape or pattern where the sides of the image do not touch the mirror line (lines all parallel or perpendicular to the mirror line). Visualise 3-D shapes from 2-D drawings and identify simple nets of solid shapes. Make patterns by repeatedly translating or reflecting shapes. Know that rows on grids are described as horizontal, columns as vertical. Make and investigate a general statement about familiar shapes by finding examples that satisfy it. Use co-ordinates to describe position. Translate and reflect shapes.
6	3	Perimeter Shape and space	To measure/calculate the perimeters of rectangles. Sketch the reflection of a simple shape in a mirror line parallel to one side (all sides parallel or perpendicular to the mirror line).

EVERY DAY: Practise and develop oral and mental skills (eg counting, mental strategies, rapid recall of + and – facts)

- Read and write whole numbers up to at least 10 000 in figures and words, and know what each digit represents.
- Count on or back in tens, hundreds or thousands from any whole number up to **10 000.**
- **Round any positive integer less than 1000 to the nearest 10 or 100.**
- Consolidate knowing by heart addition and subtraction facts for all numbers to 20.
- **Use known number facts and place value to add or subtract mentally, including any pair of two-digit whole numbers, crossing the 10 (but not the 100) boundary.**
- Know by heart multiplication facts for 2-, 3-, 4-, 5- and 10-times tables.
- Derive quickly division facts corresponding to 2-, 3-, 4-, 5- and 10-times tables.
- Derive quickly doubles of all whole numbers to 50, and the corresponding halves.
- Use known number facts and place value to multiply integers by 10.

Units	Days	Topics	Objectives
8	5	Properties of numbers and number sequences Reasoning about numbers	Recognise and extend number sequences formed by counting from any number in steps of constant size, extending beyond zero when counting back. Recognise multiples of 2, 3, 4, 5, and 10, up to tenth multiple. Explain methods and reasoning about numbers orally and in writing. Make and investigate a general statement about familiar numbers by finding examples that satisfy it. Solve mathematical problems and puzzles, recognise and explain patterns and relationships, generalise and predict. Suggest extensions by asking 'What if…'.
9	4	Understanding multiplication and division Paper and pencil procedures	Using doubling and halving from known facts. Use closely-related facts (eg to multiply 9 or 11, multiply by 10 and adjust; develop the 6-times table from 4- and 2-times tables). Extending understanding of the operations of multiplication and its relationship to addition. Develop and refine written methods for TU × U. Use informal written ways to support and explain division. Round up or down after division, depending on the context. Extend understanding of the operations of division and its relationship to subtraction.
10	5	Money and real-life problems	Develop and refine written methods for TU ÷ U. **Choose and use appropriate number operations and appropriate ways of calculating (mental, mental with jottings, pencil and paper) to solve problems.** Finding factors (NNS p. 54). Use all four operations to solve word problems, involving numbers in 'real life', time and money, using one or more steps. Check with equivalent calculations. Estimate and check by rounding up or down to the nearest 10 or 100. Solve simple problems involving ratio and proportion.
11	5	Fractions and decimals	Use fraction notation. **Recognise simple fractions that are several parts of a whole**; such as 1/3 or 5/8 and mixed numbers such as 5 ¾ . Identify two simple fractions with totals of 1 whole. Solve simple problems involving ratio and proportion. **Recognise the equivalence of simple fractions.** Begin to relate fractions to division and find simple fractions such as ½, 1/3, ¼, 1/6, 1/10 of numbers or quantities. Find fractions of shapes. Order simple fractions: for example, decide whether fractions such as 3/8 or 7/10 are greater or less one half.
12	5	Time Problem-solving involving 'real life', money and measures (including time).	**Develop and refine written methods for column addition and subtraction of two whole numbers less than 1000, extending to decimals.** **Solve mathematical problems or puzzles, recognise and explain patterns and relationships, generalise and predict. Suggest extensions by asking 'What if...?'**
13	5	Handling data Angles and co-ordinates	Solve a problem by collecting, organising, representing, extracting and interpreting data in tables, charts, graphs and diagrams. Solve a problem by collecting quickly, organising, representing and interpreting data in tables, charts, graphs and diagrams. Use bar charts labelled in intervals of 2s, 5s, 10s or 20s. Use of computers. Sorting numbers using Venn diagrams and Carroll diagrams. Recognise positions and directions, and use co-ordinates. Make turns; estimate, draw and measure angles and recognise rotations.

Place value

Children continue to multiply any whole number by 10 and to develop the process of multiplying by 100. They practise using mathematical vocabulary to estimate, approximate, compare and order numbers and they use 'greater' than and 'less than' symbols. They learn to round positive numbers (less than one thousand) to the nearest 10 or 100.

LEARNING OBJECTIVES

	Topics	Starter	Main teaching activities
Lesson 1	Place value	● Multiply or divide any integer up to 1000 by 10 (whole numbers).	● Multiply and divide any integer up to 1000 by 10 (whole number answers), and understand the effect. ● Begin to multiply whole numbers by 100. ● **Use symbols correctly, including less than (<), greater than (>) and equals (=).** ● Read and write the vocabulary of comparing and ordering numbers.
Lesson 2	Place value	● Read and write whole numbers to at least 10 000.	● Give a number lying between two given numbers and order a set of whole numbers less than 10 000. ● **Round any positive integer less than 1000 to the nearest 10 or 100.**
Lesson 3	Place value	● Give one or more numbers lying between two given numbers.	● Estimate calculations by approximating

Lessons   overview

Preparation
Use general resource sheet 'Higher or lower card game' to cut out and make sets of cards.

Learning objectives
Starter
● Multiply or divide any integer up to 1000 by 10 (whole numbers).
● Read and write whole numbers to at least 10 000.
● Give one or more numbers lying between two given numbers.

Main teaching activities
● **Use symbols correctly, including less than (<), greater than (>) and equals (=).**
● Read and write the vocabulary of comparing and ordering numbers.
● **Round any positive integer less than 1000 to the nearest 10 or 100.**
● Multiply and divide any integer up to 1000 by 10 (whole number answers), and understand the effect.
● Begin to multiply whole numbers by 100.

Vocabulary
digits, place holder, place value, thousand, ten thousand, hundred thousand, million, hundred, unit, value, greater than (>), less than (<), equal to (=), half way between, order, before/after, round, approximate, estimate, calculate, four-digit number

You will need:
CD pages
'Moving digits' core, less able, more able and template versions; 'Higher or lower card game' (see General resources); 'It helps to round up' core version.

Equipment
Whiteboards, number fans.

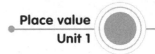
Lesson

Starter

Ask a child to use a number fan to show a two-digit number. Copy that number, for example, 23, onto the class demonstration number fan, then say aloud the result of multiplying that number by 10 (230) and alter your number fan to show it. Repeat with a couple of examples and ask: *What am I doing to the numbers? What am I doing to my number fan?* Swap roles by showing a two-digit number and asking the children to multiply it by 10. Extend to multiplying selected three-digit integers by 10 (eg 124, 210 etc.)

Main teaching activities

Whole class: Briefly remind the children about previous work on multiplication and division by 10. Revise division by 10, using the Starter activity but reversing the operation. Ask a child to show you a multiple of 10 on their number fan, then show them the result of dividing this number by 10. Repeat and ask: *What have I done to divide by 10?*

Continue giving examples until the whole class are confident.

Write '1' on the board and ask: *What is 1 multiplied by 10?* (10) Ask: *What is 10 multiplied by 10?* (100)

Introduce ten thousand, one hundred thousand and a million by continuing the pattern of shifting the digit one place to the left and putting a zero at the end. Discuss the name of each number as it arises.

Group work: Ideally, take the class outside for this activity. Alternatively, move the furniture back against the walls. Put the children into groups of four and give each child a whiteboard. Give each group a single-digit number and ask one child to write that number on her/his whiteboard. Ask all the other children to write 0 on their whiteboards. Explain to the class that you will call out a series of questions involving multiplying by 10 and dividing by 10 and that each group needs to work together as a team to display the answers by combining their whiteboards. Start with the example (left).

- Start with 5.
- Multiply by 10. *(50)*
- Multiply by 10. *(500)*
- Multiply by 10. *(5000)*
- Divide by 10. *(500)*
- Divide by 10. *(50)*
- Divide by 10. *(5)*

Now mix up the multiplication and division instructions, praising teams that work well to display the correct answers. You could introduce a competitive element by eliminating the slowest team each time. Next, include a 'multiply by 100' question and ask: *What is happening now? How many zeros are we putting at the end? How many digits are now involved?* Establish that the numbers move two places to the left and that the zeros (called place holders) fill the spaces.

Continue with mixed questions involving multiplication by 10 and 100 and division by 10.

Individual work: Back in the class, give each child a copy of 'Moving digits' to complete. Remind the children that no matter what the starting number, they must always follow the pattern, eg 110 ×100 = 11000; 12 × 100 = 1200.

Differentiation

Less able: Give each child the version of 'Moving digits' that focuses upon multiplying integers up to 1000 by 10. Work with individuals on the movement of the digits.

More able: Give each child the version of the 'Moving digits' sheet that includes examples above 1000.

Plenary & assessment

Discuss the answers to the problems and the strategies to solve them. Write on the board 234 × 11 = ☐ and ask: *How could you find an approximate answer to this question?* (234 × 10 = 2340) *Will the answer be a four-digit number?* (Yes). *What did you do to multiply by 10? How could you find the exact answer?* (Add on 234, 234 × 11 = 2574). Repeat with approximations for 348 × 12 (approximate by working out 348 × 10, exact answer 4176) and 56 × 111 (approximate by working out 56 × 100, exact answer 6216).

Lesson ②

Starter

Explain to the children how to play the 'Higher and lower' card game. Give each child a card (prepared from General resource sheet 'Higher or lower card game'). Each of these cards has a different number on it, in the range 6000 to 8000. With the whole class, read a couple of the numbers aloud, for example, 6234 (six thousand, two hundred and thirty-four). Ask: *What is the value of the 6? the 2? the 3? the 4?* Now write a four-digit number on the board. Ask the children to compare their own numbers with the number on the board and decide if their number is higher or lower. If their number is lower than that on the board, they touch the floor, if their number is equal to that on the board they remain seated and if their number is higher than that on the board they stand up. Start with 7000, then repeat with several examples, each time asking: *What is your number? Explain why you have stood up/sat down/touched the floor.*

Main teaching activities

The children will need their cards from the Starter, and whiteboards with 'greater than' (>) and 'less than' (<) symbols on them. Write 'greater than', 'less than' and 'equal to' on the board.

Whole class: Ask the children to sit in pairs. Call one pair to the front of the class and ask: *What are your numbers?* Encourage each child to read out their own number. Show the children a whiteboard with a 'less than' (<) symbol on. Ask: *What does this symbol mean? Can you make a mathematical sentence using this symbol and your two numbers?* If it helps, remind the children that the 'crocodile eats the larger number'. Now call another pair to the front and ask the pairs, together, to use the 'less than' or 'greater than' sign and a whiteboard to create a mathematical sentence.

Paired work: Ask the children, in their pairs, to make up mathematical sentences with their numbers and the 'greater than' and 'less than' symbols. Go around the class, encouraging the use of the correct mathematical language. Highlight the fact that two mathematical sentences can be made for each pair of numbers. Move on to challenge the pairs to select three numbers in the format:

❏ > ❏ > ❏ **or** ❏ < ❏ < ❏

Differentiation

Less able: Pair the children according to ability and allow these children to keep their own number cards for longer, swapping partners, so that there is more repetition.

More able: Pair the children according to ability and ask these children to swap their number cards more frequently.

Plenary & assessment

Pick out three number cards, for example 6999, 7008 and 7080. Ask: *Which is the largest/smallest number? What is the difference between 6999 and 7000? 6999 and 7008? 7008 and 7080? 7999 and 7080?* Ask: *Could you make a number sentence using all three numbers?* (6999 < 7008 < 7080, 7080 > 7008 > 6999). Write on the board: ❏ < 2769, ❏ > 2769, ❏ = 2769. Ask each child for numbers that could be placed in these boxes. Ask the children to explain their answers and establish why only one number can be put alongside the equals sign.

Lesson ③

Starter

Give the children the same number cards as in the previous lesson, to play a slightly different game. Ask two children to come to the front with their cards (start with 6001 and 7999). Now say: *If your number is between these two numbers then hold your card above your head.* All children should hold up their cards. Now use 7080 and 7800; only 7234, 7685, 7208, 7324, 7670, 7760, 7067, 7076, 7776, 7767 and 7677 should be held up. Repeat, using different pairs of starting numbers and each time encourage the children to read out their numbers in full.

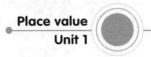

Main teaching activities

Whole class: On the board, write a selection of three-digit numbers eg 243, 231, 235 and a number line (see margin).

Now remind the children about the game they played in the Spring term, where they stand up if a number is rounded up to the nearest ten (240) and touch the floor if a number is rounded down to the nearest ten (230). Try a few examples such as 234 (down), 235 (up). Make sure they remember the convention of rounding up numbers ending in 5. Now change the numbers on the number line to 500 and 490 and repeat with 499 (up), 493 (down). Repeat until the whole class can respond instantly. For variation, ask children to pick numbers between the two starting numbers.

Write '234' on the board and ask: *What would this number be, rounded to the nearest 100? Is it closer to 200 or 300? How about 263?* How about 250? Emphasise that 250 would round up but that 249 would round down.

Repeat the game with starting numbers 400 and 500, asking the children to round 449 (down), 451 (up) and 450 (up). Repeat with numbers between the starting numbers of 900 and 1000 rounding to the nearest 10 and the nearest 100.

Group work: Ask the children, in groups of three or four, to refer to the first four questions on activity sheet 'It helps to round up' and to discuss: *Why do you think that it is important to round up or down?*

Q1. Jenna is organising a party for 29 people. She estimates that each person will eat two sandwiches and she would like a couple extra so that she does not run out. How many sandwiches should she make?

Highlight that estimation is useful to get an approximate amount.

Q2. This week Tim drove to Chester (96 miles), Coventry (82 miles) and Bath (45 miles). He wants to work out approximately how far he had travelled.

Ask: *Should you round to the nearest 10? to the nearest 100?* Explain that distances are often rounded up or down, especially long distances such as aeroplane journeys. Ask: *Why?*

Q3. In a recipe for chocolate brownies, Jamie needs 350 grams of chocolate. Should he buy a 400-gram bar or a 300-gram bar?

Highlight the need always to round up for a recipe.

Q4. Fashion Fabrics often mark the length of pieces of fabric, rounded to the nearest 10cm. Mia bought a piece of fabric that was marked 310cm long. What length could the fabric be?

It could be 305, 306, 307, 308, 309, 310, 311, 312, 313, 314cm long. Repeat this with another example, such as 560cm.

Individual work: Ask children to complete the remaining questions (5–8) on the activity sheet.

Differentiation

Less able: Group these children according to ability and give them extra support. Suggest strategies for completing the approximations involved in Questions 5–8.

More able: Group these children according to ability and challenge them to work out the exact answers for Questions 5–8.

Plenary & assessment

Write on the board '120 + 230 = ☐' and ask: *What numbers could be rounded to give the same answer?* Compile a list of possibilities as logically as possible (115/116/117/118/119/120/121/122/123/124 + 225/226/227/228/229/230/231/232/233/234). Now discuss the answers to Question 8 (19 × 10 or 20 × 11) *Which is the easier to work out? How did you work these out?*

240

230

Understanding addition and subtraction (1)

Children review a range of mental strategies and informal written methods of addition and subtraction. In Lessons 3-5, they move on to develop a written column method of addition of two whole numbers less than 1000.

LEARNING OBJECTIVES

	Topics	Starter	Main teaching activities
Lesson 1	Understanding addition and subtraction	Recall addition and subtraction facts for all numbers to 20.	Add or subtract the nearest multiple of 10, then adjust.
Lesson 2	Understanding addition and subtraction	Add or subtract a pair of two-digit numbers (crossing the 10s but not the 100s boundary).	Use known facts and place value to add or subtract mentally any pair of two-digit numbers.
Lesson 3	Understanding addition and subtraction	Add or subtract 10, 100 or 1000 from any two- or three-digit number up to 10 000.	Develop and refine written methods for column addition of whole numbers less than 1000.
Lesson 4	Understanding addition and subtraction	Identify near doubles, using known doubles.	As Lesson 3.
Lesson 5	Understanding addition and subtraction	Count on or back in 10s **Use known number facts and place value to add or subtract mentally**.	As Lesson 3.

Lessons   overview

Preparation
Use activity sheet 'Adjusting card games' to cut out and make sets of cards.

Learning objectives
Starter
- Recall addition and subtraction facts for all numbers to 20.
- Add or subtract a pair of two-digit numbers (crossing the 10s but not the 100s boundary).

Main teaching activities
- Add or subtract the nearest multiple of 10, then adjust.
- Use known facts and place value to add or subtract mentally any pair of two-digit numbers.

Vocabulary
near multiple, adjusting, partitioning, digit, align, column, carrying, thousands, hundreds, tens, written methods

You will need:

CD pages
'Adjusting card games' core, less able, more able and template versions; 'Different methods', core version.

Equipment
Squared paper, whiteboards, number fans.

Lesson

Starter

Ask quick-fire addition and subtraction questions to 20 for the children to answer orally. Use a range of addition and subtraction vocabulary. Develop a routine, for example say the name of a child, ask the question and give five seconds for the child to answer, 'Paula… What is the sum of 9 + 7?' 'Jed… What is the difference between 18 and 3?' and so on. Develop the activity to include addition facts in larger numbers, such as 29 + 7, 49 + 7… Remind the children about the use of strategies if needed.

Main teaching activities

Whole class: Remind the class that an easy way to add or subtract 9 is to add or subtract 10, then adjust the answer by 1. Use an empty number line to demonstrate the answer to the following question: 'There are 43 children in a room and then 19 more arrive. How many are there in total?'.

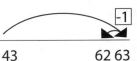

Discuss this with the children and remind them that the easiest way to add 19 to a number is to add 20 and then subtract 1 (because you have added one too many). Set another example for subtracting 19 (subtracting 20 then adding 1).

Paired work: Give each pair a stack of 'Stage 1' cards cut from activity sheet 'Adjusting card games'. The calculations on all the cards in this stage involve addition and subtraction of 9, 19, 29 or 39. Encourage the pairs to play a game: one child turns over a card and the first person to say the correct answer wins that card and explains how to work out the answer. Then the other child turns over a card and play continues. Agree that it is easier to add or subtract 10, 20, 30 or 40 then adjust by 1.

Provide similar questions involving adding or subtracting 19, 29 and 39 including crossing the 100s boundary, eg '126 peaches were delivered to the shop. 29 were rotten. How many were not rotten?' 'Paul had 57 stickers. Jamie gave him 39 more. How many stickers does he now have?'

Repeat with adding or subtracting numbers from the 'Stage 2' and 'Stage 3' cards, such as 11, 21 and 31 for example 'Super Shopper had 126 tins of peaches. They sold 31 tins on Monday. How many did they have left?'

Ask: *What is an easy way to add or subtract 18, 28 or 38?* Establish using the nearest multiple of 10, then adjusting by 2. Again provide some whole class examples as above. Repeat for 17, 27 and 37.

Differentiation

Less able: Introduce the different stage cards at the appropriate times when each child can demonstrate understanding of the 'add/subtract 10 and then adjust' method. Extra adult support may be needed to allow the children to discuss their methods.

More able: These children can be introduced to Stages 2 and 3 more quickly.

Column 1	Column 2
17 + 8 = ☐	17 + 7 = ☐
17 + 18 = ☐	17 + 17 = ☐
17 + 28 = ☐	17 + 27 = ☐
17 + 38 = ☐	17 + 37 = ☐
17 + 48 = ☐	17 + 47 = ☐

Plenary & assessment

Ask the children to explain any errors from the paired activity that they had discussed. Write two columns of additions on the board (see left). Discuss various approaches to working out the answers and stress that the answers increase by ten in each row. Compare the answers in the second column with the answers from the first column.

Finally set one or two problems involving money or measures, 'Maria has £1.35. She owes Pandit 48p. How much will she have left when she has paid her debt?' 'I bought a magazine for 79p and a bar of chocolate for 45p. How much did I spend altogether?' Collect answers and discuss strategies for solving them.

Lesson ②

Starter

Use cards cut from activity sheet 'Adjusting card games'. Ask mixed questions and let the children show their answers on number fans or whiteboards. Revise the work from the previous lesson by discussing methods for finding each answer. Write on the board '36 – 7 = ☐' and ask: *How could you use a similar method to work this out?* Discuss and highlight the fact that you could subtract 10 and then add 3. Repeat with 36 + 7 = ☐ (add ten and then subtract 3), then 36 – 17 = ☐ and 36 + 17 = ☐.

Main teaching activities

Whole class: Explain that in this lesson the children will continue adding and subtracting two numbers. Distribute activity sheet 'Different methods', which shows a series of addition and subtraction questions. Allow some time for the children to answer the questions mentally and to write down the answers. Ask them to try to explain the method that they used to work out each answer and to write it in the box provided. Stress that children may use different methods to work out the same answer.

At appropriate stages discuss the different methods as a class and decide collectively on the 'best' method and why it is 'best'. There may be more than one 'best' method.

---

1. 38 + 38 = 76 (Double 38 or (40 + 40) – 4.)

2. 50 + 70 = 120 (Use the fact that 5 + 7 = 12 and then multiply by 10, or 50 + 50 + 20 = 100 + 20.)

3. 78 – 69 = 9 (Mentally count up from the smaller number, or work out 78 – 68 = 10 and then subtract another 1.)

4. 240 + 240 = 480 (Use the fact that double 24 is 48 and then multiply by 10, or double 250 to get 500 then take away 20, or 200 + 200 + 40 + 40 = 400 + 80.)

5. 467 – 30 = 437 (Count back in tens from 467.)

6. 39 + 37 = 76 (Double 38, or double 40 then take away (1 + 3).)

7. 13 + 47 = 60 (10 + 40 = 50 and 3 + 7 = 10 so 50 + 10 = 60.)

8. 63 + 9 = 72 ((63 + 10) – 1)

9. 123 + 500 = 623 (Count on in hundreds from 123, or 500 + 100 + 23.)

10. 45 – 11 = 34 ((45 – 10) – 1)

11. 65 – 27 = 38 ((65 – 30) + 3)

12. 57 – 31 = 26 ((57 – 30) – 1)

Differentiation

Less able: Give these children extra support, especially with the explanations of their methods. Encourage them to work at their own pace and, if appropriate, set a target to complete, say, half of the questions.

More able: Challenge these children to devise more than one method of working out the answers to the questions and encourage good use of mathematical language to explain methods. Set an additional challenge to use the digits 4, 5, 6, 7, 8 and 9 to construct as many two-digit addition and subtraction questions within a time limit of 10 minutes.

Plenary & assessment

Go through the answers and ask the children to explain their methods. Prompt for alternative methods of answering each question. Write some addition and subtraction questions on the board such as 34 + 49 = ☐' and ask: *How could you work this out mentally?* ((34 + 50) – 1)
Given that 34 + 49 = 83, ask: *How would you work out 49 + 34? 83 – 49? 83 – 34?*
Repeat with 170 + 190 (Double 18 × 10 or 17 + 19 then multiply by 10, or ((17 + 20) – 1) × 10 or 200 + 170 – 10). Given that 170 + 190 = 360, ask: *How would you work out 190 + 170? 360 – 170? 360 – 190?*

Lessons   overview

Preparation
Make cards enlarged from General resources sheet 'Near doubles'.

Learning objectives
Starter
● Add or subtract 10, 100 or 1000 from any two- or three-digit number up to 10 000
● Identify near doubles, using known doubles
● Count on or back in 10s
Use known number facts and place value to add or subtract mentally

Main teaching activities
● Develop and refine written methods for column addition of two or more whole numbers less than 1000.

Vocabulary
align, digit, thousands, hundreds, tens, units, boundary, calculate, calculation, method, jotting, answer, operation

You will need:
Photocopiable pages
'Practice additions' (see page 160) for each child.

CD pages
'Near doubles', (see General resources) 'Addition over addition grid sheet', 'Addition over addition questions', 'Practice additions' and 'The Grid game', core, less able, more able and template versions (where available).

Equipment
Whiteboards, squared paper, calculator.

Lesson

Starter

Challenge the children to respond to questions involving the addition and subtraction of 10, 100 and 1000 to/from whole numbers up to 10 000, using whiteboards to record their responses. Put some questions in context. For example:

What is 10, 100, 1000 more than 258?…1234?…2756?

What is 10m, 100m, 1000m less than 3500m?

What is 10ml, 100ml, 1000ml more than 1788ml?

Main teaching activities

Whole class: Write on the board '57 + 79 = ⬚' and ask: *How would you work this out?* ((57 + 80) – 1 or 50 + 70 = 120 and 7 + 9 = 16 so 120 + 16 = 136) Now write '657 + 179 = ⬚' and ask the children to work it out in any way they can, writing their answers on their whiteboards. Discuss various methods and compare solutions. Agree that for this type of calculation it is easier to write the steps down rather than do the calculation mentally. Look at the different methods and jottings on the whiteboards.

Show one method of recording that could help.

```
   657
 + 179   (Stress that the units must align in a column and the tens must align in a column, and so on.)
   700   (600 +100 – looking at the hundreds column)
   120   (50 +70 – looking at the tens column)
    16   (7 + 9 – looking at the units column)
   836
```

Repeat with 325 + 288, again asking the children to compare the methods recorded on their whiteboard and then using the column addition method, this time adding the units column first and stressing that the order of the addition is unimportant. Agree that the column method can be helpful because it can be used for any additions.

Individual work: Give each child a copy of 'Practice additions' that includes a range of two-digit and three-digit calculations. Ask the children to decide whether they do them mentally, using jottings or as column additions.

Differentiation

Less able: Give each child the version of 'Practice additions' that includes simpler two-digit by two-digit and three-digit by two-digit additions. Give these children extra support in modelling column addition if required.

More able: Give each child the version of 'Practice additions' that includes some three-digit calculations with answers over 1000.

Plenary & assessment

```
   678
  + 76
    14   (8 + 6)
   140   (70 + 70)
   600
   754
```

Go through the practice additions and ask *Which did you do mentally?* Establish with which questions they used a mental method and which required jottings (egnumber lines) or the written column addition method. Go through alternative methods for each question. Write on the board '567 + 99 = ⬚' and ask: *Do you need to write anything down to help you answer this?* (No, as (567 + 100) – 1 = 666.) Stress that the children must look carefully at the numbers before they decide to use a written column method. Repeat with 678 + 76 and agree that this time the column method may be helpful. Be careful to emphasis the need to write the units, tens and hundreds aligned in the appropriate columns.

Ask: *How can you check, or get an approximate answer?* Explain that they will continue with this column method in the next lesson.

Lesson

Starter

Say a number and ask the children to double it. Get into a rhythm. 23, (46), 54, (108), 36, (72), 35, (70), ...
Explain that you will hold up some cards with sentences on them and you would like the children to write
the answers on their whiteboards. Hold up cards, enlarged from general resource sheet 'Near doubles', which
show calculations involving near doubles. Discuss approaches. For example: 45 + 47 = ❑ (double 46).

```
   266
 + 312
 ─────
     8   (6 + 2)
    70   (60 + 10)
   500   (200 + 300)
 ─────
   578
```

Column addition	Carrying
Stage 1	
157	157
+ 328	+ 328
───	───
15 (7 + 8)	5
	₁
Stage 2	
157	157
+ 328	+ 328
───	───
15 (7 + 8)	85
70 (50 + 20)	₁
Stage 3	
157	157
+ 328	+ 328
───	───
15 (7 + 8)	485
70 (50 + 20)	₁
400 (100 + 300)	
───	
485	

Main teaching activities

Remind the children of the method of column addition used in the previous lesson.
Write on the board '266 + 312 = ❑' and look at the place value of each of the digits in the
numbers: '266 is 2 hundreds, 6 tens and 6 units. 312 is 3 hundreds, 1 ten and 2 units.' Write
the sum vertically, reminding the children to line up the units under each other in the
units column and so on (see left). Work through one or two other examples if necessary,
but then tell the children that there is another method that will reduce the number of
lines of writing – the 'carrying' method. Talk through this process starting with the least
significant digits (the units). Then give an example that includes carrying, say 157 +
328 and compare this method with the column addition method (see left). Complete
another two examples with the children coming to the board to work through both
methods.

Paired work: Give each pair two copies of the 'Addition over addition grid sheet' and one
copy of 'Addition over addition questions'. Ask the children to work together to look at the
questions, decide on the method to use and answer each one using the grid sheet to help
them to keep the digits in the correct columns. Suggest that they might take it in turns to
complete each question and then check each answer. You might also suggest that they
use different colours on the grid sheet to explain the 'carrying' where appropriate.

Differentiation

Less able: You might prefer the children to work in mixed ability pairs for this activity.
If not, then a simplified question sheet has been supplied. A less able version of the
'grid' sheet has also been supplied on which an example of the 'column' method and
the 'carrying' method has been given. Use the core version for the children to write their
answers.

More able: Give each pair a copy of 'Addition over addition questions' that includes some questions
with four-digit answers. A more able version of the grid sheet with modified instructions has also
been supplied. You might also suggest that these pairs use both the 'carrying' and 'column addition'
methods to answer each question.

```
   234
 +  99
 ─────
   223
     ₁
```

```
   234
 +  99
 ─────
   333
    ₁₁
```

Plenary & assessment

Ask the children to explain how they added each pair of numbers and work through each
example on the sheet with them. Write on the board (see left) and ask: *What is the problem with this
calculation? What have I done wrong? How can you tell that the answer is wrong?* Establish that the
answer in the units column is correct but the 'carried' 1 in the tens column has not been added and
there should be a 1 to carry over to the hundreds column.

Lesson ⑤

Starter

Start at 234 and ask the children to count back in tens to, for example, 104, and then forward in tens up to 234. Get into a rhythm. Then ask the children to count back in nines from 234, using their whiteboards to write down the steps and show the answers. Again, try to get into a rhythm, this time allowing a little extra time, and then count forward again, up to 234. Choose a different starting number and repeat, counting up and down in steps of 9, then in steps of 19 if appropriate.

Main teaching activities

Whole class: Write on the board: '437 + 189'. Ask: *How could we add these two numbers together?* Prompt for all possible strategies – mental, mental with jottings and written methods. Review the previous lesson's work inviting children to the board to complete the example using the carrying and column methods.

Paired work: Give each pair activity sheet 'The Grid game' and a piece of squared paper for their working out. Tell them that they are going to play a game, using the addition methods that they learned in the last lesson.

In their pairs, they take turns to pick two numbers that they think that they can add together. They must pick at least one three-digit number. They can use squared paper to set out the additions and work out the answers. The other player uses a calculator to check the answer. If it is correct the first player scores a point and crosses the two numbers off the number grid. If the answer is incorrect, they do not score a point and play passes to the other player. The winner is the person with most points when all the numbers are crossed off the grid. Remind the children to use the methods that they have been practising, and stress that it will get more difficult as the game progresses as they will not have as many numbers to choose from. Encourage them to use their mental skills to approximate each answer before using a written method.

Differentiation

Less able: Give children the version of the sheet with a greater number of two-digit numbers and multiples of ten.

More able: Give children the version of the sheet with three-digit numbers only.

Plenary & assessment

Ask: *Who won your game? Were some number pairs more difficult than others?* Look carefully at the grid. Ask: *Which calculations did you do using the carrying method? Which calculations could you work out in your head? How? Which have the greatest total, which have the smallest totals? How would you work out … ?* Review this week's work and go over any difficulties that the children have experienced.

Name	Date

Practice additions

Answer the questions below.

Decide whether to work out the answer mentally, to use jottings or use the column addition method. Show how you worked out each answer.

1. What is the sum of 147 and 68?

2. How many altogether are 285 and 134?

3. Add 121 to 166.

4. 236 + 258 =

5. What is 354 add 49?

Written addition and subtraction

Children start to develop and refine written methods for column subtraction involving two numbers less than 1000. They practise number calculations in activities involving money and shopping. They investigate general statements about odd and even numbers.

LEARNING OBJECTIVES

	Topics	Starter	Main teaching activities
Lesson 1	Understanding addition and subtraction	● Count on or back in tens, hundreds or thousands from any whole number up to 10 000.	● **Develop and refine written methods for column subtraction of two whole numbers less than 1000.**
Lesson 2	Understanding addition and subtraction	● Derive quickly doubles of all whole numbers to 50 (eg 38 + 38, 38 × 2), and the corresponding halves.	As Lesson 1.
Lesson 3	Understanding addition and subtraction	● **Know by heart multiplication facts for 2-, 3-, 4-, 5- and 10-times tables.**	● Develop and refine written methods for column subtraction of two whole numbers less than 1000. ● Use knowledge of sums or differences of odd and even numbers.
Lesson 4	Understanding addition and subtraction	● **Derive quickly division facts corresponding to 2-, 3-, 4-, 5- and 10-times tables.**	● Use all four operations to solve word problems involving numbers in real life and money using one or more steps, including converting from pounds to pence.
Lesson 5	Understanding addition and subtraction	● Choose and use appropriate number operations and appropriate ways of calculating (mental, mental with jottings, pencil and paper) to solve problems.	● Money calculations (for example, £7.85 +/– £3.49). As Lesson 4.

Lesson overview

Learning objectives
Starter
● Count on or back in tens, hundreds or thousands from any whole number up to 10 000.
● Derive quickly doubles of all whole numbers to 50 (eg 38 + 38, 38 × 2), and the corresponding halves.
● **Know by heart multiplication facts for 2-, 3-, 4-, 5- and 10-times tables.**
Main teaching activities
● **Develop and refine written methods for column subtraction of two whole numbers less than 1000**
● Money calculations (for example, £7.85 +/– £3.49).
● Use addition and subtraction to solve word problems involving numbers in real life and money using one or more steps, including converting from pounds to pence.

Vocabulary
subtract, difference, counting up, column method, difference, sum, decrease, less than, odd, even

You will need:

Photocopiable pages
Subtraction pairs' (see page 167) for each child.

CD pages
'Subtraction pairs', core, less able, more able and template versions; 'Number differences questions', core, less able, more able and template versions; 'Odd or even?' cards (see General resources).

Equipment
Squared paper; whiteboards; calculators (one per pair); number fans; plastic coins; dice.

Lesson ①

Starter

Ask the children to count back in tens, starting from 4456, to 4376, then forward in tens from 4376 up to 4456. Get into a rhythm. Repeat, counting on and back in hundreds and thousands, choosing various appropriate starting numbers.

Main teaching activities

Whole class: Write on the board '79 – 57 = ☐' and ask: *How would you work this out? What is the answer?* ((79 – 60) + 3 or 70 – 50 = 20 and 9 – 7 = 2 so 20 + 2 = 22). Now write on the board '679 – 57 = ☐' and ask the children to work out the answer in any way that they choose, recording their methods on their whiteboards. Discuss various methods and compare solutions. Look at the different methods and jottings on the whiteboards.

Use the board to demonstrate methods of recording that could help. For example:

Answer: 679 – 57 = 622 (43 + 500 + 79 = 622)

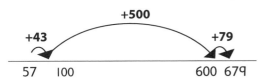

Remind the children of this strategy learned previously of counting up from the lower number to the higher number. Invite children to the board to model similar examples, such as 688 – 246, 725 – 153 and so on. Ask the children if they have any difficulties with this method (for example difficulty in adding the numbers together).

Remind children of the written calculations in columns they have used in the previous term ('counting up', which involves the same process as the number line method and 'compensation' subtracting too much and then adding back). Demonstrate the two methods using the same subtraction, for example 627 – 159. Stress the need to align numbers in columns.

Compensation	
627	
– 159	
427	(627 – 200)
+ 41	(since 100 – 59 = 41)
468	

Counting on	
627	
– 159	
1	(Counting on to make 160)
40	(Counting on from 160 to make 200)
400	(Counting on from 200 to make 600)
20	(Counting on from 600 to make 620)
7	(Counting on from 620 to make 627)
468	

Individual work: Give each child a copy of the 'Subtraction pairs' sheet in which they are given two sets of numbers – one between 500 and 1000 and the other between 100 and 250. Ask the children to select one number from each set, and then use them for a subtraction. Ask them to practise one of the written methods shown above. Allow enough time for the children to complete three examples. If necessary give the children squared paper to help them line up the numbers in columns.

Differentiation

Less able: Work with these children and help them with explanations of the two methods. If necessary, give the children a copy of 'Subtraction pairs' that includes three-digit numbers in one set and two-digit numbers in the other.

More able: Challenge these children to complete the sheet in the time allowed and to provide alternative methods where possible. If necessary, give them the copy of the 'Subtraction pairs' sheet that includes higher numbers including some four-digit numbers.

Plenary & assessment

Write on the board '567 – 99 = ☐' and ask: *Do you need to write anything down to help you answer this?* Help the children to decide that they do not, as ((567 – 100) + 1 = 468). Stress that they need to look carefully at the numbers in a question before they decide to use a column method. Repeat with 567 – 186, 567 – 239, 567 – 312 and 567 – 448. Agree that you might need to use a written column method to help you answer some of these questions. Go through the questions on the

'Subtraction pairs' sheet and one or two of the examples above, as time allows. Emphasise the need to write the units, tens and hundreds aligned in the appropriate columns.

Ask: *How can you check? Can you find an approximate answer?* Say that there will be more about this column (decomposition) method in the next lesson.

Lesson ②

Starter

Tell the children that you will say a number and you want them to show and hold up the number that is half of it on their number fans. Give several examples, such as 36 (18), 56 (28). Say: *I have 44 pencils. If I gave you half, how many would I have left?*

Main teaching activities

Explain that in this lesson you will be looking again at a written subtraction method that is even easier than the ones in the previous lesson as it will cut down the amount of working out required. Write on the board: 376 – 187. Demonstrate using decomposition.

376	=	300	+	70	+	6
– 187	=	– 100	+	80	+	7

We can exchange one ten from the 70, leaving 60 and add it to the six to make it 16:

	=	300	+	60	+	16
	=	– 100	+	80	+	7

Next, we can exchange one hundred from the 300 leaving 200 and add it to the sixty to make 160.

	=	200	+	160	+	16
	=	– 100	+	80	+	7

When we subtract each column the answer is 189.

This can also be written as the following:

Give another example, eg 543 – 256 and ask one child to write it vertically and another child to work through it on the board with help from the rest of the class. Remind them about putting the digits in the correct place and that we start from the right and work to the left.

Paired work: After completing this task, give each pair at least one copy of the 'Number differences questions'. Go through one example if necessary. The children should work together to discuss the method, lay out each question on the grid and answer it. The pairs could take it in turns to check each answer using a calculator.

Differentiation

Less able: Give the less able version of the questions sheet on which multiples of ten are subtracted from the larger number in the first few examples. A written example is included to support the children.

More able: Give the version of the questions sheet with additional questions including a four-digit by three-digit example.

Plenary & assessment

Review the subtraction vocabulary used in each question, the children's answers and the methods used. Review the decomposition method and discuss children's other ideas for answering the questions. Write the subtraction (see left) on the board. Ask: *What is the problem with this subtraction? What have I done wrong? How can you tell that the answer is wrong?* The answer in the units column is correct but in the tens column the '1' has not been taken from the 3 (it should be 12 not 13) and the same with the hundreds column (should be 100 not 200).

Stress that the subtraction could be checked, as (234 – 100) + 31 or (234 – 70) + 1.

```
 2 ¹3¹4
–   6 9
 2 7 5
```

Lesson ③

Starter

Ask quickfire questions to test the children on multiplication facts for the 2-, 3-, 4-, 5- and 10-times tables, letting them write their responses on their whiteboards. Remind the children that 3 × 5 is the same as 5 × 3 and then run through multiplications: 3 × 5, 3 × 10, 3 × 2, 3 × 4, 6 × 5, 6 × 10, 6 × 2, 6 × 4, 7 × 5, 7 × 10, 7 × 2, 7 × 4. Link the idea with money and show that three 5 pence coins are worth 15 pence, three 10 pence coins are worth 30 pence. Ask some quickfire questions involving money calculations. Each time hold up a coin and say, for example: *I have 5 of these 10 pence coins, how much do I have altogether?*

Main teaching activities

Start by revising odd and even numbers. Ask the children what they remember from the previous term. Call out some three-digit odd and even numbers and ask individuals to identify which is which. Draw two boxes on the board. After each number is correctly identified, write it in one of the boxes and label them 'odd' and 'even'.

Discuss the properties of odd and even numbers and ask the children to identify as many as they can. Write them on the board as they are identified. The list should include the following:

The sum of two even numbers is even, or even + even = even;

The sum of two odd numbers is even, or odd + odd = even;

The sum of one odd and one even number is odd, or odd + even = odd.

Display the full list of properties for adding and subtracting odd and even numbers on cards around the class (see General resources).

Tell the children that they can use their knowledge of these rules when checking answers to addition and subtraction questions. Give the children an incorrect sum such as 367 + 125 = 491. Task a class vote as to whether this calculation is correct. Agree that knowledge of the sum of odd and even numbers helps when checking whether an answer is correct or incorrect.

Paired work: Give each pair some squared paper and two dice. Ask the pairs to take it in turns to roll two three-digit numbers, which they must add together. After a period of time (eg 15 minutes), ask them to generate subtractions (reordering the two numbers as required). Ask the children to predict whether an answer will be odd or even before completing each calculation.

Differentiation

Less able: Restrict these pairs to working with three-digit by two-digit calculations. You might also supply them with a set of 'Odd or even?' cards.

More able: Extend the task to include the addition of three numbers. See if they can work out the rules for these (eg odd + odd + odd = odd).

Plenary & assessment

Ask the children to highlight some of their questions and the odd and even rules that went with them. Try to have at least one example to match each rule on the cards.

Write some calculations on the board, some of which can be seen to be incorrect by using knowledge of the properties of odd and even numbers, for example:

270 + 351 = 621; 255 + 428 = 682 (incorrect) and so on

Ask the children to explain their reasoning for each correct or incorrect answer.

Lessons   overview

Learning objectives

Starter

● **Derive quickly division facts corresponding to 2-, 3-, 4-, 5- and 10-times tables.**

● **Choose and use appropriate number operations and appropriate ways of calculating (mental, mental with jottings, pencil and paper) to solve problems.**

● Use all four operations to solve word problems involving numbers in real life and money, using one or more steps, including converting from pounds to pence.

● Use knowledge of sums or differences of odd and even numbers.

Vocabulary

add, subtract, divide, multiply, price, range, value, odd, even

You will need:

Photocopiable pages

'Totally different shopping' (see page 168) for each child; 'Party planning' (see page 169) for each child

CD pages

'Totally different shopping', core, less able, more able and template versions; 'Party planning' core, less able and more able versions.

Equipment

Whiteboards, number fans, squared paper, plastic coins, interlocking cubes, a net of four to five lemons or limes and the same number of lemons or limes bought loose, with the purchase receipt.

Lesson

Starter

Ask quick-fire questions on division facts for the 2-, 3-, 4-, 5- and 10-times tables, letting the children write their responses on their whiteboards. Remind them that $3 \times 5 = 15$ corresponds to the divisions $15 \div 5 = 3$ and $15 \div 3 = 5$. Then run through divisions: $30 \div 5$, $30 \div 10$, $30 \div 2$, $20 \div 4$, $20 \div 5$, $60 \div 10$, $60 \div 2$, $60 \div 4$.

Main teaching activities

Whole class: Discuss the column addition and subtraction methods you have been working on recently. Explain that the same methods could be applied to working out answers to money problems. Model the use of the decomposition method for money problems, eg 'Mr Shah wants to buy a plant costing £4.85. He takes £7.27 to the shop. How much would he have left if he buys the plant?'

Discuss other methods you might use to solve this, such as the compensation method – adjusting from the pence to the pounds. Explain that you will be giving them some shopping problems to solve. Discuss vocabulary such as 'more/less expensive' and finding the difference in costs.

Individual work: Distribute the 'Totally different shopping' sheet which shows objects for sale in a shop and sets some addition and subtraction questions about them. Talk about the items on the sheet and work through the first two questions as a class, reminding the children to align the decimal points, as well as the numbers, in columns. Give the children a supply of squared paper to support them with this task.

Differentiation

Less able: Give the version of the sheet that has slightly lower prices.

More able: Give the extended version of the sheet, which includes a challenge for these children to spend £12.00, deciding what to buy and how much change they would receive.

Plenary & assessment

Discuss the answers from the activity sheet, each time asking how the child worked out the answer and which method was used. Ask: *Which two objects from the shop would cost the most to buy? How much would they cost? Which two objects could you buy if you only had £5? £6? £7? Which two items have the greatest difference in price? What is the difference between the prices?*

Lesson ⑤

Starter

Explain to the children that you will write a number sentence on the board and you would like them to write down, on their whiteboards, the sign that would make the sentence correct. Start with '23 ☐ 49 = 72' (+) and then ask: *How can you tell that the sign is add? What would be a good way to work out the sum 23 + 49?* Discuss methods and then repeat with '34 ☐ 2 = 17' (÷), '23 ☐ 2 = 46' (×), '36 ☐ 19 = 17' (–). Each time, discuss appropriate methods for working out the answer. End with '123 ☐ 76 = 47' (–) and revise the vertical, 'carrying' method.

Main teaching activities

Whole class: Explain that in this lesson the children will again be looking at shopping problems. On this occasion they need to use multiplication and division to answer some of the questions they will be asked. Ask: *Think about shopping at the supermarket. Who can think of a question for which you would need to use multiplication or division?* Show the class the lemons or limes, establishing that there are the same number in the net as there are separate fruits. Read out the prices of the lemons or limes from the receipt and compare the price for the net, compared to the price for the same number of individual fruits. Discuss how much one lemon or lime from the net cost and which was the cheaper buy. Ask the children to suggest other shopping examples such as multiple packs of crisps, biscuits, cans of drink or multipacks in general.

Individual work: Give each child a copy of 'Party planning', on which they are asked a number of shopping questions involving addition, subtraction, multiplication and division with one or more steps. Remind them that although they have been practising written methods of addition and subtraction, they might find it quicker to work out some of these questions mentally. They might also check the results of their calculations by using a written method of calculation or other checking strategies such as knowledge of sums and differences of odd and even numbers. Remind them of work done on this in the previous term/lessons.

Differentiation

Less able: Use the version of the activity sheet that includes lower prices.
More able: Use the extended version of the activity sheet, which includes a challenge for these children to organise a birthday party for ten people, with a budget of £15.

Plenary & assessment

Discuss the answers to the questions on the activity sheet, each time asking how the child worked out the answer and which method they used. Ask: *Which two objects from the shop would cost the most to buy? How much would they cost? How many chocolate bars could you buy for £1? How many apples? How many packets of biscuits could you buy for £5? How many cakes?* Illustrate logical workings on the board to help the children answer such questions. Include examples from the differentiated activity sheets. Finally, discuss the methods the children used to check their answers.

Name   Date

Subtraction pairs

Choose one number from each set, and then use them for a subtraction.

Use one of the column methods that your teacher showed you.

Set 1

562	672	634
643	746	823

Set 2

159	215	137
236	161	248

Name	Date

Totally different shopping

Emily has been saving up her pocket money and has decided to go shopping.
Help her work out how she could spend her money. Set out the questions below on squared paper and work out the answers.

Book 2 £3.70

Tape 2 £2.65

CD 2 £4.10

£5.00

£4.90

Mag 2 £1.30

Tape 1 £4.20

Mag 1 £1.75

Book 1 £4.20

CD 1 £3.85

1. How much would it cost Emily to buy the two magazines?

2. If she had £2.90 and she bought Magazine 1, How much change would she have left?

3. How much would it cost her to buy both of the books?

4. How much more expensive are the headphones than the DVD?

5. What is the cost of the two CDs?

6. What is the difference in the cost of the CDs?

7. How much more expensive is Tape 1 than CD 1?

8. If she had £4.45 and she bought Book 2, how much change would she have?

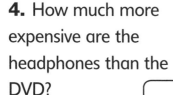

SCHOLASTIC
photocopiable

Party planning

Mrs Jones is planning a party for my birthday.

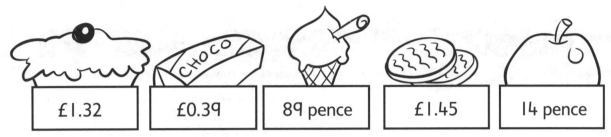

| £1.32 | £0.39 | 89 pence | £1.45 | 14 pence |

Set out each of the questions below on the squared paper and work out the answers, to help me with my planning.

1. How much would it cost to buy one cake, one chocolate bar and one apple?

2. If I had £1.90 and I bought two ice creams, how much would I have left?

3. How much would it cost to buy three chocolate bars?

4. How many apples could I buy for £1?

5. What is the cost of two ice creams and a packet of biscuits?

6. How much change would I have if I bought the chocolate bar than if I bought the ice cream?

7. How many chocolate bars could I buy for £5?

8. If I had £4.45 and I bought a cake and an apple, how much would I have left?

9. How many packets of biscuits can I buy for £10?

10. If I buy ten chocolate bars and ten apples, how much will I spend altogether?

Measures

...duced to capacity as the amount something holds. They become familiar with the relationship ...res and litres and learn to estimate and measure capacity.

LEA... ...ECTIVES

	Topics	Starter	Main teaching activities
Lesson 1	Capacity	● To consolidate understanding of 1/2, 1/4 and 3/4.	● **Suggest suitable units and measuring equipment to estimate or measure capacity.** ● Use, read and write standard metric units (l, ml) and imperial (pints). ● Begin to recognise the equivalent of one half, one quarter, three quarters and one tenth of 1 litre in millilitres.
Lesson 2	Capacity	● Use known number facts and place value to multiply and divide integers, including by 10 and then 100 (whole-number answers).	● Convert up to 1000ml to litres and vice versa. ● **Write the equivalent of one half, one quarter, three quarters and one tenth of 1 litre in millilitres.** ● **Record measures using decimal notation and mixed numbers.**
Lesson 3	Capacity	● As Lesson 2.	● **Know and use relationships between familiar units of capacity.** ● Record readings from scales.
Lesson 4	Capacity Problem-solving	● Derive quickly doubles of multiples of 100 to 5000 (eg 2400 × 2), and corresponding halves.	● Use all four operations to solve measurement word problems.
Lesson 5	Capacity Problem-solving	● Derive quickly all number pairs that total 100 (eg 62 + 38, 75 + 25, 40 + 60).	● **As Lesson 4.**

Lesson overview

Preparation
Draw scales on A1 paper (or copy on OHT), including ones that go up in 100 ml, 50ml and 25ml divisions (or copy template of 'Liquid measures' onto OHT).

Learning objectives
Starter
● To consolidate the children's understanding of 1/2, 1/4. and 3/4.
● Use known number facts and place value to multiply and divide integers, including by 10 and then 100 (whole-number answers).
● Derive quickly doubles of multiples of 100 to 5000 (eg 2400 × 2), and corresponding halves.
● Derive quickly all number pairs that total 100 (eg 62 + 38, 75 + 25, 40 + 60).
Main teaching activities
● **Suggest suitable units and measuring equipment to estimate or measure capacity.**
● Use, read and write standard metric units (l, ml) and imperial (pints).
● Begin to recognise the equivalent of one half, one quarter, three quarters and one tenth of 1 litre in millilitres.
● Convert up to 1000ml to litres and vice versa.
● **Write the equivalent of one half, one quarter, three quarters and one tenth of 1 litre in millilitres.**
● **Record measures using decimal notation and mixed numbers.**
● **Know and use relationships between familiar units of capacity.**
● Record readings from scales.
● Use all four operations to solve measurement word problems.

Vocabulary
millilitre (ml), litre (l), holds, full, empty, pint, metric, imperial, unit, halves, quarters, tenths, more than, less than, scale, intervals, measuring cylinder

You will need:
Photocopiable
'A capacity for questions' (see page 175) for each child.

CD pages
'Capacity table' core, less able, more able and template versions; 'Reading from scales' (see General resources); 'Liquid measures' core, less able, more able and template versions; 'The witch's cauldron clues', and 'The witch's cauldron'; 'Waldo the Wizard's scarf', core version only and 'A capacity for questions', core, less able and more able versions.

Equipment
OHP; number fans; whiteboards; Post-it Notes; string; scissors; stiff paper; transparent ruler; 30cm rulers for the class; metre stick; can of cola; litre carton of orange juice; tablespoon; bucket; various jugs and cylinders to measure capacity (1 litre or 1000cm³ capacity); a cereal bowl; a teacup; a pint bottle; soluble food colouring; rice.

Lesson

Starter

Hold up a metre ruler. Point at 50cm and say: *What fraction of the whole stick is this?* (one half) *How many centimetres would I need to add to make 1 metre? What fraction would I need to add to make 1 whole?* Repeat, pointing to 25cm (1/4 metre) and then 75cm (3/4 metre). Now show the children a litre bottle or measuring cylinder filled to 500ml and ask: *What fraction of the whole bottle/cylinder is this?* (one half) *How many millilitres would I need to add to make one litre? What fraction of a litre would I need to add to make one whole litre?* Repeat, pointing to 250ml (1/4 litre) and then 750ml (3/4 litre).

Main teaching activities

Whole class: Use a measuring cylinder to illustrate the capacity of 1 litre and, if appropriate, have available a can of soft drink, a litre carton of fruit juice, tablespoon and a bucket, a cereal bowl and a tea cup. Revise that 1 litre = 1000 ml. Discuss different ways of recording equivalents, eg 1/2 l = 500 ml, 1/4 l = 250 ml etc. Write these measures on the board. Discuss with the class the approximate capacities of the above each time starting by asking: *Is this capacity more than or less than one litre?*

Show a range of measuring equipment including 1 litre, 500ml, 250ml and 100ml measures. Ask: *Which of these measures would be best to find out how much the fruit juice carton holds? Why?* Repeat with the other containers above.

Ask children to come to the front and match one of the unmarked containers (such as the tea cup) with one of the pieces of apparatus with which it would be appropriate to measure its capacity. Repeat with two or three other containers. Discuss the choices made and extend by asking the children to estimate the capacities of the unmarked containers on their whiteboards.

Paired work: Give the children sheets of stiff paper, scissors and rulers and challenge them to make a container that they think will hold 1 litre. Tell them that 1 litre = 1000cm³ and that when they have made their containers you will measure out 1 litre of rice to test them.

Differentiation

Less able: These children may require extra discussion and assistance. Give each pair a container with a capacity of approximately 1 litre so they can make comparisons.
More able: Discuss ways of calibrating their containers, marking 500ml, 250ml and 750ml.

Plenary & assessment

Compare the capacities of the containers and ask: *If I had a container that had a capacity of 980ml, what would its capacity be to the nearest 100ml?* (1000ml) Illustrate with the rice and a suitable container. Repeat with 940ml (900ml) and 950ml (1000ml). Show a pint bottle and ask the children to estimate its capacity. Check by measuring and establish that it is roughly half a litre. Explain that a pint is an imperial measure and ask the children: *What might have been measured in pints?* (milk, beer…)

Lesson

Starter

Write a number on the board and ask the children to multiply it by 100. Start with 23 (2300) then 6 (600), stressing that each time the digits are moving two places to the left and two zeros are written as place holders. Repeat, now choosing multiples of a hundred, and ask the children to divide by 100 each time. Start with 500 (5) then 1000 (10), stressing that each time the digits are moving two places to the right and two zeros are removed. Now write on the board '100cm = 1 metre'. Call out several measurements in metres and ask the children to write down, on their whiteboards, the same length in centimetres and show you. Call out 2m (200cm), 4m (400cm), 7m (700cm) then repeat, this time calling out lengths in centimetres and asking the children to write down and show you the same lengths in metres. Call out 500cm (5m), 800cm (8m), 1000cm (10m).

Main teaching activities

Whole class: Fill a litre measuring cylinder with coloured water and ask: *How many millilitres are there in a litre?* Write on the board '1 litre = 1000 millilitres'. Ask: *How many millilitres are there in two litres? Three litres? How many in half a litre? A quarter of a litre? A tenth of a litre?*

Focus on a tenth of a litre. Point to the 100ml mark on the measuring cylinder and ask an individual child to count up, in tenths, from one tenth to one whole as you point to 100ml, 200ml, 300ml, and so on. Now ask: *If I had three tenths (3/10) of a litre, how much would I need to add to make 1 litre?* Repeat with 4/10, 5/10 (making the link with 1/2), 6/10, 7/10, 8/10 and 9/10.

Ask: *How many millilitres in 2½ litres? 3½ litres? 4¼ litres?* Discuss and record the answers in millilitres and then discuss the different ways of recording the capacities, for example, 2½ litres can be written as 2.5 litres, 2 litres and 500ml or 2500ml.

Say a measurement in litres and ask the children to use their whiteboards to write the same capacity in a different way. Start with 1½ litres (1.5 litres, 1 litre and 500 ml or 1500ml) Compare answers and, for each example, encourage the children to try all three ways of recording.

Write these measurements on the board: 500ml, 250ml, 750ml, 100ml, 200ml, 300ml, 400ml. For each measurement ask: *What fraction of a litre is it? How could you write this as a decimal? How much more liquid do you need to make it up to one whole litre?*

Focus on 250ml, 500ml, 100ml and 200ml and ask: *How many of these could I fit into one litre? How did you work that out?* Deal with 750ml, 300ml and 400ml in a similar way, discussing the possibility of remainders, or not having quite enough to make a complete litre.

Individual work: Give each child a copy of 'Capacity table' to complete.

Differentiation

Less able: Give each child a copy of the sheet that focuses on fractions of a litre and their equivalents. You might work with this group and demonstrate the amounts required to make a litre practically using a marked measuring cylinder and some coloured liquid.

More able: Give each child the version of the sheet which gives greater capacities and asks the children for the amounts required to make two litres.

Plenary & assessment

Use the table on activity sheet 'Capacity table' to assess children's understanding of millilitres and their fraction equivalents. Reinforce the conversion of capacities from one format to another. Write some capacity measurements on the board and ask children to come out and write the same measurements in a different way. Start with examples from the sheet but move on to more difficult ones, such as 3½l = ☐ ml and then introduce some decimal numbers such as 0.45l = ☐ ml.

Lesson

Starter

Repeat the Starter from Lesson 2, this time focusing on decimals. Write on the board '100cm = 1m'. Call out several measurements in metres and ask the children to write down, on their whiteboards, the same length in centimetres and show you. Say 0.5m (50cm), a quarter of a metre (25cm), 0.75m (75cm), one tenth of a metre (10cm) and so on. Then repeat, saying a length in centimetres and asking the children to write down and show you that length in metres. Say: 50cm (1/2 m), 10cm (1/10m), 1000cm (10m), 25cm (0.25m) and so on.

Main teaching activities

Show the children how scales are marked on the side of measuring cylinders. Display the enlarged (or OHT) version of the scales sheet, 'Reading from scales' (see General resources). Illustrate how scales can vary, not only in the amount they measure but also how they are divided up. Point out that when we measure we sometimes have to record to the nearest mark.

Group work: Prepare some measuring containers with different volumes of coloured water and ask children in groups to read the scales, then to record their measurements to the nearest division.
Individual work: Give each child a copy of 'Liquid measures' to complete.

Differentiation
Less able: Give each child the version of the sheet that consolidates reading scales to the nearest 100ml.
More able: Give each child the version of the sheet that includes 20ml and 25ml examples.

Plenary & assessment
Review their readings. Discuss any problems in reading the scales – either in the practical or worksheet examples.
Select one or two examples of unmarked containers used in Lesson 1 (for example tea cup and drinks can). Ask the children to estimate how much the containers hold in ml and to write on their whiteboards. Next, fill the containers, then empty them into marked measuring containers. Ask one child to read the scales. Ask: *How close were your estimates?*

Lesson 4

Starter
Call out a measurement and ask the children to double that length or capacity, write the answer on their whiteboards and show you. They may use whichever unit of measurement they wish. Start with 500cm (1000cm or 1m), 500ml (1000ml or 1 litre), 300cm (600cm or 0.6m), 700m (1400m or 1km 400m or 1.4km), 250ml (500ml or 1/2 a litre), 5mm (10mm, 1cm), 80cm (160cm, 1m and 60cm, 1.6m). Discuss the various ways of writing the answers, using different measurements for each example shown above.

Main teaching activities
Group work: Split the children into groups of three or four. Give each group a piece of paper, a pencil and a set of cards cut from activity sheet 'The witch's cauldron clues'. Ask them to use these clues to solve the problem called 'The witch's cauldron' together. Within their groups, the children shuffle the clue cards and deal them out equally, without looking at them. Once the children have been dealt their cards they can look at them but they may not show them to anyone else in the group. Write the two questions on the board.
● How much of the potion is the witch making? (Assume there is no evaporation.)
(2875ml, encourage the children to look for pairs of numbers that total 1 litre or 1000ml when adding up their measures.)
● Would the potion fit into six bottles, each able to hold 1/2 litre? (yes)
Explain that they can talk about the information on the cards with the other members of their group but they must not show anyone their cards or they will be out of the game. Suggest that they use the table to help them answer the questions. Remind them to keep all the measures in the same unit, such as millilitres. The first group that answers the two questions correctly wins.

Differentiation
Less able: Use the 'Witch's cauldron' activity sheet. If necessary, after a few minutes this group could lay the cards down and look at them together.
More able: Use the 'Waldo the Wizard's scarf' activity sheet that has an extra problem. How long is Waldo's scarf?

Plenary & assessment
Go through the core version of the activity sheet together as a class. Ask: *What operations did you use when calculating the answers? Which calculations did you need to write down? What was the best strategy to use when working as a group? Which clues were helpful? Were any clues unhelpful? Why?* (Listen to each other!) *Did it help to use the table?*

Lesson ⑤

Starter

Revise work on number pairs totalling 100. Call out a two-digit number, eg 61 and ask for children to write on their whiteboards the number that needs to be added to make 100 (39). Continue with a few examples. Next, call out a length and ask the children to work out how much has to be added to make 1 metre. They write their answers on their whiteboards and show you. Start with 39cm (61cm), 38cm (62cm), 3/4 m (1/4 m) and so on. Repeat but this time use capacities. Ask the children to show the capacity that they would add to make up to 1 litre. Start with 750ml (250ml), 1/4 litre (3/4 litre).

Main teaching activities

Whole class: Explain that in this lesson the children will be solving problems involving capacity. Hold up a 2-litre bottle and ask: *How many glasses of 100ml can I pour from this bottle? How could you work it out? What type of calculation should you use?* (2000 divided by 100 = 20 glasses). Repeat, asking how many quarter-litre glasses you could pour (8 glasses).

Individual work: Give the children activity sheet 'A capacity for questions', which sets a series of questions involving capacity in real-life situations.

Differentiation

Less able: Use the version of the activity sheet that includes simpler questions. These children could be encouraged to convert all of their measurements into millilitres. Sticky notes with the measurements written on them would also be useful for this group.

More able: Use the version of the activity sheet that includes more demanding questions.

Plenary & assessment

Discuss the questions on the activity sheet. Ask: *What method did you use to help you? Which questions did you find easiest to answer? Were there any that were very difficult?* Talk about any problems that arose and encourage the children to share their methods.

A capacity for questions

Look at these problems and answer in the space provided.
Show any working that you use on the back of the sheet.

1. A bucket holds 10 litres of water and a large jug holds 500ml. If I fill the bucket with water, how many jugs can I fill from it? _____

2. A bottle of medicine holds 250ml. The doctor says that Jane has to take 10ml per day until the bottle is finished. For how many days does Jane have to take the medicine? _____

3. A carton of orange juice holds 2 litres. How many 300ml glasses can I pour from it? _____

4. Cans of cola hold 330ml and cost 23 pence. Bottles of cola hold 1 litre and cost 60 pence. Which is the better value for money? _____

5. The label on the bottle suggests that I use one part orange squash to five parts water. If I put six cups of orange squash into a jug, how much water should I add? _____

6. A bottle holds 1.5 litres of water. Jim opens a new bottle and drinks half. How much water is left in the bottle? _____

7. Mrs Summer uses 50 grams of cheese to make half a pint of cheese sauce. How much cheese sauce could she make with 750 grams of cheese? _____

8. To make a fruit punch I add together half a litre of orange juice, 200ml of apple juice and 100ml of pineapple juice. How much punch will this make? If this is enough for four people, how much would I need to make for six people?

_____

_____

9. Look at these measurements. Put them in order of size, starting with the smallest.

3 litres   3.5 litres   700ml   750ml
$\frac{1}{4}$ litre   200ml   5 millilitres   5 litres

_____

_____

_____

Challenge

Can you find the total capacity of the measurements in question 9?

_____

Reasoning about shape

Children perform various practical activities to support their understanding of line symmetry and to help them identify lines of symmetry. They use this knowledge to classify polygons. They also sketch reflections and translations of shapes.

LEARNING OBJECTIVES

	Topics	Starter	Main teaching activities
Lesson 1	Reasoning about shape	● Begin to know multiplication facts for 9-times table.	● Identify lines of symmetry in 2-D shapes. Understand and use the associated vocabulary.
Lesson 2	Reasoning about shape	● Recall multiplication facts for 6- and 8-times tables.	● **Classify polygons using criteria such as number of right angles, whether or not they are regular, symmetry properties.** ● Make shapes: for example, construct polygons by paper folding. ● Classify 2-D shapes according to lines of symmetry.
Lesson 3	Reasoning about shape	● Recall multiplication facts for 6-, 8- and 9-times tables.	● Describe and visualise 3-D and 2-D shapes, including the tetrahedron and heptagon. ● Sketch the reflection of a simple shape or pattern where the sides of the image do not touch the mirror line (lines all parallel or perpendicular to the mirror line).
Lesson 4	Reasoning about shape	● Begin to know multiplication facts for 7-times table.	● Visualise 3-D shapes from 2-D drawings and identify simple nets of solid shapes. ● Make patterns by repeatedly translating or reflecting shapes. Know that rows on grids are described as horizontal, columns as vertical.
Lesson 5	Reasoning about shape	● Recall multiplication facts for 6-, 7-, 8- and 9-times tables.	● Make and investigate a general statement about familiar shapes by finding examples that satisfy it. ● Use co-ordinates to describe position. ● Translate and reflect shapes.

Lesson overview

Preparation
Prepare a display of tiling patterns and other repeating patterns, eg, Islamic patterns, wallpaper etc. Copy 'Mirror image' and 'Co-ordinates grid' sheets on to OHT. Lesson 4 might require access to the computer suite. Cut out shapes from 'Shape sorting' (see General resources).

Learning objectives
Starter
● Begin to know multiplication facts for 6-, 7-, 8- and 9-times tables.
Main teaching activities
● Identify lines of symmetry in 2-D shapes. Understand and use the associated vocabulary.
● **Classify polygons, using criteria such as number of right angles, whether or not they are regular, symmetry properties.**
● Make shapes: for example, construct polygons by paper folding.
● Classify 2-D shapes according to lines of symmetry.
● Describe and visualise 3-D and 2-D shapes, including the tetrahedron and heptagon.
● Sketch the reflection of a simple shape or pattern where the sides of the image do not touch the mirror line (lines all parallel or perpendicular to the mirror line).
● Visualise 3-D shapes from 2-D drawings and identify simple nets of solid shapes.
● Make patterns by repeatedly translating or reflecting shapes. Know that rows on grids are described as horizontal, columns as vertical.
● Make and investigate a general statement about familiar numbers and shapes by finding examples that satisfy it.
● Use co-ordinates to describe position.
● Translate and reflect shapes.

Vocabulary
line of symmetry, mirror line, symmetrical, reflect, reflection, co-ordinates, movement, translate, translation, horizontal, vertical

You will need:
CD pages
'Symmetrical shapes?' core, less able, more able and template versions; 'Shape sorting' (see General resources); Shape sorting diagram'; 'Mirror image' (see General resources), 'Reflections' core, less able and more able versions; 'Reflections and translations' (see General resources); 'Co-ordinates grid' and 'Co-ordinates instructions' (see General resources)

Equipment
Mirrors; sorting rings; Post-it Notes; whiteboards.

Lesson

Starter

Stand in front of the class and say the 9-times table. As you do this, hold your hands up, palms towards the class and encourage the children to copy you. As you say: *One times nine*, hold down the smallest finger on your right hand, then lift it up. As you say: *Two times nine*, hold down the next finger along, then lift it up and so on. Continue in this way until you say: *Ten times nine*, and hold the little finger on your left hand down. Ask: *What do you notice about all the answers in the 9-times table? What would happen if you added the digits of the answers together?* (They always add up to 9.)

Main teaching activities

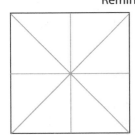

Remind the class of previous work they have done on symmetrical shapes. Take a square and fold it in half. Use a mirror to show that each half is a mirror image of the other. Ask: *How is the reflected half of the shape different from the other half?* Establish that it is reversed. Point out that some shapes have more than one line of symmetry. With the square, invite the groups to find all four lines of symmetry.

Paired work: Give each child a copy of 'Symmetrical shapes?' and ask the children to draw all the lines of symmetry they can find in each shape. Explain that some may not be symmetrical. Their partners can check by placing a mirror vertically on the line.

Differentiaition

Less able: Give children the version of the sheet that includes shapes with no more than two lines of symmetry (apart from the circle).

More able: Give children the version of the sheet that includes an additional challenge.

Plenary & assessment

Discuss the activity and address any difficulties that the children experience. Ask: *Which shapes had more than one line of symmetry? Which shapes were not symmetrical? How do you know?* Model one or two examples from the sheet on the board and ask children to draw in the line(s) of symmetry.

Lesson

Starter

Ask the class to count to 60 in 6s. Ask: *What is an easy way to multiply by 6?* Establish that ×6 is double ×3. Ask the class now to count in 8s to 80. Again, ask: *What is an easy way to multiply by 8?* (doubling ×4). Ask quick-fire multiplication and division questions involving ×6 and ×8. Ask the children to write the answers on the whiteboards.

Main teaching activities

Remind the children of work done in the previous lesson on lines of symmetry. Emphasise the positions of the lines on the square, ie they include diagonal, horizontal and vertical lines of symmetry.

Group work: Give out a set of symmetrical shapes cut from the 'Shape sorting' sheet (see General resources). Discuss the names of the various shapes. Ask the children to fold the shapes to check if they have no lines of symmetry, one line of symmetry or more than one line of symmetry. In groups, the children should sort the set of shapes using a sorting method of their choice (see Spring term Unit 12 for examples). If necessary supplement the shapes on the sheet with other prepared polygons or with the polygons on the 'Symmetrical shapes?' sheet.

Differentiation

Less able: Provide children with a copy of activity sheet 'Shape sorting diagram' or supply with sorting rings and labels to let them complete the task practically.

More able: Further sort the shapes by the numbers of lines of symmetry. If time is available, you might also allow them to define their own criteria for sorting.

Plenary & assessment

Ask the children to explain the criteria they used for sorting the shapes with more than one line of symmetry. Ask: *What did you notice about regular shapes?*

Lesson

Starter

Using vocabulary such as 'multiply', 'product', 'double' and 'groups of', ask quickfire questions to test the 6-, 8- and 9-times tables, with the children recording their answers on their whiteboards. For example, ask: *Find 9 multiplied by 8. Find the product of 8 and 5. What is double 6? I have 8 groups of 4 children, how many children do I have altogether?* Check responses and relate back to the Starters in Lessons 1 and 2. Write any still unfamiliar multiples in the corner of the board to return to later.

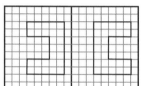

Main teaching activities

Display the 'Mirror image' sheet on an OHT. Colour in different squares to aid understanding as necessary. Invite a child to come to the front and indicate where the reflection of the shape should be placed. Draw in the reflection of the shape in an incorrect position (see left).

Ask: *Is this correct? Why not? How many squares to the right of the line should the shape start?* Establish that it should be the same number of squares from the line as the original shape. Ask a child to draw its reflection on the OHT. Ask the class if it is correct and prompt for any misconceptions.

Paired work: Give out the 'Reflections' activity sheet and explain to the children that they should draw or colour the reflection of each shape.

Differentiation

Less able: If necessary, give them the version of the 'Reflections' sheet in which the children have to sketch the reflection of simple shapes along one edge.

More able: If time is available, allow them to draw their own mirror line patterns on squared paper or use the blank version of the 'Reflections' sheet.

Plenary & assessment

Let children show their patterns and reflections. Use this session to clarify any misconceptions with the main activity. Display the second example from the 'Mirror image' sheet. Remind the class how to use co-ordinates and ask individuals to identify and record co-ordinates of the reflected shape. Discuss each co-ordinate and draw the agreed co-ordinates of the shape.

Lesson

Starter

With the class, say the 7-times table together twice. Then ask questions such as: *What is 6 times 7? What is 42 divided by 6?* Ask the children to show their responses on number fans. Write any problem statements in the corner of the board and repeat these several times.

Main teaching activities

Review work from the previous lesson. Show one of the mirror line examples and ask: *What is the word used to describe this type of movement?* ('reflection'). Draw an L-shape on the board and repeat the shape to the right of it. Ask: *How has this shape been moved?* Encourage the use of correct vocabulary and agree that it has been moved horizontally to the right. Repeat 'sliding' the shape horizontally and vertically. Explain that this is called 'translation'. Draw some more shapes on the board, eg circle, square, rectangle. Invite individuals to the board and give them clear instructions to translate the shapes, eg 'Translate the square vertically upwards', 'Move the circle horizontally to the left' etc. Show the children some examples of repeating patterns including Islamic patterns and tiling patterns. Discuss these with the children and ask them to predict how they would continue.

Group work: Give each mixed ability group a copy of the 'Reflections and translations' sheet. Ask them to discuss and describe each pattern on the sheet. Provide a supply of squared paper, pencils and rulers to enable the groups to make their own translations and reflections. This fits in with the QCA ICT Scheme of Work, Unit 4B 'Developing images using repeating patterns' so if appropriate, move the groups onto the computer to produce their repeated translations or reflections.

Plenary & assessment

Review the children's selection of patterns and ask other children from each group to describe each pattern. If possible, display all the children's patterns in the classroom after the lesson.

Lesson

Starter

Ask the children to write the answers to some table fact questions on their whiteboards. Ask, for example: *What is 3 times 6? What is 9 times 7? What is 8 times 4?* Include some word problems such as: *If I have 6 teams of 5 children, how many children would I have altogether?*

Main teaching activities

Whole class work: Show the 'Co-ordinates grid' (see General resources) on an OHT. Explain that each point is defined by co-ordinates and that the horizontal or x co-ordinate comes first followed by the vertical or y co-ordinate. The co-ordinates mark the point where the lines cross. Demonstrate some points on the grid, asking children to locate different points from given co-ordinates and vice versa. Give each child a copy of 'Co-ordinates grid' and read the following instructions:

● Find the point (1,1) and mark it with a small cross. Find the point (9,1) and draw a line joining these two points.

● Find (9,7) and draw a line to join it to the point (9,1).

● Find (5,10) and draw a line from (9,7) to that point.

● Then draw a line from (5,10) to (1,7), then back to (1,1).

Ask: *What has been drawn?* (a house). Review the work in the previous lesson on translations and reflections. Explain that the children in pairs should draw the shapes on the instructions sheet onto the grid and then follow the instructions to translate or reflect them.

Paired work: Give each pair a copy of the 'Co-ordinates instructions' sheets as well as two copies of the 'Co-ordinates grid'. One child in each pair should draw each shape on the grid while the other child records the co-ordinates. They then swap roles with one child describing the translation or reflection (and recording the co-ordinates) with the other child drawing the shapes on the grid.

Less able: Limit the children to drawing the shapes and simple translations to the left and right. If necessary, work with the pairs and give them additional practice of recording co-ordinates – for example by drawing windows and a door on the house.

More able: Ask the pairs to reflect each shape both horizontally and vertically. If time is available, ask them to write out their own set of co-ordinates for a different shape, such as symmetrical letters of the alphabet.

Plenary & assessment

Ask the children to share their work. The more able pairs could give instructions for the rest of the class to follow on the 'Co-ordinates grid'. Review children's understanding of the key vocabulary and of the use of co-ordinates: *What do we call the movement of a shape in a straight line? What are the co-ordinates of a point that is 3 squares vertically above (5,4)?* and so on.

Angles and position

In this unit children are introduced to the protractor and perform some basic angle measuring tasks. They also consolidate their understanding of 'angle' as a measurement of turn and combine this with work on position and movement including developing their understanding of the eight compass directions (N, S, W, E, NW, SW, NE, SE).

LEARNING OBJECTIVES

		Topics	Starter	Main teaching activities
Lesson	1	Perimeter	● Consolidate knowing by heart addition and subtraction facts for all numbers to 20. ● Derive quickly doubles of all whole numbers to 50.	● Begin to know that angles are measured in degrees and that one whole turn is 360° and a quarter turn is 90°. ● Start to order a set of angles less than 180°.
Lesson	2	Perimeter	● Derive quickly doubles of multiples of 100 to 5000 (eg 3400 × 2).	● Begin to know that angles are measured in degrees. ● Make and measure clockwise and anti-clockwise.
Lesson	3	Shape and space	● Begin to know that angles are measured in degrees and that one whole turn is 360° or four right angles, a quarter turn is 90° or one right angle, half a right angle is 45°.	● Make and measure clockwise and anti-clockwise. ● Recognise position and directions. ● Recognise simple examples of horizontal and vertical lines.

Lessons overview

Preparation
Prepare a copy of the 'Compass angles' sheet (template version) and 'Co-ordinates grid' (from Unit 5) on OHT.

Learning objectives
Starter
● Consolidate knowing by heart addition and subtraction facts for all numbers to 20.
● Derive quickly doubles of all whole numbers to 50
● Derive quickly doubles of multiples of 100 to 5000 (eg 3400 × 2).
● Begin to know that angles are measured in degrees and that one whole turn is 360° or four right angles, a quarter turn is 90° or one right angle, half a right angle is 45°.

Main teaching activities
● Begin to know that angles are measured in degrees and that one whole turn is 360° and a quarter turn is 90°.
● Start to order a set of angles less than 180°.
● Make and measure clockwise and anti-clockwise.
● Recognise position and directions.
● Recognise simple examples of horizontal and vertical lines.

Vocabulary
angle, degrees (°), protractor, clockwise, anticlockwise, turn, half turn, quarter turn, horizontal, vertical, rotate

You will need:
Photocopiable pages
'Angle measuring' (see page 183) for each child; 'Compass angles' (see page 184) for each child.

CD pages
'Angle measuring', core, less able and more able versions; 'Compass angles' core, less able, more able and template versions; 'Co-ordinates grid' (see General resources); 'Mr Jolly's journey' core, less able and more able versions; 'Mr Jolly's journey' planner' (see General resources) .

Equipment
A set of protractors (one per group); an OHP protractor (optional); geo-rods.

Lesson

Starter

Call out two numbers, less than 20, and ask the children to add the numbers together and then double the answer. They can show any necessary working and their answers on their whiteboards. Start with 4 and 11. ((4 + 11) × 2 = 30) Discuss how difficult this was for the children and explain that this is the same calculation as 11 + 4 + 11 + 4 or 4 + 4 + 11 + 11 or (2 × 11) + (2 × 4). Repeat with several other examples.

Main teaching activities

Tell the children that they are going to look at angles. *What is an angle?* (a measurement of turn) *What unit do we measure angles in?* (Degrees or °). *How many degrees are in one whole turn?* (360°).

Give each group a protractor and ask them to discuss what they can see and what the instrument is used for. If one is available, show an OHP protractor and describe what it is. A protractor placed on an OHP also works well. Ensure that all the children realise that it is used to measure angles and that it includes values marked from 0-180°. Highlight the centre point of rotation and the straight line along the bottom.

Explain how the protractor works from left to right or from right to left or 'clockwise' and 'anticlockwise'. Ask the children to find 0° on the protractor and to move round 90°. Ask: *What does this make?* (a right angle). Next ask them to move 45° anticlockwise. *Where are you now?* (45°). *What fraction of a right angle is 45°?* (½). Repeat the question for 30° (1/3) and 60° (2/3). From 60° ask: *How many degrees to get to 180° (or a straight line)?* (120). Ask the pupils to check using their protractors. Ask: *What fraction of a straight line is 60°?* (1/3). Consolidate children's understanding of 'clockwise', 'anticlockwise' further moving them round the protractor to different points. Stress the need to line up the protractor correctly when measuring angles.

Group work: Give each group a copy of the 'Angle measuring' sheet in which children have to measure a set of angles and put them in size order.

Differentiation

Less able: Give this group the version of the sheet with four larger angles from left to right.
More able: Give this group the version of the sheet with an extra challenge with vertical angles.

Plenary & assessment

Check answers and identify any difficulties in measuring or ordering the angles. Sort the angles into two groups with the children: 'Less than a 1/4 turn' and 'More than a 1/4 turn'. Discuss the vocabulary with the children. Establish with them that a quarter turn = 90° (or one right angle), a half turn = 180° (or two right angles), a three-quarter turn = 270° (or three right angles), and a whole turn = 360° (or four right angles).

Lesson

Starter

Call out a multiple of 100 and ask the children to double it. They can show any necessary working and their answers on their whiteboards. Start with 2400, 3400, 4400, then 2300, 3300, 4300. Repeat with several examples.

Main teaching activities

Check the children understand the meaning of quarter turn, half turn, three-quarter turn and whole turn. Show children the template for the 'Compass angles' sheet. Highlight the horizontal and vertical lines through the centre of each circle. Mark in a quarter turn clockwise from N to E with a coloured pen. Establish that the children understand that this is a quarter turn, one right angle or 90° clockwise. Ask: *What does the N mean at the top of the circle?* Remind them of the points of the compass directions. Go through the eight compass directions (including NE, NW, SE and SW).

Individual work: Give each child a copy of 'Compass angles' and ask them to work on their own to complete the sheet. They have to establish the amount of turn, whether the movement is being made clockwise or anticlockwise and from which directions.

Differentiation

Less able: Give each child the version of the sheet that includes only 1/4 and 1/2 turns and only four compass directions. Also, focus the children on measuring the angles and support the children with describing the turns.

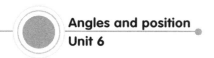

More able: Give children the version of the sheet that includes turns over 180° and eight compass directions.

Plenary & assessment

Show the template of 'Compass angles'. Point to S and move clockwise to W. Draw this turn and ask: *What size of angle is this?* Repeat with other angles including questions involving the eight compass directions, eg *'I want to move 45° clockwise from NW. Where do I finish?'* Continue to use the OHT to check answers and discuss any misunderstandings. Make sure the children understand and can use the correct mathematical language.

Lesson

Starter

Use two connected geo-rods to make an acute angle. Ask: *Is this angle more than 90°?* Make a larger angle and ask: *Is this angle more than 90°?* Repeat with several more examples. Now tell the children that you will make an angle. If it is less than 90° they should touch the floor. If it is more than 90° they should stand up. Give several examples. With the last few examples, keep the separate geo-rods angles, tacking them to the board. Finally, put these angles in order of size.

Main teaching activities

Review all the key vocabulary from the previous lesson and check the children's understanding of position and direction. Remind the children of the co-ordinate system for identifying points used in the previous unit. Show the copy of the 'Co-ordinates grid' on an OHT and put a cross on (3, 1). Ask: *What are the co-ordinates of this point?* Ask: *What if I were to move 3 squares horizontally?* (6, 1). Prompt if anyone needs reminding that the horizontal or x co-ordinate comes first. *From this point what points would I move through if I moved, directly north (6,2), (6,3) etc. Why do all of these co-ordinates begin with the number 6?* Agree that moving north will create a vertical line above 6. Ask: *If I moved horizontally, what directions could I move?* (east or west).

Continue the session demonstrating routes from (6, 1) using all four compass directions, eg *'Which squares would I move through if I moved north west from (6, 1)?* and so on.

Paired work: Give out two copies of 'Mr Jolly's journey' and 'Mr Jolly's journey planner'. Explain that the children have to describe a route for Mr Jolly to get to the train station. In Route 1, Mr Jolly can only move in right angles (ie one square horizontally, then one square vertically or vice versa). In Route 2, Mr Jolly can move in any direction including diagonally – though making sure he avoids any obstacles. Explain that you want them to use compass directions and co-ordinates to describe their routes. Each player should complete one route then give it to their partner who follows the route and draw it on the grid.

Differentiation

Less able: Limit the children to Route 1. You might also supply the version of 'Mr Jolly's journey' that includes an identified route. The children then have to supply a description of the route.
More able: Provide the version of the sheet that includes Mr Jolly's house. The children have to create a set of instructions to get Mr Jolly to his house and then down to the train station. You might also ask them to think of some rules for the journey, eg vary the compass points used and/or the number of steps.

Plenary & assessment

Go through some of the different routes with the children and review all of the possible options for Route 1. Review all the key words and give some whole class instructions, such as *Stand up. You are all facing north. Move round 180°. Which direction are you now facing?* (south) *Move round 45° anticlockwise. Which direction are you now facing?* (west) and so on.

Name	Date

Angle measuring

Measure the angles below using your protractors.

Write the angle in degrees (°) below each one then put them in size order at the bottom of the sheet.

Remember to line up the angles correctly using your protractor.

Your teacher will show you how to do this.

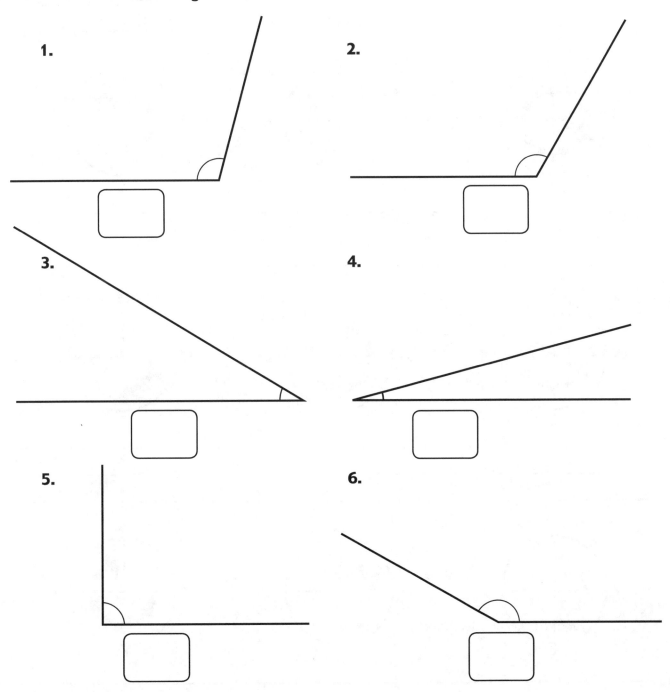

1.

2.

3.

4.

5.

6.

Order the angles below:

Name	Date

Compass angles

Write underneath each diagram:

- the type of turn that is being made (e.g. 90° or $\frac{1}{4}$ turn)
- whether the movement is clockwise or anticlockwise
- the direction of turn (e.g. from N to E)

The first example has been completed for you.

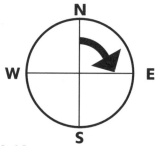

90° (Quarter turn)

Clockwise

From North to East

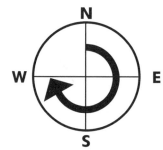

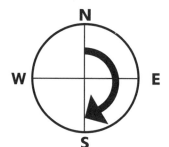

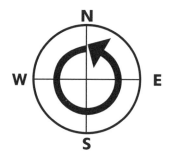

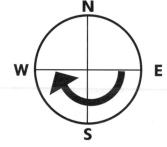

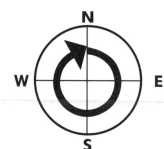

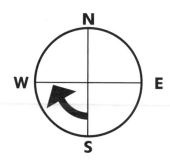

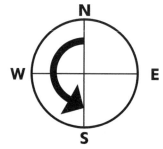

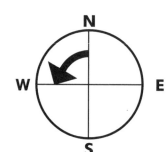

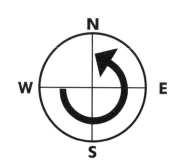

Properties of number and number sequences

Children continue to recognise and extend number sequences formed by counting from any number, in steps of constant size, extending beyond zero when counting backwards. They make and investigate statements about odd and even numbers and multiples of 2, 3, 4, 5 and 10.

LEARNING OBJECTIVES

	Topics	Starter	Main teaching activities
Lesson 1	Properties of numbers and number sequences	● Add or subtract 1, 10, 100 or 1000 to or from any integer, and count back in tens, hundreds or thousands from any whole number up to 10 000. ● Count on or back in steps of constant size, including beyond zero	● Recognise multiples of 2, 3, 4, 5, and 10, up to tenth multiple. ● Explain methods and reasoning about numbers orally and in writing.
Lesson 2	Properties of a numbers and number sequences	● As Lesson 1.	● Recognise multiples of 2, 3, 4, 5 and 10 up to the tenth multiple. ● Solve mathematical problems or puzzles, recognise and explain patterns and relationships, generalise and predict. Suggest extensions by asking 'What if…?' ● Explain methods and reasoning orally and in writing.
Lesson 3	Reasoning about numbers	● Recognise multiples of 2, 3, 4, 5, and 10, up to tenth multiples.	● Solve mathematical problems or puzzles, recognise and explain patterns and relationships, generalise and predict. Suggest extensions by asking 'What if…?' ● Explain methods and reasoning orally and in writing.
Lesson 4	Reasoning about numbers	● Recognise and extend number sequences formed by counting from any number in steps of constant size, extending beyond zero when counting back.	● Make and investigate a general statement about familiar numbers by finding examples that satisfy it.
Lesson 5	Reasoning about numbers	● As Lesson 4.	● Solve mathematical problems or puzzles, recognise and explain patterns and relationships, generalise and predict. Suggest extensions by asking 'What if…?' ● Explain methods and reasoning orally and in writing.

Lessons   overview

Preparation
Cut out and prepare cards from resource sheet 'Multiple cards' (enough for a set of five cards per child or pair of children). Photocopy several copies of resource sheet 'Grid of multiples' onto OHTs. You will also need to prepare a number grid computer program with a facility to highlight multiples in different colours. OHT of '100 square' (General resource).

Learning objectives
Starter
● Add or subtract 1, 10, 100 or 1000 to or from any integer, and count back in tens, hundreds or thousands from any whole number up to 10 000.
● Count on or back in steps of constant size, including beyond zero.
● Recognise multiples of 2, 3, 4, 5, and 10, up to tenth multiple.
Main teaching activities
● Recognise multiples of 2, 3, 4, 5, and 10, up to tenth multiple.
● Explain methods and reasoning about numbers orally and in writing.
● Solve mathematical problems or puzzles, recognise and explain patterns and relationships, generalise and predict. Suggest extensions by asking 'What if…?'

Vocabulary
sequence, pattern, multiple, vertical, diagonal, predict, row, column, consecutive, rule

You will need:
Photocopiable pages
'Multiples of 5 and 10' (see page 190) for every child

CD pages
'Grid of multiples' (see General resources); 'Multiples of 5 and 10' core, less able and more able versions; '100 square' (see General resources); 'Multiple cards' (see General resources); 'Consecutive challenge' core, less able, more able and template versions

Equipment
OHP; OHP pens in three different colours; whiteboards; computer with large display screen (or interactive whiteboard); a computer program to demonstrate number grids; 0–9 dice; 0–6 dice.

Lesson ①

Starter

Write 'Stop' on the board. Give the children a starting number and ask the children to count on together, in ones, tens, hundreds or thousands, from that number, stopping when you point to 'Stop' on the board. Start with 578 and ask them to count on in ones, then back in ones, then on in tens and back in tens. Repeat with hundreds and thousands. Ask: *Starting with 578, how many jumps of ten do I need to reach 1000? How many jumps of a hundred do I need to get a negative number?* Finish by starting at 3 and asking the children to count with you, in ones, down past zero to negative 5.

Main teaching activities

Whole class: Explain that the topic for this lesson is numbers and their patterns. Use a number grid computer program, or display an OHT of resource sheet 'Grid of multiples'. On the grid, highlight the multiples of 2. Ask: *What is the difference between consecutive even numbers?* (2) *Look at the even numbers. What are the last digits of the even numbers?* (2, 4, 6, 8 and 0) *How can you describe the pattern that they make on the grid?* Display a new grid and repeat with a different number, showing that the grids can produce vertical or diagonal patterns. Depending on time and computer access, children could investigate the patterns formed by highlighting the multiples of 2 on various grids of numbers.

Now return to the OHT 'Grid of multiples' with multiples of 2 shaded. Use a different colour to circle every other even number, starting with 4 (4, 8, 12, 16). Ask: *What is the difference between pairs of these circled numbers?* (4) *How could you describe these numbers?* (multiples of 4) *Look at the multiples of 4. What are the last digits of the numbers? Is there a pattern?* (2, 4, 6, 8 and 0, yes) *Are the multiples of 4 always even? How can you describe the pattern that they make on the grid?*

Individual work: Give the children activity sheet 'Multiples of 5 and 10' and ask them to shade all the multiples of 5 in one colour, then to make observations in the box provided. Then ask them to use a different colour to circle alternate multiples of 5, starting with 10 (10, 20, 30 – multiples of 10). Ask the children to record any observations that they make.

Differentiation

Less able: Use the version of the activity sheet that will guide the children in their observations.
More able: Use the version of the activity sheet that challenge these children to make links, such as:
● every fifth even number is a multiple of 10;
● every fifth multiple of 4 is a multiple of 10.

Plenary & assessment

Discuss the children's observations and summarise.
● The last digit of a multiple of 5 is always 5 or 0 and the last digit of a multiple of 10 is always 0.
● Every other (even) multiple of 5 is a multiple of 10.
● Multiples of 10 are always even numbers.

Lesson ②

Starter

Ask quick-fire questions such as: *What is 1 more than 4567? 7864? 876? –3? –2? –1? What is one less than 345? 7864? 876? –3? –2? –1? What is 10 more than 4567? 7864? 876? 0? –1? –9? What is ten less than 345? 7864? 876? – 10? 1? –1? What is 100 more than 4567? 7864? 876? –100? –200? –1? What is one hundred less than 345? 7864? 876? 0? 1? –1? What is 1000 more than 4567? 7864? 876? –1000? –1? What is one thousand less than 3745? 7864? 1000? 0? 1? –1?*

Main teaching activities

Whole class: Review the patterns of multiples discovered in Lesson 1. Use the computer program (or an OHT of '100 square') to highlight multiples of 2, 5 and 10. Write on the board four columns headed 'Multiple of 2,…4,…5,…10'. Call out a number and the children have to tell you whether it can be added to any of the columns on your chart.

Ask the children to tell you the multiples of 3 and add another column to your chart. Ask: *Can you see a pattern?* The sum of the digits for numbers in the 3-times tables follows the pattern 3, 6, 9, 3, 6, 9. Say: *Let's test for other numbers to see if this is always true.* Try 63. Ask the children to demonstrate their methods for dividing 63 by 3 to give the answer 21 with no remainder. Then add the digits: 6 + 3 = 9, so the rule works in this example.

Paired work: Ask the pairs to use 0–9 dice to generate two-digit numbers. For each number, ask the children to sum the digits and decide whether they think it is a multiple of 3. They should check by dividing by 3 and record the results in two lists: those that are multiples of 3 and those that are not.

Differentiation

Less able: Limit the pairs to 0–6 dice
More able: Challenge the children to generate three-digit numbers.

Plenary & assessment

Review the children's lists of multiples of 3 and use the computer program or 100 square to highlight each number. Call out some other numbers and ask the children to determine whether it can be added to the 100 square. Look for other patterns that these multiples make (eg they produce diagonal patterns). If time is available discuss the other patterns made on the 100 square (eg multiples of 2 and 10 produce vertical patterns).

Lesson

Starter

Give each child a set of five cards cut from resource sheet 'Multiple cards'. Each set consists of the five numbers 2, 3, 4, 5 and 10. Explain that you will call out numbers and if the children think that your number is a multiple of 2 (even) they must hold up the 2, if your number is a multiple of 3, they must hold up the 3, and so on. Explain that sometimes they may need to hold up more than one card, for example, 6 is a multiple of both 2 and 3.

Main teaching activities

Display the 100 square on OHT or use a 1–100 square grid computer program. Cover three consecutive numbers, eg 55–57 and ask: *Which numbers are covered? How do you know?* Establish that the covered numbers can be identified from the patterns in the grid. If necessary, explain that numbers that come one after the other are called 'consecutive numbers'.

Select three consecutive numbers below 20, eg 6 + 7 + 8 = ❑ and ask: *What is the total of these consecutive numbers?* Repeat with other sets of three numbers. Ask: *Can anyone suggest a rule for finding the total of consecutive numbers?* Discuss that by adding 1 from the largest number to the smallest number results in three numbers that are all the same.

Paired work: Challenge the children to use this rule to find the target numbers on the 'Consecutive challenge' activity sheet. Observe the strategies that the pairs use as they work.

Differentiation

Less able: Give children the version of the sheet with lower target numbers.
More able: Give the children the version of the sheet without any target numbers. Instead Player 1 selects a target number and Player 2 finds three consecutive numbers to make the target number.

They record their target numbers and answers on the sheet. They also have an additional challenge: to highlight all of the numbers to 30 that they are able to find using three consecutive numbers.

Plenary & assessment

Bring the children together to review the target numbers. Mark off the children's consecutive numbers on the OHT (or computer grid). Review the children's strategies for finding the consecutive numbers and establish that dividing by 3 is a helpful strategy to use.

Lessons   overview

Preparation

Use resource sheet 'Statements to evaluate' to prepare enough cards for every child or pair of children to have one.

Learning objectives

Starter
- Recognise and extend number sequences formed by counting from any number in steps of a constant size, extending beyond zero when counting back.

Main teaching activities
- Make and investigate a general statement about familiar numbers by finding examples that satisfy it.
- Solve mathematical problems and puzzles, recognise and explain patterns and relationships, generalise and predict. Suggest extensions by asking 'What if…?'
- Explain methods and reasoning orally and in writing.

Vocabulary

consecutive, predict, continue, relationship, odd, even, multiple investigation

You will need:

CD pages
'Statements to evaluate' (see General resources); 'Investigations' core, less able, more able and template versions.

Lesson

Starter

Ask the children to count back in 4s from 40. Get into a rhythm. When you reach zero ask: *What would happen now? Can we go on?* Repeat, this time starting at 39, then at 38.

Main teaching activities

Whole class: Explain that in this and the next lesson the children will investigate some statements. Say that you would like them to look at some general statements and to try out different numbers to find whether the statements are true or false. Write on the board 'Multiples of 4 end in 2, 4, 6, 8 or 0.' Invite individual children to think of some numbers and to say whether they support the statement. Encourage discussion and ask children to explain the relationships between the numbers and expressions and to decide whether the written statement is true or false. The suggested statement is true, as any multiple of 4 will be even.

Individual or paired work: Give the children, working individually or in pairs, cards made from activity sheet 'Statements to evaluate' and ask them to investigate. When they have finished one card they can have another, but limit the number of statements they work on, keeping some for the next lesson.

Differentiation

Less able: Let these children work in pairs or groups, with some extra assistance. Supply a list of numbers for them to test as a starting point. Allocate a helper or classroom assistant to whom they can explain their reasoning, when they have reached a conclusion about a statement.

More able: Ask these children to develop written statements that fully explain their findings.

Plenary & assessment.

Discuss and develop vocabulary for the children to explain their ideas and findings about the statements they have tackled. Refer only to those statements that children have evaluated. Some of the following may be held over for the next lesson.

● Half-way between any two multiples of ten is a multiple of five. (True, for example, 20 and 50 are multiples of 10, and half-way between them is 35, which is a multiple of 5). Ask: *Would it be helpful to use a number line to find the midpoint? Could somebody give me another example to show that this statement is true?*

● Multiples of 4 end in 2, 4, 6, 8 or 0. (True, as any multiple of 4 will be even, double a multiple of 2.)

● Multiples of 8 end in 2, 4, 6, 8 or 0. (True, as any multiple of 8 will be even, double a multiple of 4.)

● Multiples of 3 end in 3, 6 or 9. (False)

● The sum of three odd numbers is odd. (True, for example, 1 + 3 + 7 = 11 which is odd.)

● The sum of three even numbers is odd. (False, for example, 2 + 6 + 8 = 16 which is even.)

● Half-way between any two multiples of 4 is a multiple of 2. (True, for example, 8 and 12 are multiples of 4, and half-way between them is 10, which is a multiple of 2.)

● The sum of 3 consecutive numbers is always a multiple of 3 (true).

Lesson

Starter

Repeat the Starter for Lesson 4, this time stating that the rule is 'subtract 4' and using 37, 36 and 35 as starting numbers. Include examples that extend beyond zero, eg 'Count back in 4s from 5.' Ask: *How far can you go?*

Main teaching activities

If necessary, continue working through the 'Statements to evaluate' from the previous lesson.

Go through the core 'Investigations' questions in turn to explain what is involved. Tell the children in pairs to discuss methods that they could use, then record their workings.

Paired work: Give each pair the version of the 'Investigations' sheet that includes 'Making numbers', 'Using 9s' and 'Missing numbers – subtractions'.

Differentiation

Less able: Give each pair the version of the sheet that includes ' Making numbers' and 'Missing numbers – additions'.

More able: Give each pair the version of the sheet that includes 'Numbers for letters' and two 'Make 100' challenges.

Plenary & assessment.

Go through all of the investigations and ask the children to share their methods for working out each one.

Name	Date

Multiples of 5 and 10

Use a coloured pencil to colour in all the multiples of 5.

1	2	3	4	5	6
7	8	9	10	11	12
13	14	15	16	17	18
19	20	21	22	23	24
25	26	27	28	29	30
31	32	33	34	35	36
37	38	39	40	41	42
43	44	45	46	47	48
49	50	51	52	53	54
55	56	57	58	59	60
61	62	63	64	65	66

1. What do you notice about all of the multiples of 5?

_____

Now, starting with 10, use a second colour to circle every alternate multiple of 5.

2. What do you notice about every alternate multiple of 5?

_____

Understanding multiplication and division

The children review the distributive law as it applies to multiplication (eg $12 \times 7 = (10 \times 7) + (2 \times 7)$) and use this and other strategies to answer a range of multiplication questions. They go on to review a range of division strategies (both mental and informal written strategies) and refine estimation and checking strategies. Finally, they use all four operations to solve problems on a fairground theme.

LEARNING OBJECTIVES

	Topics	Starter	Main teaching activities
Lesson 1	Understanding multiplication and division	● Know by heart multiplication facts for 2, 3, 4, 5 and 10-times tables.	● Understand the principle (not the name) of the distributive law as it applies to multiplication.
Lesson 2	Understanding multiplication and division	● Begin to know multiplication facts for 6-, 7-, 8- and 9-times tables.	● Use known facts including doubling to multiply, including by 10 and 100 Use closely-related facts (eg to multiply 9 or 11, multiply by 10 and adjust; develop the 6 times table from 4 and 2 times tables).
Lesson 3	Understanding multiplication and division Pencil and paper procedures	● Use known number facts and place value to multiply and divide integers, including by 10 and then 100 (whole-number answers).	● **Derive quickly division facts corresponding to 2, 3, 4, 5, 10** ● Use the relationship between multiplication and division
Lesson 4	Understanding multiplication and division Pencil and paper procedures	● Derive quickly division facts corresponding to 2-, 3-, 4-, 5- and 10-times tables.	● Round up or down after division, depending on the context.
Lesson 5	Understanding multiplication and division	● As Lesson 4.	● Use all four operations to solve word problems involving numbers in real life, money and measures, using one or more steps.

Lessons overview

Preparation
OHT of 'Triangles', template version. Copy 'Division examples' on OHT. Enlarged copy of 'Multiplication grid' (see General resources).

Learning objectives
Starter
● Know by heart multiplication facts for 2-, 3-, 4-, 5- and 10-times tables.
● Begin to know multiplication facts for 6-, 7-, 8- and 9-times tables.
● Use known number facts and place value to multiply and divide integers, including by 10 and then 100 (whole-number answers).
● Derive quickly division facts corresponding to 2-, 3-, 4-, 5- and 10-times tables.
Main teaching activities
● Understand the principle (not the name) of the distributive law as it applies to multiplication.
● Use known facts including doubling to multiply, including by 10 and 100
● Use closely-related facts (eg to multiply 9 or 11, multiply by 10 and adjust; develop the 6 times table from 4 and 2 times tables).
● **Derive quickly division facts corresponding to 2, 3, 4, 5, 10**
● Use the relationship between multiplication and division
● Round up or down after division, depending on the context.

Vocabulary
sum, total, multiply, product, multiple, double, inverse, division, divide, how much is it?, what could we try next?

You will need:
Photocopiable pages
'Multiplication breakdown' (see page 196) for every child; 'Many methods of multiplication' (see page 197) for each pair; 'Division dilemmas' (see page 198) for each pair.

CD pages
'Multiplication breakdown', 'Many methods of multiplication' and 'Triangles' core, less able, more able and template versions; 'Multiplication grid' and 'Division dilemmas' (see General resources); 'Division dilemmas' core, less able, more able and template versions.

Equipment
Number fans; whiteboards.

Lesson ①

Starter

Ask quick-fire multiplication questions such as: *Six fives, three times four, ten times zero, two multiplied by one. Multiply seven by four. Find the product of five and three.* Ask the children to respond quickly, showing their answers on their number fans or whiteboards.

Main teaching activities

Tell the children that you will be showing them a way to work out multiplications. Write 12×7 on the board. Ask: *How can you work out the answer?* Collect responses, then write the question in a different way, as follows:

$12 \times 7 = (10 \times 7) + (2 \times 7)$. Ask the children to use this model for other multiplications in the 7-times table, eg 16×7, 17×7 up to 20×7. Establish that the children understand this pattern and that they can apply it to multiplication questions that they cannot work out in their heads, eg $26 \times 7 = (10 \times 7) + (10 \times 7) + (5 \times 7) + (1 \times 7)$.

Individual work: Give each child a copy of 'Multiplication breakdown'. Ask the children to show this partitioning method for each answer. If time is available, you might challenge them to break down the first number in two different ways.

Differentiation

Less able: Give each child the version of the sheet with single-digit and lower two-digit starting numbers. Work with the children to establish that they understand and can use the distributive method.
More able: Give the children the version of the sheet with higher starting numbers and with an additional challenge to partition or distribute both numbers in each question.

$(3 \times 4) + (9 \times 4) = \square$
or $(12 \times 2) + (12 \times 2) = \square$
or $(3 \times 2) + (9 \times 2) + (4 \times 2) + (8 \times 2) = \square$

Plenary & assessment

Use the children's answers to establish how comfortable they are with this method. Explore breaking down both numbers with a simple example such as '12×4' (see left). Ask: *What happens? Does the method still work?*

Lesson ②

Starter

Repeat the Starter from Lesson 1, this time using numbers from the 6-, 7-, 8- and 9-times tables.

Main teaching activities

Whole class: Explain that in this lesson the children will learn different methods to work out multiplication problems mentally, or using jottings. Encourage the children to use their whiteboards as you go through these examples.

Write on the board '$13 \times 4 = \square$' and ask: *How can we work this out?* Discuss various methods: $((10 \times 4) + (3 \times 4), (13 \times 2) \times 2)$.

Repeat with '$13 \times 8 = \square$' and discuss methods: $(((13 \times 2) \times 2) \times 2)$.

Now try '$13 \times 5 = \square$' and discuss methods: $((10 \times 5) + (3 \times 5), (13 \times 10) \div 2)$. Ask: *Will multiplying by 10 and then halving always work? Why?* (Yes, as $10 \div 2$ is 5.)

Challenge the children to find a similar method for multiplying by 20. (Multiply by 10 and then double.)

Now write up '$11 \times 14 = \square$' and ask: *How could we work out this product?* $((10 \times 14) + (1 \times 14)$, or $11 \times (7 \times 2)$, or using doubling $(1 \times 14) + (2 \times 14) + (8 \times 14))$

Now challenge the children to find two methods of finding '$14 \times 9 = \square$'. $((14 \times 10) - (14 \times 1)$ or $(14 \times 8) + (14 \times 1)$ or $9 \times (7 \times 2))$

Paired work: Give the children activity sheet 'Many methods of multiplication' and ask them to work out a variety of multiplications and to record their methods. Encourage the children to find as many different methods as possible.

Differentiation

Less able: Ask these children to find one method and explain it aloud before continuing to the next multiplication. Where possible, ask another adult to support the pairs with their explanations.
More able: Encourage these children to provide three methods for each multiplication.

Plenary & assessment

Write on the board '15 × 4 = ❏" and ask: *How would you work out this multiplication?* Discuss methods and approaches, asking individuals to share their ideas. Include (10 × 4) + (5 × 4), (15 × 2) × 2. Repeat with:

- 17 × 8 = ❏   (((17 × 2) × 2) × 2) or ((10 × 8) + (7 × 8))
- 19 × 5 = ❏   ((10 × 5) + (9 × 5), (19 × 10) ÷ 2)
- 23 × 20 = ❏   ((23 × 10) × 2)

Each time, repeat the question: *How would you work out this multiplication?*

Lesson ③

Starter

Ask quick-fire questions such as: 20 × 4, 40 × 5, 90 × 10, 70 × 2, double 30, double 35, 56 × 10, 34 × 100, 13 × 5, 14 × 5 and ask the children to respond quickly, showing their answers on their number fans or whiteboards. extend the questioning to include division by 10, then by 100.

Main teaching activities

Ask the children how they can check if a multiplication is correct. If necessary, remind the children that multiplication is the inverse of division and that is useful when checking answers, eg you can check 49 ÷ 7 = 7 by using 7 × 7 = 49.

Establish that by knowing one fact, you can work out another three that are directly related to it, for example, 5 × 4 = 20 means that you know that 4 × 5 = 20, 20 ÷ 4 = 5 and 20 ÷ 5 = 4.

Show an OHT of the template 'Triangles'. Demonstrate how we can find four facts using these triangles by writing these numbers in the triangle (see left).

Go through the format of the triangle and ask the children what does 5 × 4 equal etc. Write another example on the OHT, this time leaving one of the spaces blank. Emphasise that this format reinforces the fact that knowing one fact will help you establish three other facts.

Individual work: Give each child a copy of the 'Triangles' sheet, which includes examples in which two numbers are given in each triangle. The children have to add the third number then write the four multiplication and division facts for each triangle in the space provided. If necessary, model the first example with the children.

Differentiation

Less able: Give children the version of the sheet in which all numbers are given.
More able: Give children the version of the sheet that includes only one number in each triangle. The sheet also includes three 'blank' triangles for the children to generate their own examples.

Plenary & assessment

Go through the completed triangles with the children and establish where some alternative answers are possible (with the more able sheet). Ask: *Which numbers would give you only two facts?* Establish that some square numbers would only give two facts, for example 49 ÷ 7 = 7; 7 × 7 = 49. Display an enlarged copy of resource sheet 'Multiplication grid' and use it to reinforce the fact that multiplication and division are inverses.

Lesson ④

Starter

Ask quickfire questions such as: *Divide 36 by 4. What is 25 shared by 5? How many threes in 24? Find half of 34 pence, 46 pence, 66 pence. Find a quarter of £8, £16, £32.* Ask the children to respond quickly, showing their answers on their number fans or whiteboards.

Main teaching activities

Remind the children that remainders are what is left over after dividing and that they are always written as whole numbers. Work through some 'Division examples' (see General resources). Invite children to write estimates for each answer on the board and ask them to explain the methods used (any reasonable mental method will do such as halving and halving again). When you have probed the children's mental methods and agreed the answer to each example, explain that in many practical situations it is necessary to round down or up to get a sensible answer. Read some questions out from the 'Division dilemmas' sheet. Discuss rounding up or rounding down for a sensible answer to each one. Ask: *Why should we round down/round up?*

Agree that rounding down is appropriate when you need to know the number of completed groups and rounding up is appropriate when you need to know the number of all groups, including the final incomplete group.

Paired work: Ask the children to work together to solve the problems on the 'Division dilemmas' sheet. They should estimate their answers first, then discuss methods to solve each problem and decide whether to round up or round down. Finally, they are challenged to write their own division problems – one that requires rounding up and one that requires rounding down.

Differentiation

Less able: The 'Division dilemmas' activity could be tackled in mixed ability pairs. However, a 'less able' version has been provided which includes division facts from the 2-, 3-, 4-, 5- and 10-times tables only. The final challenge has also been left out.

More able: Give pairs the version of the sheet that includes more difficult complex examples including context-based questions involving money and measures.

Plenary & assessment

Check through the questions. Ask the children to discuss their estimates and methods of working out each answer. Ask: *Which questions did you need to round up/down? Why?* Finish by asking each pair to read one of their own division dilemmas. Review the reasons for rounding up or down again if necessary.

Lesson overview

Preparation
OHT of 'At the fair'.

Learning objectives
Starter
● Derive quickly division facts corresponding to 2-, 3-, 4-, 5- and 10-times tables.
Main teaching activities
● Use all four operations to solve word problems involving numbers in real life, money and measures, using one or more steps.

Vocabulary
product, multiple, divide, factor, inverse, double, half, approximate, estimate, remainder, factor

You will need:
Photocopiable pages
'At the fair' (see page 199) for each group.

CD pages
'At the fair' core, less able, more able and template versions.

Equipment
Number fans; whiteboards.

Lesson

Starter
Repeat the Starter from Lesson 4, this time focusing on dividing by 1, 2, 4 and 8 to practise halving. Start by asking: *Find 32 ÷ 1. Find half of 32. Find a quarter of 32. Find one eighth of 32* and so on.

Main teaching activities
Display the 'At the fair' activity sheet on an OHT. Invite the children to select one item from each section from the list and work out the total cost using a method of their choosing.
Ask: *How did you work out your total?* Discuss strategies and highlight examples such as rounding up to £1 then adjusting, using multiples of 10p and so on.
Group work: Next, give the whole class in groups some target totals, such as 'I have £5.00 to spend on two rides and a drink. What options do I have?' Set each group the three challenges on the 'At the fair' sheet. You might differentiate this activity by giving lower or higher target totals or split the class into mixed ability groups. After completing this first challenge the children have to complete a second challenge, which involves working out costs for five children. A final challenge sets them a budget, which might require them to adjust their total spend.

Differentiation
Less able: If you split the groups by ability, then provide the version of the 'At the fair' activity sheet that includes lower prices and lower target totals. Work with this group to discuss strategies for carrying pence and pounds. If they cannot make the target totals, ask them: *What could we try next?*
More able: Provide the version of the 'At the fair' activity sheet with higher prices and higher target totals.

Plenary & assessment
Review all of the different challenges and discuss different strategies for solving them. Set some additional challenges involving all four operations if time is available, for example:
Addition: How much would it cost to have one go on each fairground ride? (£7.85)
Subtraction: I have £5.00. I buy a hotdog and a milkshake. How much do I have left? (£3.16)
Multiplication: You and your four friends go on the Screamer ride. How much would it cost altogether? (£12.50)
Division: You have just spent £2.97 on one of the stalls. You played the game three times. Which stall was it? ('Prize Every Time!')

Name	Date

Multiplication breakdown

For each multiplication question, use the method shown by your teacher.

Example:

12 × 7 =   (10 × 7) + (2 × 7) = 70 + 14 = 84

14 × 6 =

17 × 7 =

22 × 8 =

18 × 9 =

31 × 4 =

Challenge:

If you have time, try to break down the numbers
in different ways.

Show your working out.

SCHOLASTIC

photocopiable

Name	Date

Many methods of multiplication

In your pairs, find different methods to work out these multiplications.
Record each method and discuss it with your partner. Use some extra squared paper
if you need more space.

13 × 20

11 × 15

16 × 9

12 × 8

23 × 4

16 × 5

14 × 20

17 × 9

12 × 15

Challenge

Find and write down as many methods as you can to multiply 21 × 8.

| Name | Date |

Division dilemmas

1. Mrs Higgins has made 66 cakes for the school fair.
Boxes hold six cakes. How many boxes could she fill?

Answer: _____

Rounding up or down? _____

2. There are 37 people waiting for a ski lift.
The ski lift can take a maximum of 4 people.
How many times must the ski lift go up to take all the people?

Answer: _____

Rounding up or down? _____

3. Sim has saved £50. She wants to buy computer games
with her money, which cost £9.00 each.
How many computer games could she buy?

Answer: _____

Rounding up or down? _____

4. Joe has 59 CDs. CD holders can take up to 8 CDs.
How many holders will he need?

Answer: _____

Rounding up or down? _____

Challenge: $57 \div 5 = ?$ _____

Answer the question above, then use this question to write a word problem for
rounding up and one for rounding down.

Rounding up problem _____

_____

Rounding down problem _____

_____

Name	Date

At the fair

Rides

Screamer	£2.50
Spooky Ride	£1.80
Waltzer	£1.50
Tea Cups	£1.10
Ladybird	95p

Stalls

Prize Every Time!	99p
Hook a Duck	80p
Coconut Shy	75p

Food

Cheeseburger	£1.29
Hotdog	99p
Chips	70p
Toffee Apple	65p

Drink

Milkshake	85p
Can of pop	49p
Slush	60p

Challenge 1

You have £6.25 to spend on two rides, one stall, two items of food and a drink. What

options do you have? _____

_____

How much change would you have left? _____

Challenge 2

You have invited four friends to come to the fair with you and you are paying!
How much would it cost for you and your four

friends to have everything you selected in Challenge 1? _____

Challenge 3

You have only £30 to spend. Can you afford it? _____

If not, try to replace some of your selections with cheaper options. _____

_____

Multiplication and division 2

Children develop and refine written methods for multiplication and division. They choose and use appropriate number operations and ways of calculating (mental, mental with jottings, pencil and paper) to solve problems. They use various strategies to check their calculations including checking using inverse operations and using approximations.

LEARNING OBJECTIVES

	Topics	Starter	Main teaching activities
Lesson 1	Mental calculation strategies (× and ÷)	**Round any positive integer less than 1000 to the nearest 10 or 100.**	Use known number facts and place value to multiply and divide integers, including by 10 and then 100 (whole number answers).
Lesson 2	Pencil and paper procedures (× and ÷) Checking results	Know by heart multiplication facts for 2-, 3-, 4-, 5- and 10-times tables.	Develop and refine written methods for TU × U. Approximate first.
Lesson 3	As Lesson 2	Derive quickly doubles of multiples of 100 to 5000 (eg 3400 × 2), and the corresponding halves.	Develop and refine written methods for TU ÷ U. Check with the inverse calculation.
Lesson 4	As Lesson 2	**Derive division facts in the 2-, 3-, 4-, 5- and 10-times tables**	Use known number facts and place value to multiply and divide integers. Develop and refine written methods for TU ÷ U.
Lesson 5	As Lesson 2	Use all four operations to solve word problems, involving numbers in 'real life', and money.	Develop and refine written methods for TU × U. **Choose and use appropriate number operations and appropriate ways of calculating.**

Lessons   overview

Preparation
Cut out and prepare cards from resource sheet 'Multiple cards' (enough for a set of five cards per child or pair of children). OHTs of 'Place value grid' and 'Method of division' (General resources).

Learning objectives
Starter
- **Round any positive integer less than 1000 to the nearest 10 or 100.**
- Know by heart multiplication facts for 2-, 3-, 4-, 5- and 10-times tables.
- Derive quickly doubles of multiples of 100 to 5000 (eg 3400 × 2), and the corresponding halves.
- **Derive division facts in the 2, 3, 4, 5 and 10 times tables**
- Use all four operations to solve word problems, involving numbers in 'real life', and money.

Main teaching activities
- Use known number facts and place value to multiply and divide integers, including by 10 and then 100 (whole number answers).
- Develop and refine written methods for TU × U.
- Approximate first.
- Develop and refine written methods for TU ÷ U.
- Check with the inverse calculation.
- Use known number facts and place value to multiply and divide integers.
- Develop and refine written methods for TU ÷ U.
- Develop and refine written methods for TU × U.
- **Choose and use appropriate number operations and appropriate ways of calculating.**

Vocabulary
times, multiply, multiplication, approximate, multiplied by, grid method, approximate, division, remainder, chunking, divisor, inverse, factor

You will need:
Photocopiable pages
'Bigger or smaller?' (see page 206) for each child.

CD pages
'Place value grids' and 'Bigger or smaller grid' (see General resources), 'Bigger or smaller?' core version only; 'Grids for multiplication' core, less able, more able and template versions; 'Methods of division' (see General resources), 'Written division' core, less able, more able versions; 'Definitely division' core, less able, more able and template versions. Multiplication or division?' core, less able, more able and template versions.

Equipment
OHP; number fans; whiteboards.

Lesson

Starter

Call out different amounts of money and ask the children to round each amount up or down to the nearest pound. Start with £3.51 (£4), £3.21 (£3) ... . Repeat, but ask the children to round up or down to the nearest 10 pence. Start with £3.51 (£3.50), £3.21 (£3.20) ... .

Main teaching activities

Whole class: Remind the children that when a whole number is multiplied by 10 the digits move one place to the left, so $35 \times 10 = 350$. Similarly when a whole number ending in 0 is divided by 10 the digits move one place to the right, so $350 \div 10 = 35$. Use the 'Place value grid' on OHT to demonstrate this pattern and extend to other examples. Next, ask: *What number is 100 times bigger than 10?* (1000) *What number is 100 times smaller than 1000?* (10) Remind the children that this time the digits move two places to the left or right to correspond with the number of zeros. So $35 \times 100 = 3500$ and $3500 \div 100 = 35$.

Point out that multiplying by 100 is the same as multiplying by 10 and then by 10 again. Complete the 'Bigger or smaller grid' together to reinforce the pattern. Finally, give the children quick-fire questions multiplying and dividing by 10 and 100. The children can respond individually or as a whole class using number fans.

Individual work: Give each child a copy of activity sheet 'Bigger or smaller?' to complete in her/his own. If time is available, ask the children to write some number sentences using ×10, ×100, ÷10 or ÷100.

Differentiation

Less able: Provide copies of the 'Place value grid or structured equipment to support children with this activity. The children might also benefit from completing the 'Bigger or smaller grid' with adult support.

More able: Set a time limit (eg 10 minutes) to complete this activity. If time is available, ask the children to multiply the first set of numbers by 1000.

Plenary & assessment

Go through the answers and correct any misunderstandings. Revise the rules for multiplying and dividing by 10 and 100. Get the children to explain them using the 'Place value grid' where possible.

Lesson

Starter

Ask quick-fire questions such as: 20×4, 40×5, 90×10, 70×2, double 30, double 35, 56×10, 34×100, 13×5, 14×5 and ask the children to respond quickly, showing their answers on their number fans or white boards. Extend the questioning to include division by 10, then by 100.

Main teaching activities

Whole class: Remind the children that in the previous unit they wrote down multiplications to help them work out products. Draw a grid on the board for the multiplication 21×8. Ask: *How could you work this out, using a few jottings?* $(10 \times 8) + (10 \times 8) + (1 \times 8)$; $(3 \times 7 \times 8)$; $(21 \times 2 \times 2 \times 2)$; $(2 \times 10 \times 8) + (1 \times 8)$. Focus on the first method (the distributive law). Ask the children for other examples using these methods. Remind the children of the 'grid method' they have used before.

×	20	1	
8	160	8	= 168

Fill in the grid together (see left) and discuss whether this method is helpful. Repeat for 24×6. Point out the similarity to 12×12, since 12 is double 6 and half 24. Look at 25×6 and ask: *How could you approximate this answer?* (between 20×6 and 30×6).

Would the answer be nearer to 120 or 180? Why? How could you find the half-way number? (Multiply 6 by 100 and then halve and halve again to find a quarter: 600, 300, 150, and 150 is half-way between 120 and 180.)

Individual work: Give the children activity sheet 'Grids for multiplication' and ask them to use the grid method to work out the multiplications in the boxes provided. Challenge them to approximate their answers to check their calculations.

Differentiation

Less able: Use the version of the activity sheet that has only six questions and involves less challenging tables calculations. Help these children to identify where to put the numbers in the grid.

More able: Use the version of the activity sheet that has eleven questions that become increasingly more challenging.

Plenary & assessment

Write on the board '29 × 6' and ask: *How could you approximate this answer?* (somewhere between 20 × 6 and 30 × 6). *Would it be nearer to 120 or 180? Why?* Discuss methods to work out the multiplication: (30 × 6) – (1 × 6) or 29 × 2 × 3. Compare with the answer from the grid method (see below left).

Write '39 × 6' and ask individual children to find an approximate answer, then use a grid to work out the actual answer.

Set one or two word problems, 'A spider has eight legs. How many legs do 26 spiders have?' Discuss how the calculations could be set out using the grid method. Ask: *Is the grid helpful? When would you use it?*

×	20	9	
6	120	54	= 174

Lesson 3

Starter

Say a number and ask the children to double this number and keep doubling, in a rhythm, until you say: *Stop.* Start with 100. (100, 200, 400, 800, 1600, 3200, 6400) Then say a number and ask the children to halve it and keep halving, in a rhythm, until you say: *Stop.* Start with 5000. (5000, 2500, 1250, 625) Ask: *How do you know that 625 will not divide by two without a remainder?* (It is odd, ends in 5.) Repeat with £4800 (£4800, £2400, £1200, £600, £300, £150, £75, £37.50) Ask: *How do you know that £75 will not divide by two without a remainder?* (It is odd.) Discuss how to find half of £75 and £37.50.

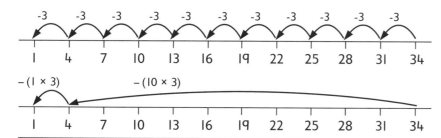

Main teaching activities

Whole class: Explain that the topic for this lesson is division. Write on the board '34 ÷ 3 = ☐' and draw a copy of this number line or prepare an OHT of the 'Methods of division' sheet.

```
  11
3)34
– 30   (10 × 3)  We know that 10 × 3 is 30
   4            Subtract 30 from 34, which leaves 4.
–  3   (1 × 3)   We know that 1 × 3 is 3.
   1            Subtract 3 from 4
                Answer: 11 remainder 1
```

Agree with the children that this method takes too long. Say that you can cut down on the written workings (see left). Colour code numbers in columns, if necessary, explaining that at each step you are looking for a multiple of 3 that you can subtract.

Individual work: Give the children activity sheet 'Written division'. They should use two written methods for division, and there is a box provided for each. Ask them to use whichever method they want to in the first box and then try out a different written method in the second box (such as repeated subtraction, using multiples of the division or 'chunking' short division). Discuss and compare methods and answers. Establish that the children can use their knowledge of multiplication facts to answer division questions such as these.

Differentiation

Less able: Use the version of the activity sheet with questions that involve less challenging tables. Be prepared to give them extra assistance in choosing their method and selecting the number line to use for counting back. The 'Methods of division' sheet (see General resources) is also useful for this purpose.
More able: Use the version of the activity sheet with five more challenging questions. Ask these children to use approximations and find ways to check their work by any of the methods discussed in earlier lessons.

Plenary & assessment

Go through the worksheet examples and address any misconceptions. Invite some of the children to show some of their calculations and explain their reasoning.

Write on the board 53 ÷ 5 = 10 R3

Ask the children to read and interpret this. Ask: *How can we check that this is correct?* If necessary, prompt the children to use multiplications facts to check the answer, ie we know that $10 \times 5 = 50$ and add the remainder 3.

Write a set of division calculations on the board such as:

29 ÷ 7 = 4 R1
38 ÷ 3 = 12 R2
64 ÷ 5 = 10 R1
49 ÷ 10 = 4 R9

Ask if all of these statements are correct. If not, ask which ones are incorrect (two are correct; two are incorrect). Ask the pupils to check each statement using their knowledge of multiplication facts, and then ask individuals to explain their reasoning.

Lesson 4

Starter

Ask quickfire questions such as: 'Divide 36 by 4. What is 25 shared by 5? How many threes in 24? Find half of 34 pence, 46 pence, 66 pence. Find a quarter of £8, £16, £32'. Ask the children to respond quickly, showing their answers on their number fans or white boards. Repeat this time focusing on dividing by 1, 2, 4 and 8 to practise halving. Start by asking: *Find 32 ÷ 1. Find half of 32. Find a quarter of 32. Find one eighth of 32,* and so on.

Main teaching activities

Whole class: Explain that in this lesson the children will revise all the different methods for working out division problems mentally, or using jottings that they know. Encourage the children to use their whiteboards as you go through the examples.

Write on the board '32 ÷ 4 = ❑' and ask: *How can you work this out?* Discuss various methods. (Halve 32 and then halve again, or use a number line to keep subtracting 4). Explain that a quarter of 32 is the same as 32 ÷ 4. If appropriate, ask 32 children to arrange themselves into four groups of eight. Repeat for '56 ÷ 2 = ❑', discussing how to find half of 56 by finding half of 50 and half of 6.

Next write '73 ÷ 5 = ❑' and ask: *Can you divide 73 exactly into five equal parts?* (No, as it does not end in a 5 or 0.) *How could you approximate this?* (The answer lies somewhere between 100 ÷ 5 = 20 and 50 ÷ 5 = 10.) Discuss whether to work out 73 − 5 − 5 − 5 … and establish that it would take too long. Agree to try another method.

73 ÷ 5 = (50 + 23) ÷ 5
        = 10 + 4 remainder 3
        = 14 remainder 3

Clarify by asking: *If I have 73 pence to share among five people, how much will each of them get?* (Each person would receive 14p and there would be 3p left over.) Repeat for 35 ÷ 3.

35 ÷ 3 = (30 + 5) ÷ 3
        = 10 + 1 remainder 2
        = 11 remainder 2

Remind the
children that
this can also
be written as:

$$
\begin{array}{r}
11 \\
3\overline{)35} \\
-30 \ (10 \times 3) \\
\hline
5 \\
-\ 3 \ (1 \times 3) \\
\hline
2
\end{array}
$$

Therefore 35 ÷ 3 is (10 × 3) + (1 × 3) + 2 which is 11 remainder 2 (see left). Challenge the children to make up a 'real-life' problem that can be solved by that calculation.

Remind the children that in the second calculation it is important to align the tens and units columns correctly.

Paired work: Give the children activity sheet 'Definitely division' and ask them to work out and record their methods for the division questions. Encourage them to find as many different methods as possible. Discuss and compare methods.

34 ÷ 4 = ☐   (34 is halved and then halved again.)
28 ÷ 3 = ☐   (Approximate by finding 30 ÷ 3 and recognise that it will be just less than 10.)
23 ÷ 5 = ☐   (Discuss 23 – 5 – 5 – 5 – 5 = 3 (4 remainder 3), approximate by finding 25 ÷ 5 and find that it will be just less than 5.)
67 ÷ 10 = ☐ (Approximate by finding 60 ÷ 10 and 70 ÷ 10.)
101 ÷ 2 = ☐ (Find half of 100, there will be one left over.)

Differentiation

Less able: Pair according to ability. Ask these children to find as many different methods as possible and explain it aloud before continuing to the next question. Use the version of the activity sheet that has easier calculations.

More able: Pair according to ability. Encourage these children to provide as many methods as possible. Use the version of the activity sheet that has more challenging calculations.

Plenary & assessment

Work out 64 ÷ 8 with the children by halving (32), halving again (16) and then halving again (8). Explain that you have found one eighth of 64. Now ask: *If I have £65 and want to share it among eight people, how much will each person receive? How much will I have left?* (£8 each and £1 left over) Discuss rounding answers up and down after a division, depending on the question. Discuss these questions.

● A school wants to take 65 children on a trip. Each bus holds eight children, How many buses will the school need? (9)

● A school wants to take 65 children on a trip. Each bus holds eight children, How many buses will be full? (8)

Collect answers and discuss methods. Correct any errors and misunderstandings.

Lesson ⑤

Starter

Write on the board '£3.60' and ask quickfire questions such as: *How would you write £3.60 in pence? How many lots of 10 pence are there in £3.60? How many lots of 5 pence? 2 pence? 1 penny? 20 pence? How much change would you receive if you gave a £5 note to pay for something costing £3.60? What combinations of coins could you receive? How many things worth £3.60 could you buy for £10? What is half of £3.60? A quarter? An eighth?* Let the children write their answers on their whiteboards or answer the questions individually.

Main teaching activities

Whole class: Remind the class that this week they have been focusing upon written methods for multiplication and reviewing a range of division methods.

Provide a couple of multiplication and division questions for the whole class to work out such as: 37 × 8 = ☐; 84 ÷ 5 = ☐. Collect up all the answers and work through the two calculations with the children.

Write the following problem on the board:

'A minibus holds 18 people. How many people could 7 minibuses take?' Ask: *What calculation do we need to answer this question?* Encourage the children to imagine one full minibus. Ask: *Will there*

be more than 18 people? If so, how many times more? Establish that the calculation is 18 × 7 and ask the children to complete the calculation. Establish that 7 minibuses could take a maximum of 126 people. Record this answer on the board.
Paired work: Give each pair a copy of activity sheet 'Multiplication or division?' Explain that you want the pairs to read each problem, decide whether it is a multiplication or division and then calculate the answer. Finally, they should write a statement in words to explain the calculation similar to the example above. Tell them to watch out for examples with a reminder in which they will have to decide whether to round up or down.

Differentiation

Less able: Give the pairs the version of the sheet with less challenging problems.
More able: Give the pairs the version of the sheet with more challenging problems including those involving TU × TU.

Plenary & assessment

Collect the children's statements and discuss their methods for solving each problem. Correct any errors or misunderstandings. If time is available, set some additional problems, such as:
'A tent holds 6 people. There are 77 scouts in a scout camp. How many tents will they need?'
'Joel has 50p. How many 6p stickers can he buy?'

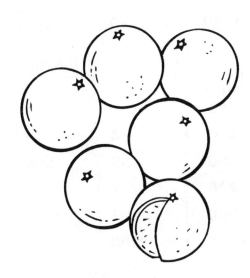

Name	Date

Bigger or smaller?

1. Circle the number on the right that is ten times bigger than the number on the left

x10

7	77	700	70	17	777
29	129	229	292	290	920
48	480	448	484	4800	440
187	1887	1877	8710	1807	1870
263	2360	2603	2630	6302	2600

2. Circle the number on the right that is 100 times bigger than the number on the left

x100

6	66	600	606	660	6000
15	150	155	500	115	1500
38	338	3800	380	3830	3338
84	8400	884	8480	840	4800
92	992	9290	9002	902	9200

3. Circle the number on the right that is ten times smaller than the number on the left

÷10

60	16	26	66	6	106
140	14	4	104	41	40
230	223	23	2300	203	32
1800	188	1880	18	118	180
2230	230	2030	223	232	23

4. Circle the number on the right that is 100 times smaller than the number on the left.

÷100

400	4	44	440	40	104
500	55	5000	5	50	550
700	7	77	70	117	17
1000	101	10	100	1	11
2000	200	210	120	20	2

Fractions and decimals

The children continue to use fraction notation, recognising simple fractions and identifying two fractions with totals of one whole. They use equivalent fractions and they order fractions, deciding whether they are less than or greater than one half. They solve simple problems involving ratio and proportion. They use money, mass, length and capacity to understand decimal notation and place value for tenths and hundredths.

LEARNING OBJECTIVES

	Topics	Starter	Main teaching activities
Lesson 1	Fractions and decimals	● Recognise the equivalence of simple fractions (eg ½)	● Use fraction notation. ● Recognise the equivalence of simple fractions.
Lesson 2	Fractions and decimals	● Identify two simple fractions with a total of 1.	● Use fraction notation. ● **Recognise simple fractions that are several parts of a whole, such as 1/3 or 5/8 and mixed numbers such as 53/4.** ● Find fractions of shapes. ● Order simple fractions: for example decide whether fractions such as 3/8 or 7/10 are greater or less than one half.
Lesson 3	Fractions and decimals	● Recognise the equivalence of simple fractions (eg 1/2, 1/4, or 3/4).	● Begin to relate fractions to division. ● Find simple fractions of quantities.
Lesson 4	Fractions and decimals	● Recognise the equivalence between decimals and fractions.	● To begin to relate fractions to division and find simple fractions such as 1/2, 1/3, 1/4, 1/10 of numbers or quantities.
Lesson 5	Fractions and decimals	● Understand decimal notation. Order decimals including money.	● To find simple fractions such as 1/2, 1/3, 1/4, 1/5 or 1/10 of numbers or quantities. ● To begin to relate fractions to division and find simple fractions such as 1/2, 1/3, 1/4, 1/10 of numbers or quantities.

Lessons   overview

Preparation
Copy activity sheet 'Equivalent fractions' onto an OHT.

Learning objectives
Starter
● Recognise the equivalence of simple fractions (eg 1/2).
● Identify two simple fractions with a total of 1.

Main teaching activities
● Use fraction notation.
● Recognise the equivalence of simple fractions.
● **Recognise simple fractions that are several parts of a whole, such as 1/3 or 5/8 and mixed numbers such as 5¾.**
● Find fractions of shapes
● Order simple fraction: for example, decide whether factions such as 3/8 or 7/10 are greater or less than one half.

Vocabulary
equivalence, fraction, whole number, equal parts, denominator, numerator, multiples, mixed numbers, greater than (>), less than (<), division

You will need:

Photocopiable pages
'Equivalent fraction teams' (see page 212) for each group

CD pages
'Number lines' (see General resources); 'Equivalent fraction teams' core, less able and more able versions, 'Equivalent fractions' (see General resources); 'Fraction shapes' core, less able and more able versions.

Equipment
Coloured pencils.

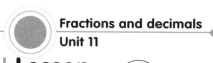

Lesson ①

Starter

Call out a fraction and say that if it is equivalent to a half then the children are to sit on their chairs, if it is less than a half they are to touch the floor and if it is greater than a half they are to stand up. Use several examples: 1/3, 1/4, 5/6, 1/8, 7/8, 5/5, 7/7, 1/10, 3/10, 9/10.

Main teaching activities

Whole class: Draw six dots on the board and cover up three of them. Ask: *What fraction can you see?* (3/6 or 1/2) Explain that 3/6 and 1/2 are equivalent fractions and demonstrate this on the board (see left). Emphasise the fact that the same is happening to the top and the bottom. Ask: *Can anyone else give me a fraction that is the same as one half?* Discuss the responses. Draw a 0–1 number line on the board and ask the children to suggest some fractions. Ask each child to write her/his fraction on the number line and where possible to suggest an equivalent fraction to write above it. Focus in particular on halves, quarters and eighths and write any equivalences on the board.

Group work: Split the class into groups of three or four and assign to each group a fraction (eg 1/2, 1/4, 3/4, 1/5, 1/3, 2/3). Explain that they have 5 minutes to work together and to write down as many fractions that are equivalent to their fraction as they can. Compare and discuss the equivalent fractions from each group.

Individual work: Give each child a copy of the 'Equivalent fraction teams' activity sheet and ask them to colour code the 'fraction teams' into wholes, halves or quarters.

Differentiation

Less able: Group these children together and set them to find fractions equivalent to 1/2 in the group activity. They can keep their lists to use with the individual activity. Use the version of the activity sheet that includes wholes and halves only.

More able: Group these children together and set them to find fractions equivalent to 3/4 or 2/3 in the group activity. Use the version of the activity sheet that includes thirds and three-quarters. These children could find 'substitutes' for each team with more equivalent fractions.

Plenary & assessment

Display the OHT of activity sheet 'Equivalent fractions' (see General resources) or copy the chart onto the board. Discuss it with the children and fill in the blanks together. Ask questions.

- *What is happening to the bottom number (denominator) in the fraction?*
- *What could you do to the top number (numerator) in the fraction to make the fractions equivalent?*
- *Why do you need to multiply the numerator and denominator by the same amount?*
- *What would happen if you didn't?*
- *Can you think of another equivalent fraction for 1/4? 1/2? 1/3? 2/3? 1/5? 3/4?*

Lesson ②

Starter

Draw five dots on the board. Cover up some of the dots and say the fraction you have covered. Ask the children to say the fraction that is left, for example, 4/5 and 1/5. Repeat with six dots and eight dots. Ask: *What is 7/8 + 1/8?* (1 whole) Now explain that you will say a fraction and ask the children to say the other part of the fraction pair that makes one whole, for example, 5/6 (1/6) and 3/4 (1/4). Repeat with several more examples.

Main teaching activities

Whole class: Remind the children of yesterday's work on equivalent fractions. Draw a 3 × 4 rectangle divided into 12 squares. Invite the children to colour in a number of squares on the rectangle. Each time ask them to work out the fraction, eg 5/12 in red and 7/12 in blue. Point out that these two fractions make one whole. Repeat with other fractions then ask individual children to order the fractions on a number line.

Paired work: Give each pair a copy of activity sheet 'Fraction shapes'. Ask the pairs to colour a fraction of each shape, write this fraction underneath each shape and then decide whether it is less than (<) or greater than (>) one half. Give them a copy of the 'Number lines' sheet (see General resources) to help them with this final task.

Differentiation

Less able: Support the children with the ordering activity. If necessary, give each pair the version of the sheet that includes simpler shapes.

More able: After completing the core sheet, give them the more able sheet that includes more complex shapes. They should then record these additional shapes on their 'ordering grid'.

Plenary & assessment

Share some of the children's work. Ask questions such as: *You have coloured in 3/8. What fraction of the shape is left?* Repeat for other fractions. Ask: *How do you know 3/8 < 1/2?* Again, repeat for other examples. Write 1½ on the board. Draw one and a half squares on the board. Ask: *What would 1¾ circles look like? What will 3⅓ rectangles look like?* Draw a 0–3 number line on the board and ask individual children to place mixed numbers on the line explaining their reasoning (eg 1¾, 1 ³/₈, 2 ½ , 2³/₅ etc.)

Lessons   overview

Preparation
Use resource sheet 'Equivalent fraction grids' (see General resources) to prepare enough grids so that every child has one.
Prepare a copy of the 'Fraction hunt board' for every group of children and use activity sheet 'Fraction cards' to prepare sets of cards, 2–3 sets for each group.

Learning objectives
Starter
- Recognise the equivalence of simple fractions (eg 1/2, 1/4 or 3/4).
- Recognise the equivalence between decimals and fractions.
- Understand decimal notation. Order decimals including money

Main teaching activities
- To begin to relate fractions to division and to find simple fractions such as 1/2, 1/3, 1/4, 1/5, 1/10 of numbers or quantities.
- To find simple fractions of quantities.

Vocabulary
tenths, hundredths, decimal point, decimal place, decimal fraction, proportion, in every, for every, twentieth, fifth, sixth, eighth, integer

You will need:
CD pages
'Equivalent fraction grids' (see General resources); 'Fractions of measures' core, less able and more able versions; 'Fraction hunt board' (see General resources); 'Fraction cards' core, less able and more able versions; 'Fraction problems' core, less able, more able and template versions.

Equipment
Whiteboards; Post-it Notes; Blu-Tack; interlocking cubes; a litre bottle of water; a cylinder or jug to measure 1000ml; 4 glasses; metre ruler; plastic money; clock face.

Lesson

Starter

Give each child a grid from resource sheet 'Equivalent fraction grids'. Call out fractions (1/3, 1/4, 1/2, 1/5 or 3/4) and let the children cross off the equivalent fractions on their grids as they hear the fraction being called. Ask them to stand up if they get a line or when they get 'full house'.

Main teaching activities

Whole class: Review the work in the previous lesson. Ask the children to draw some diagrams to show 1¾, 2½ and 3¼ . Ask questions such as: *Does your diagram show parts of the whole?* Ask the children to hold up their diagrams and discuss any misunderstandings.

Give each child or group 12 interlocking cubes. Ask them each to make the cubes into a tower and then to break their tower in half. Ask: *How many cubes are there in each half?* Write on the board '12 ❏ ❏ = 6' and ask: *What operation and number could you put in these boxes?* (÷, 2) Establish that '× 1/2' is the same as 'divide by 2'.

Repeat, dividing the cubes by 3, 4 and 6, each time making the link between the fraction and division. Show the children a litre jug filled with water and ask, *If I divided this equally into four glasses, how much liquid would there be in each of them?* (¼ litre or 250ml, 1000 ÷ 4) Repeat, dividing by 2 and then 10.

Individual work; Give the children activity sheet 'Fractions of measures' on which they are asked to find fractions of various quantities. As the children complete the sheets make sure that they link their calculations of fractions to the relevant division sentences.

Differentiation

Less able: Use the version of the activity sheet that asks children only to find half, quarter or one fifth of amounts. Ask them to give answers in only one unit of measurement and to focus on finding half of each of the eight measures and then quarter and finally, if time allows, one fifth. Provide these children with a litre bottle, a metre ruler, some plastic money and a clock face.

More able: Use the version of the activity sheet that asks children to find more complex fractions. Challenge these children to find these fractions and to write them using as many different units of measurement as possible. Most can be written in three ways, eg half of 3 litres = 1½ litres, 1500ml or 1 litre and 500ml.

Plenary & assessment

Discuss the findings and different methods of recording using various units of measurement. Ask individual children for ideas and to describe their findings. Invite individuals to share one of their results and to explain how they worked out the quantity. Each time ask: *Why did you choose to use that unit ? Can you write the answer another way?* Check the children's understanding by asking some quick-fire fractions questions: *What is ¼ of 16 cubes? 'What is ½ of 3 metres? What is 1/10 of 500 grams?' and so on.* Ask the children to show their answers on whiteboards.

Lesson ④

Starter

Write on the board '1/2' and ask: *What decimal is equivalent to one half?* (0.5) Link 0.5 to other quantities: 50p in £1 (£0.50), half of 1m is 50cm (0.5m), half of a litre is 500ml (0.5l). Repeat and discuss for other fractions: 0.25 = 1/4, 0.75 = 3/4 and 0.1 = 1/10. Call out a decimal fraction and ask the children to show the equivalent fraction on their whiteboards. Repeat, this time calling out the fraction and asking children to show the decimal fraction.

Main teaching activities

Whole class: Review simple fractions of quantities. Ask: *What is 1/3 of 30 cubes?* (10 cubes). Discuss sharing: 'If we have half each we divide by two, if there are three of us we divide by 3'. Write:

1/2 ⟶ divide by 2   1/3 ⟶ divide by 3   1/4 ⟶ divide by 4

Review some examples from the previous lesson or ask: *What is 1/4 of £1.00 (25p); What is 1/3 of 45?* (15). Extend to 2/3 (×2 then ÷3) or (÷3 then ×2), 3/5 and so on.

Group work: Explain that the children will play a game of 'Fraction hunt'. Give each group (of 4–6 children) a copy of the 'Fraction hunt' board and 2 to 3 sets of 'Fraction cards', which should be shuffled and placed in a pile. The children take turns to take one card from the 'Fractions cards' pile. If they are able to complete a calculation by using the fraction card and a number from the 'Fraction hunt board' they score a point and the number is crossed off the board. For example, they may pick 1/2 and 100 from the board (50). If they cannot make a fraction, the player should shout 'Pass' and play moves on. All players should record and check each calculation.

Differentiation

Less able: Organize the game in mixed ability groups. Alternatively, provide this group with the version of the cards that do not include any fractions that are several parts of one whole.
More able: Provide this group with the additional set of cards that include a greater range of fractions.

Plenary & assessment

Discuss the outcomes of the game. Go through a couple of examples with the children, eg
1/4 of 40 is 10 because 40 ÷ 4 = 10 etc.
2/5 of 60 is 24 because 60 ÷ 5 = 12 and then 2 × 12 = 24 and so on.
Share any interesting or difficult questions and discuss solutions.

Lesson

Starter

Write three lists on the board.
● 9.8, 6.2, 5.9, 7.6, 2.2, 2.1 ● 99p, £0.90, £9.00, £90, £1.99 ● 1.2 litres, 120ml, 0.2 litres, 20ml
Ask the children to look at each list in turn then, on their whiteboards, write the largest on the left, the smallest on the right and then order the remaining measures between them. When they have ordered all three lists, check their responses.

Main teaching activities

Whole class: Review the work from the previous lesson. Write on the board:
'1/2 ——————▶ divide by 2' etc. and set the class some fractions problems similar to those in the previous lesson, for example: *What is 1/4 of 80? What is 1/5 of 100 cm? What is 3/4 of £5.00?* Work through each problem and establish the relationship between fractions and division.
Give the whole class a multi-step fractions problem:
'Hannah has 64 sweets, but gives 3/4 of them to her friends. How many does she have left?'
Give the class time to solve the problem and go through the solution with them as follows:
1/4 of 64 sweets = 16 sweets or
3/4 of 64 sweets = 3 × 16 = 48 sweets
            64 – 48 = 16 sweets left.
'Hannah has 1/4 of the sweets left. Hannah has 16 sweets left.'
Go through the children's own methods for solving the problem and establish that they can use their knowledge of adding pairs of fractions to make one.
Paired work: Give each pair a copy of 'Fraction problems' and ask them to work out solutions by using the link between fractions and division. The pairs must also provide statements for each solution like the example above.

Differentiation

Less able: Provide the version of the sheet, which includes the worked example. The sheet also includes some single step problems. Ask another adult to support the children with these problems – for example by drawing diagrams to support their understanding of the problem.
More able: Provide the version of the sheet with a greater range of fractions.

Plenary & assessment

Discuss and review the problems from the sheet. Ask: *Can you describe the method you used?* Establish that the children understand the link with division and that they can use their knowledge of adding pairs of fractions to make 1. Write another example on the board such as the following:
'A clothes shop offers two suits. The first suit costs £160 but is reduced in the sale by 3/8. The second suit costs £150, but is reduced by 2/5. Which is the cheapest suit? Why?' (Suit 1 now costs £100; Suit 2 costs £90. Suit 2 is cheaper). Work through the example step by step and address any misunderstandings with the children.

Name	Date

Equivalent fraction teams

The fractions on the shirts show which equivalent fraction team these footballers play for.

Look at the fractions, then colour in the footballers' shirts to show which team they are in.

Colour the halves yellow.
Colour the quarters blue.
Colour the wholes green.

Time, addition and subtraction

Children learn to estimate time and use am and pm notation. They are also asked to complete some simple timetables and identify some facts from them. In lesson 3, they move on to consolidate methods for column addition and subtraction before refining these methods for money calculations in Lessons 4 and 5.

LEARNING OBJECTIVES

	Topics	Starter	Main teaching activities
Lesson 1	Time	• Read the time from an analogue clock to the nearest minute.	• Read and write from an analogue clock to the nearest minute, and from a 12-hour digital clock. • Use am and pm notation. • Read simple timetables.
Lesson 2	Time	• Use, read and write the vocabulary related to time.	• Estimate/check times using seconds, minutes, hours. • Read simple timetables.
Lesson 3	Addition and subtraction	• Round a sum of money to the nearest pound.	• **Develop and refine written methods for column addition and subtraction of two whole numbers less than 1000.**
Lesson 4	Problems involving 'real-life', money and measures (including time)	• Use known number facts to add and subtract mentally (money calculations)..	• **Develop and refine written methods for:** **- column addition and subtraction of two whole numbers less than 1000.** - money calculations (for example, £7.85 +/- £3.49).
Lesson 5	Solving problems	• Consolidate all mental strategies for addition and subtraction.	• As Lesson 4.

Lessons   overview

Preparation
Collect television guides (one per group) and prepare copies of the school timetable (one per pair)

Learning objectives
Starter
• Read the time from an analogue clock to the nearest minute
• Use, read and write the vocabulary related to time
• Use known number facts and place value to add or subtract mentally, including any pair of two-digit whole numbers.
Main teaching activities
• Read and write from an analogue clock to the nearest minute, and from a 12-hour digital clock.
• Use am and pm notation.
• Read simple timetables.
• Estimate/check times using seconds, minutes, hours.

Vocabulary
day, week, fortnight, month, year, century, millennium, minute, second, am, pm

You will need:
Photocopiable pages
'Money adds' (see page 218) one per child.

CD pages
'Tricky timetables' core, more able and template versions.

Equipment
Analogue clock face; whiteboards; TV guide (one per group); 'copy of school timetable; supermarket till receipts (with totals cut off).

Lesson ①

Starter

Hold up an analogue clock face (set to 12:00) in front of the class and explain that you will move the hands and that you would like them to write down the time on their whiteboards each time. Move the time forward in steps of 5 minutes. Alternate the language, describing, for example, 6:15 as six fifteen and a quarter past six.

Main teaching activities

Whole class: Write on the board 9:00am, 11:30am, 1:00pm, 3:30pm and 6:00pm. Explain that these times are departure times for trains, then ask: *If I was at the station at five to nine in the morning, how long would I have to wait for a train? If the 3:30pm train is running 20 minutes late, what time will it leave?* etc. Draw a time line on the board to help you with this and similar problems (see below). Also, establish that the children understand am and pm times.

| 9:00 am | 10:00am | 11:00am | midday | 1:00pm | 2:00pm |

Individual work: Give each child a copy of 'Tricky timetables' to complete.

Differentiation

Less able: Provide these children with clock faces to support them with the 'Tricky timetables' sheet.

More able: Give children the version of 'Tricky timetables' with more difficult time differences and with additional challenges involving the adjustment of the timetable for late and early running buses.

Plenary & assessment

Review the 'Tricky timetables' answers and address any misconceptions about time differences. Discuss children's own experiences of time and ask them to estimate times in practical contexts such as: *How long does it take you to travel to school? How long does it take to eat lunch? How many days to the end of term?* and so on. Explain that the class will be doing more on estimating time in the next lesson.

Lesson ②

Starter

Ask individual children to complete the following list:
Continue by asking other children: *How many days in 3 weeks? How many weeks in 2 years? How many minutes in 10 hours? How many seconds in 5 minutes?* etc.

1 millennium =
1 century =
1 year =
1 month =
1 week =
1 day =
1 hour =
1 minute =

Main teaching activity

Group work: Provide groups of children with a copy of a television guide and look specifically at the dates for that week. Rewrite the dates in different ways, for example 28/09/05 or 28 October 2005. Ask questions for the groups to solve such as: *How long is this programme? If there are ten episodes of this series, how long will it be altogether? How many episodes of this soap opera are there this week? If there are five minutes of adverts, what will be the duration of each episode? How many hours/minutes of this soap opera are there in the whole week?'*

Paired work: Give each pair a copy of the school timetable. Challenge the children to work out how much mathematics they have to do in a day, week, month, term or year. Ask them to write down estimates first then check their answers. If time is available, ask them to repeat this for other subjects, eg *Do you think you will have more or less time for music? Explain why/why not?*

Differentiation

Less able: Limit the task to finding the amount of time they spend doing maths in a day, week and month. Support the children with their estimations.

More able: Challenge the children to come up with as many facts about the amount of time they spend doing maths. Prompt with some additional questions if necessary, such as *What percentage of your day/week do you spend doing maths?*

Plenary and assessment

Compare the various results of the main activity. Check how close the children were with their estimates. Pick an individual's birthday, write it on the board and ask: *What will the date be when you are 16? 21 years old? How many days to your birthday?* Repeat with other children.

Lessons overview

Preparation
Copy, cut up and, if possible, laminate the cards from the activity sheet 'Operation follow-on', making enough complete sets so that every child can have at least one card. Prepare '0–10 digit cards' (General resources).

Learning objectives

Starter
- Round a sum of money to the nearest pound.
- Use known number facts to add and subtract mentally (money calculations).
- **Choose and use appropriate number operations and appropriate ways of calculating.**

Main teaching activities
- Develop and refine written methods for column addition and subtraction of two whole numbers less than 1000, extending to decimals.
- Solve mathematical problems or puzzles, recognise and explain patterns and relationships, generalise and predict. Suggest extensions by asking 'What if...?'

Vocabulary
align, digit, hundreds, tens, units, justify, increase, decrease, make a statement

You will need:

CD pages
'Money adds' core and less able versions; 'Money adds 2' more able version; 'Operation follow-on' (see General resources); 'Money subtractions' core, less able and more able versions; '0–10 digit cards' (General resources) for pairs of pupils.

Equipment
Whiteboards; squared paper; supermarket till receipts (with totals cut off).

Lesson

Starter
Call out different amounts of money and ask the children to round each amount up or down to the nearest pound. Start with £3.51 (£4), £3.21 (£3), ... Repeat, but ask the children to round up or down to the nearest 10 pence. Start with £3.51 (£3.50), £3.21 (£3.20) ... .

Main teaching activities
Whole class: Give the children a three-digit subtraction sentence such as 344 – 162 = ☐.
Ask the children how they might tackle this question. Discuss the empty number line method and demonstrate as required.

$$8 + 30 + 100 + 40 + 4 = 182$$
$$344 - 162 = 182$$

Write another question on the board such as 336 – 177 = ☐. Ask: *Can anyone demonstrate a written method for answering this question?* If necessary, demonstrate a written method (see left).

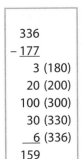

```
  336
- 177
    3 (180)
   20 (200)
  100 (300)
   30 (330)
    6 (336)
  159
```

Paired work: Ask the children to work together with a set of 0–10 digit cards. Turn over the cards and ask each child in turn to select six cards, which they should arrange into a three-digit by three-digit subtraction calculation. The children should decide what method to use and record their calculations.

Differentiation

Less able: Work with the children when recording written subtractions, using graph paper to support them if necessary.

More able: Extend the activity by asking each pair to select seven digits, which they should arrange into a four-digit by three-digit subtraction calculation.

Plenary & assessment

Review the different written calculation methods used by the children. Compare and contrast the methods used, for example *Which method was easier for this calculation – the number line or written method? Why?* Ask: *How could we check the answers?*

Lesson

Starter

Write on the board '54p + £0.67 = £1.21'. Ask quick-fire questions and let the children write the answers on their whiteboards. Ask: *If I had £1.21 in my purse and spent 54p, how much would I have left? (67p) If I had £1.21 in my purse and spent 67p, how much would I have left? (54p) If I bought a pencil for 54p and a pen for 67p, how many pence would I spend altogether? (121 pence) If I bought a cake for 67p and a chocolate bar for 54p, how much would I spend altogether? (£1.21)* Remind the children that these related operations can be used to check the problems. Repeat for £0.81 + 121p = £2.02.

Main teaching activities

Whole class: Write on the board the amounts £8.75, £7.85, £5.78 and £5.07.

$$\begin{array}{r} \text{£ } 8.75 \\ + \text{£ } \underline{5.78} \\ \text{£14.53} \\ {\scriptstyle 1\ 1} \end{array}$$

Ask the children to find sums of pairs of these numbers. Set the calculation in columns and reiterate the importance of positioning digits carefully with the decimal points written 'in line' one below the other. Write one example on the board (see left).

Begin by adding the pence first (£0.75 + £0.78). Ask the children for the total: 153 pence or £1.53 in pounds and pence. Say: *We can write the .53 under the pence and carry the £1.00.* Focus on the correct positioning of the decimal point in the answer. Add the pounds £8.00 + £5.00 = £13.00 *plus the £1.00 we have carried over.* Describe the method and talk through each step.

Individual work: Challenge the children to find the sum of as many pairs of amounts of money (written on the board) as they can in a set amount of time (5 or 10 minutes). Ask them to set out their work on squared paper, leaving a square for the decimal point. Discuss responses and the number of combinations. (£8.75 + £7.85 = £16.60, £8.75 + £5.07 = £13.82, £7.85 + £5.78 = £13.63, £7.85 + £5.07 = £12.92, £5.78 + £5.07 = £10.85). Give each child a copy of the 'Money adds' activity sheet. Ask them to work out the answers in their heads or use the method they have been shown.

Differentiation

Less able: Give these children the version of the sheet in which the first two examples are set out with the decimal points aligned.

More able: After completing the 'Money adds' core activity sheet move them on to the 'Money adds 2' sheet. The children will need till receipts – ideally with at least ten items. Cut up the receipt and give them the total at the end after they have added and checked the amounts.

Plenary & assessment

Go over the main teaching points, stressing the correct positioning of the decimal point using the written method. Prepare another shopping list example, write the items up on the board and ask the children to keep a running total of the amounts. Ask the children to write the 'grand total' on their whiteboards. Check how many children worked out the correct total.

Lesson ⑤

Starter

Shuffle the pack of 'Operation follow-on' cards and distribute all of them to the class. There are 35 cards in total, so some children may need to have two cards, depending on the size of the group. All the cards follow on from each other, for example, the answer (17) to the question '26 take away nine' will be found at the top of another card. Tell the children that they have to work out the calculation and then the child who has the card with that number at the top must stand up, say the answer and then read out the question on their own card. Note that you will need to remember the starting number (you can start anywhere in the loop) and that everyone should have a turn before play returns to the beginning of the loop.

Main teaching activities

Whole class: Write the same amounts on the board as the previous lesson.

£8.75   £7.85   £5.78   £5.07

Explain that this time you will be asking them to find the difference between pairs of these numbers. Demonstrate with 'Subtract £5.78 from £7.85'. Remind the children that if they use the column written method they should write the larger number on the top line. As before, tell them to deal with the pence first: *85 pence subtract 78 pence is 7 pence*. Children should be able to use a variety of strategies to calculate this. Go through suggestions. Point out that 7 pence can be written as £0.07 and write it under the pence, after the decimal point. Then, subtract the pounds to give the answer £2.07.

Individual work: Challenge the children to find as many combinations from the numbers above in a set amount of time (5 or 10 minutes). Remind them that they can check the results of calculations by using the inverse operation (addition), eg £5.78 + £2.07 = £7.85.

Next, give each child a copy of the 'Money subtractions' activity sheet. Ask them to work out the answers in their heads or use the method they have been shown.

Differentiation

Less able: Give these children the version of the sheet in which the first two examples are set out with the decimal points aligned.

More able: Give these children the version of the sheet with higher-level examples and with a final shopping problem.

Plenary & assessment

Review the results from the two activities. Ask: *Did you find all the possible combinations?* (£8.75 – £5.78 = £2.97, £8.75 – £7.85 = £0.90, £8.75 – £5.07 = £3.68, £7.85 – £5.78 = £2.07, £7.85 – £5.07 = £2.78, £5.78 – £5.07 = £0.71). Point out that you cannot work out £5.07 – £5.78 and get a positive number. Ask: *How could you check your calculations? Can you justify your workings and your answer?* Discuss responses.

Name   Date

Money adds

Work out the answers to the following 'Money problems' in your head or using the method you were shown.

---

1. Add £2.95 and £1.80.

---

2. Find the total of £3.99 and £2.50.

---

3. What is the sum of £5.76 and £3.38?

---

4. What is the total cost of a £3.65 book and a £5.86 computer game?

---

5. Sunitta has saved £6.86. She is given another £2.55. How much does she now have altogether?

Handling data

The children collect, organise and represent data, extracting and interpreting it in tables, charts, graphs and diagrams. They use these to solve a range of problems relating to numbers and shapes. They also sort information by means of Venn diagrams and Carroll diagrams.

LEARNING OBJECTIVES

		Topics	Starter	Main teaching activities
Lesson	1	Handling data	● Make and investigate general statements about familiar numbers.	● Collect, classify, represent and interpret data in Venn diagrams (two criteria)
Lesson	2	Handling data	● Use the eight compass directions. ● Begin to know that angles are measured in degrees.	● Solve a given problem by collecting, classifying, representing and interpreting data in Venn diagrams ● Classify polygons, using criteria such as number of right angles, whether or not they are regular, symmetry properties.
Lesson	3	Handling data	● Recall multiplication and division facts in 2-, 3-, 4-, 5- and 10-times tables. ● Begin to recall facts in 6-, 7-, 8- and 9-times tables.	● Solve a given problem by collecting, classifying, representing and interpreting data in Carroll diagrams.
Lesson	4	Handling data	● Derive quickly all number pairs that total 100 (eg 62 + 38, 75 + 25, 40 + 60).	● Collect, classify, represent and interpret data in pictograms: symbols representing 2, 5, 10 or 20 units.
Lesson	5	Handling data	● Derive quickly all pairs of multiples of 50 with a total of 1000 (eg 850 + 150).	● Collect, classify, represent and interpret data in tally charts and pictograms: symbols representing 2, 5, 10 or 20 units.

Lessons   overview

Preparation
Make sure you are familiar with the data-handling program on the computer and can demonstrate it to the class. Copy activity sheets 'Favourite days' and 'Exercise counts' on to OHTs. Prepare grids from activity sheets 'Number grids 110' and 'Number grids 1000', producing enough for every child to have one of each grid. Ask the children to collect bottles, cans or packets that hold liquid, as found in the local supermarket. Prepare Post-it Notes to use as labels for the Venn diagrams in Lesson 4. OHTs of 'Venn diagram' and 'Carroll diagrams' (see General resources). Prepare and cut out some shapes for use with 'Carroll diagrams'.

Learning objectives
Starter
● Make and investigate general statements about familiar numbers.
● Use the eight compass directions.
● Begin to know that angles are measured in degrees.
● Recall multiplication and division facts in 2-, 3-, 4-, 5- and 10-times tables.
● Begin to recall facts in 6-, 7-, 8- and 9-times tables.
● Derive quickly all number pairs that total 100 (eg 62 + 38, 75 + 25, 40 + 60).
● Derive quickly all pairs of multiples of 50 with a total of 1000 (eg 850 + 150).

Main teaching activities
● Collect, classify, represent and interpret data in Venn diagrams (two criteria).
● Solve a given problem by collecting, classifying and representing and interpreting data in Venn diagrams.
● Classify polygons, using criteria such as number of right angles, whether or not they are regular, symmetry properties.
● Solve a given problem by collecting, classifying and representing and interpreting data in Carroll diagrams.
● Collect, classify, represent and interpret data in pictograms: symbol representing 2, 5 or 10 units.
● Collect, classify, represent and interpret data in tally charts and pictograms: symbols representing 2, 5, 10 or 20 units.

Vocabulary
Venn diagram, set, sort, property, digit, multiples, greater than, less than, properties, faces, vertices, edges, regular, Carroll diagram, criteria, data, region, survey, symbol, represent, pictogram, bar chart, scale

You will need:
CD pages
'Venn diagram', 'Sorting shapes', 'Carroll diagrams', 'Number grids 100' and 'Favourite days' (all General resources); 'Interpreting pictograms' core, less able and more able versions; 'Exercise counts' and 'Number grids 1000' (see General resources); 'Capacity for tallies' core version only.

Equipment
Post-it Notes; empty bottles; cans and packets in which liquids were sold; computer; interactive whiteboard connected to the computer (if one is available); data-handling package; 1–6 dice; Place value cards to 50.

Lesson

Starter

Say that you are thinking of a two-digit number and that you would like the children to guess your number, using as few questions as possible. Explain that you will only answer 'yes' or 'no'. Discuss the vocabulary that may help narrow down their search: 'factor', 'multiple', 'odd', 'even', 'greater than' or 'less than'. Play this game twice and each time at the end of the game draw up a list of the numbers that it could be, encouraging sensible questions that allow the children to narrow down the search.

Main teaching activities

Whole class: Draw two overlapping circles on the board and say: *I am going to use this to sort numbers onto a two-way Venn diagram.* (a 'Venn diagram' general resource sheet has also been included for this purpose). Write '12' in the intersection of the Venn diagram and invite the group to suggest what the labels for each of the circles might be. For this demonstration use 'even numbers' and 'multiples of 3'. It may be useful to have these written on sticky notes ready to attach to the board quickly at the end of the activity.

Ask the children to guess where other numbers would be placed, according to the rules of your Venn diagram. For example, they might ask: *Could I place the number 18 into the intersection?* (Yes) *Why?* If necessary, explain that where the two circles overlap both criteria must apply. Would 2 appear in one of the two circles? (Yes) Place numbers in the correct sections as children identify them. Then encourage the children to develop questions such as:

- 12 is a multiple of 3, it is in the intersection, so could one of the labels be multiples of 3?
- 12 is an even number, it is in the intersection, so could one of the labels be 2-times table/even?
- 12 is a multiple of 6, it is in the intersection, so could one of the labels be multiples of 6 (in both the 2- and 3-times table)?
- 12 is less than 20, it is in the intersection, so could one of the labels be less than 20?

When the children have guessed the correct labels, attach the sticky notes to complete the Venn diagram. Ask: *Would 11 fit in either circle?* (No). Explain that if a number does not fit the criteria of either circle it is placed outside the circles.

Paired work: Give each pair a copy of the 'Venn diagram' sheet (see General resources) and tell the children to choose from the following criteria and sort the given set of numbers on their own Venn diagrams.

1. Odd numbers					Multiples of 5	
7	15	22	30	33	47	60
2. Multiples of 10					Even numbers	
20	40	30	27	44	82	15
3. Numbers greater than 20			Numbers less than 30			
44	29	30	12	54	27	11

Differentiation

Less able: Limit the children to the first two examples. Work with the children on the examples and ask for explanations after each number is positioned.

More able: Challenge the children to think of their own criteria using < and > symbols, numbers and shapes.

Plenary & assessment

Children should present their diagrams. Ask additional questions about each diagram, eg *Where would the number 31 go? Why?* Ask the more able pairs to show their own prepared diagrams but to cover the labels on them. Ask: *Look at the left-hand circle. What could the criteria be that defines all the numbers/shapes in the left-hand circle?* Take answers. Repeat the question for the right-hand circle.

Lesson ②

Starter

Place a Post-it Note to mark North and point this out. Ask the children to stand, facing that direction. Call out a direction, for example south, east, north-west, and ask the children to turn clockwise to that direction. Repeat, this time asking them to turn anticlockwise. Each time ask: *How much did you turn? Did you turn more than half a turn? 180 degrees? If 180 degrees is a half turn, how many degrees in a quarter turn?* (90) *What other name is there for a 90 degree turn?* (Right angle) Write down an instruction that would turn you through 45 degrees. (For example, north to north-east) Ask individual children for examples. Establish that an angle of 45 degrees is half of a right angle.

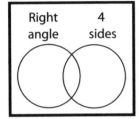

Main teaching activities

Whole class: Review the work on Venn diagrams in the previous lesson. Ensure children understand that the overlap area of the circles contains items in which both criteria apply (the 'both' region). Also, make sure that they understand that the 'empty' area contains items that do not fit the criteria of either circle (the 'neither' region). Suggest that we could sort shapes on to a Venn diagram. Ask: *How could we label the sets?* Take suggestions and draw a Venn diagram (or use an OHT of the 'Venn diagram' general resource sheet) (see left).

Show one or two 2–D shapes or take suggestions from the class, eg square, rectangle… and position them on the grid.

Group work: Give each group a copy of the 'Venn diagram' sheet and a set of 'Sorting shapes'. Ask them to place the letter of each shape in the appropriate position on the diagram. (Alternatively, enlarge the diagram to A3 and provide each group with a set of shapes cut out from the sheet.) When they have completed this task, ask them to think of their own criteria for sorting shapes relating to the number of sides, vertices, symmetry and so on.

Differentiation

Less able: Support the children with the first task and provide suggestions for the second task sets, eg 'Right angles/Four sides'…
More able: Extend the activity to include 3-D shapes and ask the group to select suitable criteria relating to the number of faces, vertices, right angles and so on.

Plenary & assessment

Children should present their diagrams. Ask additional questions about each diagram, eg *Where would we position a hexagon? Why?* Ask the more able pairs to show their diagrams, but to cover the labels on them. Ask: *Look at the left-hand circle? What could the criteria be that defines all the numbers/ shapes in the left-hand circle?* Take answers. Repeat the question for the right-hand circle.

Lesson ③

Starter

Ask quick-fire questions of individual pupils to build up the 10-times table on the board, as far as 200. Ask quick-fire questions about the 7-, 8- and 9-times tables, for example $3 \times 9 = 27$, each time relating it to the nearest multiple of 10 (3×10) to illustrate that this would be a good method for approximating if they were not sure of the product. Repeat by listing the 5-times table as before, to 100, and then making a link with the 4, 6 and 7-times tables, for example, $3 \times 7 = 21$ is greater than 3×5 but less than 3×10.

Main teaching activities

Whole class: Remind children about work on Carroll diagrams in the previous term. Ask: *What is a Carroll diagram?* Discuss the uses of Carroll diagrams.

	At least one line of symmetry	No lines of symmetry
Regular		
Irregular		

Remind the children about work on shapes in the previous lesson and draw the following Carroll diagram on the board (see left), or use the general resource sheet on an OHT.

Talk through the construction of the diagram – in particular, that it allows more options than the Venn diagrams – and ask children to position some prepared shapes on the diagram.

Paired work: Extend the activity to numbers – this time using the criteria 'Numbers that have three tens/Numbers that do not have three tens' and 'In the ×5 table/Not in the ×5 table'. Ask the children to prepare a Carroll diagram using the general resource sheet and to generate a set of two-digit numbers using two 1–6 dice or a set of place value cards to 50. They should then write the numbers that they generate into the correct quadrant of the diagram. If time is available, ask the children to complete the other Carroll diagram on the sheet with a new set of criteria, eg 'Numbers that have four tens/Numbers that do not have four tens' and 'In the ×7 table/Not in the ×7 table'.

Differentiation

Less able: Limit the activity by giving the children a prepared set of numbers to place on the grid, eg 20, 25, 27, 30, 33, 35, 37, 40. You might also support the children in labelling the diagram correctly.

More able: Extend the activity by challenging the children to think of their own numerical criteria, eg using even or odd numbers, three-digit numbers etc.

Plenary & assessment

Choose a few different pairs and discuss the numbers they generated and their positions on the diagram. Ask: *What number could I put into this box? How many numbers was I able to put in the top-left box?* Discuss why no other numbers can be fitted into this box.

If time is available, complete another Carroll diagram to check children's understanding of Carroll diagrams. This could be numerical, eg 'Odd numbers/Even numbers' and 'In the ×7 table/Not in the ×7 table' or non-numerical, eg 'Children with black hair/Not black hair' and 'Green eyes/Not green eyes'.

Lesson ④

Starter

Give each child a grid cut from activity sheet 'Number grids 100'. Explain that you will call out numbers, one at a time, and each time the children should cross off the number on their grid that would make a total of 100 with the number called out. When they have a line or full house, the children must stand up. Call out the numbers: 21, 22, 23, 24, 25, 26, 27, 28, 36, 63, 64, 65, 66, 68, 75, 77, 78, 81, 82, 86, in any order. These match up with the numbers on the grids. You could add in a few extras, as red herrings.

Main teaching activities

Whole class: Explain that in this lesson the children interpret information from charts and pictograms, using that information to answer questions. Display the OHT of activity sheet 'Favourite days' (see General resources) so that the class can read and discuss the bar chart. Then ask:

● *What was the most popular day of the week?* (Wednesday)

● *Why do you think Wednesday could be a popular day of the week?*

● *16 children voted for Tuesday as their favourite day of the week. How many children voted for Monday as their favourite day?* (9) *For which day of the week did 10 children vote?* (Thursday)

● *What is the difference between the number of votes on Thursday and the number of votes on Wednesday?* (30)

● *How many children took part in the survey?* (100)

Add the numbers to the vertical scale, remembering to include zero. The children will find it easy to read off the tens (20, 30 or 40) but will find it more difficult to read Monday (9) and Tuesday (16), which do not coincide exactly with grid lines. Next ask: *How could you display this information*

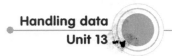
as a pictogram? Discuss what symbols to use and decide that it would be better to use symbols that represent 5 or 10 children. Discuss how you could represent one, two, three or four children by splitting up the symbols clearly. You will need to do this for Monday and Tuesday. Draw the pictogram on the board (see below left). Ask individual children to draw the symbols for each day.

Individual work: Give the children activity sheet 'Interpreting pictograms' and ask them to answer the questions about pictograms. The symbols represent two and ten units.

Favourite days of the week

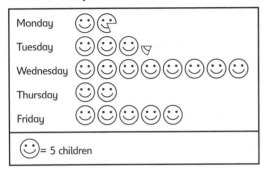

Monday	☺ ☺
Tuesday	☺ ☺ ☺ ☺
Wednesday	☺ ☺ ☺ ☺ ☺ ☺ ☺ ☺
Thursday	☺ ☺
Friday	☺ ☺ ☺ ☺ ☺

☺ = 5 children

Differentiation

Less able: Provide the version of the sheet in which the symbols represent 2 units only. Ensure that the children understand how the key works before answering the questions.

More able: Provide the version of the sheet that includes pictograms representing 20 units.

Plenary & assessment

Display the OHT of activity sheet 'Exercise counts' or copy the tally chart onto the board (see left).

Fill in the '4 hours or more' together and discuss the results. Ask: *If you drew a pictogram, which units could you use to represent this data?* Establish that using a symbol to represent two hours would be one possible representation. Discuss other possible representations, eg *Each symbol represents five hours. Ten hours.* (All the numbers are multiples of 5 apart from the 12 and 18.) *How could you represent these numbers?* (With part symbols) *Each symbol represents 20 hours.* Establish that it would be difficult to interpret some numbers, such as 12.

Tally chart to show the number of hours of exercise that 100 children took in 1 week

Less than 1 hour	₩₩ ₩₩ //
More than 1 hour but less than 2 hours	₩₩ ₩₩ ₩₩ ₩₩
More than 2 hours but less than 3 hours	₩₩ ₩₩ ₩₩ ₩₩ ₩₩
More than 3 hours but less than 4 hours	₩₩ ₩₩ ₩₩
4 hours or more	

Lesson ⑤

Starter

Repeat the Starter from Lesson 4 but use cards cut from activity sheet 'Number grids 1000', with the children pairing the numbers to make 1000. Call out: 1000, 950, 900, 850, 800, 750, 700, 650, 600, 550, 500, 450, 400, 350, 300, 250, 200, 150, 100, 50 in any order.

Tally chart of the capacities of packaging for drinks

Capacity	Number of bottles, cans and packets
Less than 1 litre	
1 litre	
More than 1 litre	

Main teaching activities

Group work: Put the children into mixed-ability groups of four or five. Explain that they will investigate the statement: 'Most drinks in a supermarket are sold in litre containers.' Ask: *Do you think that this is true?* Look at the bottles, cans and packets that the children have collected over the last few days. Share them among the groups and ask the children to sort them out. Observe how the children sort the containers and give some guidelines: 'more than 1 litre', 'less than 1 litre' and 'exactly 1 litre'. When they have finished sorting, ask: *How can we put all the information together?* Suggest a tally chart on the board (see left).

Ask: *How could you check the information?* (Count the total number of containers and check against the total number of tallies.) *Are most of the capacities one litre? How could you display this information more accurately?* Decide to round the capacities to the nearest 100ml.

Ask the children to complete the first part of activity sheet 'Capacity for tallies' filling in the tally chart, in their groups, then to combine the information from all the groups to complete the tally chart for the whole class.

Differentiation

Less able: Group accordingly and provide these children with containers that are already rounded to the nearest 100ml or give extra support to this group while they round up the capacities at the start of the session, and then help to check the tallies together at the end of the session.

More able: Provide these children with more challenging capacities to round to the nearest 100ml. Challenge these children to sort the containers further by naming the cans or bottles and using a Carroll Diagram, for example sort by 'less than ½ litre', 'more than ½ litre', 'fizzy drinks' and 'still drinks'. Ask: Can you use your Carroll Diagram to support another statement which could be true? For example: fizzy drinks are usually sold in containers holding less than 1 litre.

Plenary & assessment

Ask: *Do you think that the statement is true? How could you show this information on a pictogram? What scale could you use to make the information clear?* Discuss units of two, five, ten or 20 and their limitations and possibilities. Ask: *If you want to use a scale of multiples of five or ten what would you have to do with the data?* eg round to the nearest five or ten. *Would this give a fair representation of the data? If you use the bar chart, what would be the best way to fit the numbers onto this axis? Do you need to put in every number?* A computer software program could be used in a follow-up session to construct these pictograms or bar charts. The task could be differentiated by varying the scales the children work with. The 'Capacity for tallies' activity sheet will also be useful in planning this task.